Cover image is
South Africa, a
(See pp. 32-33 to learn more.)

Sincere believers are asking:
As we watch the dying of the West and demise of the free world,
how should Christians respond?
Should the Church have any prophetic voice in society
against tyranny and for freedom?

How should Christians respond to coercion and mandates
(masks, vaccines) in the workplace, at school, and elsewhere?
Should believers defend human rights and civil liberties
as co-workers, neighbours and citizens?
If so, when and how do we resist tyranny
without confusing the mission of the Church
or harming our Christian witness?

How do we know when political agendas
have wrongly polarised us or not?
What is the place of godly patriotism in the Great Commission,
without confusing the cross and the flag?
Is 'For God and country' a biblical motivation?

What does being 'gospel-centred' mean when applying the gospel and
Christ's lordship to moral and ethical issues of our day?
How do we think biblically about a theology of the face,
and about free speech and dissent?
What happens when the 'tyranny of the weaker brother'
or the 'greater good' rules a church, a society?
In seeking biblical answers to the above questions,
what can we also learn from church history and modern examples?

Read on for answers to these questions and more!

It has been such an encouragement to watch the Lord strengthen and lead Antioch Bible Church and Tim Cantrell and his fellow pastors down in South Africa during the past two years of Covid insanity. While I miss being with the saints there, this book is wonderful testimony to the fact that the Gospel will continue to have a bright and shining light in that place. You will find great resources and references contained in this work, and solid biblical argumentation for the supremacy of Christ and His truth.

– James R. White, Director of Alpha & Omega Ministries, Author of more than 24 books, Apologist who has done over 175 moderated debates, does his twice-weekly Dividing Line podcast

For most of us Christians who have resided in western democracies, freedom to worship is something we have taken for granted. Having restrictions placed on our gathering together as believers has largely been relegated to the history books or viewed as a theoretical (but unlikely) possibility. The emergence of Covid-19 in 2020, however, has changed all of that. What was once theoretical has now become reality.

Romans 13 has been used by some in the evangelical world as a proof-text for submitting to the government when it tells the church it cannot gather for worship so as to protect our "health and safety." My friend Tim Cantrell has written an extraordinarily helpful and practical book to aid faithful churches navigate these confusing waters. Resisting Tyranny is thoroughly biblical and serves as a clarion call for churches to courageously obey Her Head, the Lord Jesus Christ, above all. I am profoundly grateful for this important contribution and cannot commend it to you enthusiastically enough."

– Justin Peters, Author, Evangelist; produced *Clouds Without Water* teaching series

As a Christian virtue, freedom brings out the dignity and prosperity of a people. Cantrell builds an argument built on the rock of Scripture, but also calling scores of the most thoughtful pastors, historians, scientists, politicians, and even a few philosophers to march in defense of liberty in all its glory and potential.

If you are troubled with the government's response to COVID, or if you need a fresh charge of courage, Resisting Tyranny *is lively, readable political science. In other words, you are holding a précis of Samuel Rutherford's Lex Rex. Centuries of political freedom oiled the wheels in the modern missionary movement. No wonder Satan wants those gears to clog.*

– Seth Meyers, Missionary to the Tsongas; Pastor of Grace Bible Church, Makhado, South Africa

All too quickly pastors have handed over the keys to their church doors to the secular powers, waiting on them to (hopefully) give them back again. Some of us were never happy with this and felt our government had transgressed and that the churches had capitulated. Slowly we started speaking to each other and shared our biblical reasons for standing for the independence and freedom of our congregations. This book by Pastor Cantrell comes at a timely moment in South African church history and captures clearly and firmly for many of us what needs to be said. Thank you Tim for giving us a voice!

– Paul Hartwig, Senior Pastor of Lakeside Chapel, Bettys Bay, Cape Town, South Africa

RESISTING TYRANTS:

Covid, the Church & Christian Duty

Tim Cantrell

Kress Biblical Resources
www.kressbiblical.com

Resisting Tyranny: Covid, the Church & Christian Duty

ISBN 978-1-934952-73-3

Cover, interior design and typeset by Nel Scheepers. Image from: https://commons.wikimedia.org/wiki/File:Huguenot_Monument_Franschhoek.jpg

CONTENTS

Preface 1

Essay #1 – "Live Not by Covid Lies!" (by Mark Christopher) 13

Essay #2 – "Give Me Liberty Or Give Me Death!:
A Theology of Human Freedom" (A Biblical Case Against Coercion) 31

Essay #3 – "When to Disobey:
A Theology of Resistance for Reluctant Protestants"
(Romans 13, Sphere-Sovereignty & the Lesser Magistrate) 69

Essay #4 – "Face to Face:
Against Disembodied and Defaced Christianity"
(A Theology of the Human Face) 117

Essay #5 – "Assembly Required:
A Case for Churches Standing Up, Not Locking Down" 145

Postscript 163

Appendix A – "Christ, Not Caesar, is Head of the Church"
(by MacArthur and the GCC elders) 177

Appendix B – "Facing Covid-19 Without Fear"
(by MacArthur and GCC pastoral staff) 185

Appendix C – Sample Religious Exemption Letter 203

Appendix D – Religious Exemption Appeal for a Student 207

Appendix E – Declaration of Christian and Civil Liberties 219

Appendix F – What is the Way of Salvation? 225

In 1776 in New England, one month after the Continental Congress had drafted the Declaration of Independence, one of its architects, Benjamin Franklin, sketched out a brief description of his design for the Great Seal of the new nation. Franklin wanted the seal of the United States to feature, “Moses in the dress of a high priest standing on the shore, and extending his hand over the sea, thereby causing the same to overwhelm Pharoah.”

Franklin wrote that the seal should depict, “rays from a pillar of fire in the clouds reaching to Moses, to express that he acts by command of the Deity”. This illustrates how America’s founding fathers, even when unsaved, were the product of a scripturally rich, Protestant and Puritan legacy that prized human dignity and despised tyranny. Encircling this seal is a biblical conviction and motto of the 16th century Reformers, “Rebellion to Tyrants is Obedience to God.”[1]

---

[1] https://www.tabletmag.com/sections/arts-letters/articles/pilgrims-american-jewish-holiday

PREFACE

"Some people wouldn't know tyranny if it covered their faces, locked them in their homes, enacted the biggest wealth transfer in history, censored them, made them show papers, and force-medicated them."[2] Such is the blindness and insanity of our age, as the last two years have proven.

Even the Church, once a champion of human dignity and civil liberties, has become an indifferent, compliant doormat for dictators and an agent of the state. Biblical and historical ignorance, combined with nominalism and worldliness, has caused Christians voluntarily to surrender to Caesar the very hard-earned freedoms for which our forefathers fought and died.

The blessings of limited government, and the absence of persecution, have lulled us asleep and caused the muscle of godly resistance to atrophy. Covid has merely been a dress rehearsal it seems. The storm clouds are building on the horizon as we move from a post-Christian to an anti-Christian society.

As Al Mohler writes:

> *The rising fear…since the early days of the COVID pandemic has been that we would emerge from the crisis significantly less free. …It's an unease rooted in the historic reality of one of the most powerful laws of human governance, the Ratchet Effect. Once introduced, rules almost always get more expansive, seldom more limited.*

---

[2] Jack Wolman on Twitter.

Mohler then offers these two foundational propositions:

> *(1) Without robust Christian faith, totalitarianism is inevitable*
>
> *(2) In an increasingly secularized culture, totalitarianism, both in its subtle and less-than-subtle forms becomes a far more powerful temptation.*
>
> *...The big question [in the West] is whether or not we can now see the emergence of an even new form of totalitarianism, something that was unexpected and could only have arrived with Silicon Valley and the technologies of the digital revolution. ...It is a seductive totalitarianism.*[3]

How then do we ensure we're not seduced but grounded in a robust faith? That's why we will need many more books like this one in the coming days.[4]

Origin of this Book

This book is a compilation of four essays adapted from sermons to my own congregation, plus an important essay from a pastor-friend of mine in Cape Town, Mark Christopher. In the past year, my church has had the distinct honour of the police showing up on three separate Sundays, and we've had to go underground five times already; and who knows what's next?

The Lord has also enabled our little Gideon's band of a church to launch a court case in the Johannesburg High Court appealing for our constitutional

---

[3] https://albertmohler.com/2022/02/03/briefing-2-3-22; https://www.wsj.com/articles/covid-overreach-brings-america-toward-a-libertarian-moment-bill-maher-biden-lockdown-mask-vaccine-mandate-backlash-youngkin-11643646923

[4] Here are four excellent new resources I wish I'd had two years ago pre-Covid: (1) Bret Laird, *Family, Government and Church: Relating Three Jurisdictions of Divinely Delegated Authority* (2021, Shepherd Press; https://www.shepherdpress.com/products/family-government-and-church/); (2) Forsyth, *Caesar and the Church: A Biblical Study of Government and the Church* (2022, Kress); (3) Harrison & Walker, *Just Thinking About the State* (2021, Founders); (4) Busenitz & Coates, *God vs. Government: Taking a Biblical Stand When Christ & Compliance Collide* (2022, Harvest House)

rights to religious liberty and gatherings without state interference.[5] Compared to what Christians have suffered throughout church history and in hostile countries today, this is a small trial. Yet still it tried us, and we want to share what the Lord has taught us.

Were it not for my faithful fellow elders/pastors (and our steadfast wives) and our stalwart flock, this book would not exist. Thank you, dear brothers, and beloved church family! More than half of the footnotes, quotes, resources, and insights contained in this book come from the host of brilliant friends and church members the Lord has surrounded me with lavishly. "What do you have that you did not receive?" (1 Cor. 4:7)

Thank you also to my pastor-brothers in South Africa, Virl Tait and Mark Christopher, for their contributions and assistance. My thanks also to my talented brothers, Nel Scheepers and Charles Russel, for all their help in typesetting; and to my longtime friend Rick Kress for taking on this project. My precious sons and daughters (with their classical Christian education) also assisted me (and tolerated me!) often in hammering out these issues around the family table, and I praise God for each of them.

Most of all, God has used my beautiful bride, Michelle, on top of all her tireless mothering, homemaking, home educating and role as a pastor's wife, also to edit this entire book with her eagle eye and keen insight. She is my helper *par excellance*!

I've put these five essays in logical order, instead of chronological. The one I preached last is placed before all my other essays, as I came to see that a biblical case for human freedom is foundational.[6] Yet you may pick and choose to read in whichever order you like – it is a loose collection (with

---

[5] Now headed to the national Supreme Court of Appeals, the 2nd highest court in the land.

[6] Note that you will find occasional overlap in these essays, as I've sought to "stir up our people by way of reminder" (2 Pet. 3:1), especially regarding some basic truths that have been long-forgotten in our day, e.g., church-state doctrine. (Note also we have retained the original South African English and day-month format.)

dates given for original context and timing[7]). See also Appendix E, "Declaration of Christian and Civil Liberties", for an excellent international statement that captures much of the argument of this book.

Other pastors and theologians, past and present, have articulated these truths better than me. Yet I pray that our Captain, the Lord of Hosts and Head of His Church, would be pleased to use this meagre contribution to further equip His army for the battle.

Last Sunday, one of our church members shared with me how a top executive in his company called him in and demanded, "Tell me about your faith! What is it that makes you willing to stand up to the vaccine mandates?" His blameless record and firm-but-respectful stand had given him a gospel opportunity he might never have had otherwise. May God use the truths in this book to equip many other believers to love God and country in such a way.

Looking Back

Francis Schaeffer was one of the 20th century's finest defenders of the Christian faith. After the catastrophic Roe versus Wade legalising of abortion in 1973, Schaeffer was deeply burdened over the apathy of the American evangelical church towards infanticide. He defines tyranny for the Church in every age:

> *If there is no final place for civil disobedience, then the government has been made autonomous, and as such, it has been put in the place of the living God. ...And that point is exactly when the early Christians performed their acts of civil disobedience, even when it cost them their lives.*
>
> *Acts of State which contradict God's Law are illegitimate and acts of tyranny. Tyranny is ruling without the sanction of God. To resist*

[7] With occasional updates on further research and additional sources, usually in my footnotes.

tyranny is to honour God. ...The bottom line is that at a certain point there is not only the right, but the duty to disobey the State.[8]

Looking Forward

Totalitarianism shows no signs of waning on many fronts.[9] Islam has reclaimed Afghanistan and continues out-reproducing across Europe. China's surveillance state keeps rising, largely unopposed as they tighten their grip on Hong Kong and Taiwan and continue their genocide of the Uyghurs. Putin is perched on the porch of Ukraine and is confident that "the West will protest but it will not pay a price to resist."[10] What is a Christian response to all of this?[11]

---

[8] https://www.peopleforlife.org/francis.html

[9] Another key resource: *Covid-19 and the Global Predators: We Are the Prey*, by Peter & Ginger Breggin (Sept. 2021). For over 40 years, the Breggins have been using relentless empirical research to expose the psychiatric industry, through such best-sellers as *Talking Back to Prozac*, and many other volumes. Now they've employed their medical expertise in unmasking the ten-year plan of global powers to reorganise the world in the name of public health (the Great Reset). Many are saying this is the most comprehensive book yet, proving what is behind the draconian lockdown measures crushing civil liberties around the world. The authors state, "our research…moved us inexorably toward the conclusion that Covid-19 has always been about making fortunes from rushed-through vaccines while weakening America and strengthening globalism. …it was about forcing humanity to submit to experimental, dangerous and costly vaccines, and to use that justification for increasing totalitarian power. …Every global predator we could identify is financially wedded to and filled with admiration for…Communist China and totalitarianism." See also these recent, solemn warnings: https://rumble.com/vn3r38-dr-roger-hodkinson-destroys-covid-in-4-mins..html?s=09; https://jlronning.substack.com/p/the-ten-commandments-of-our-pandemic; https://www.dailywire.com/news/cnbc-host-we-should-have-military-enforce-universal-vaccination; https://townhall.com/columnists/benshapiro/2021/12/01/an-abundance-of-caution-mentality-leads-to-tyranny

[10] "Make no mistake, Vladimir Putin's ultimate aim is to end…the very idea of representative democracy and Western constitutionalism and the Western-dominated understanding of a democratic and peaceful world order." https://albertmohler.com/2022/02/09/briefing-2-9-22; https://www.allisrael.com/with-putin-poised-to-invade-ukraine-this-week-he-could-ignite-biggest-land-war-in-europe-since-ww-ii-i-m-heading-to-eastern-europe-to-cover-the-crisis: "Europe thus suddenly finds itself on the verge of the biggest land war since World War II."

[11] "…there seem to be no brakes on any of the deep historical, cultural, and spiritual forces that lead to authoritarian governments, random exercises in bio-power, and anti-scientific purity cults....Only the libertarian right has stood fairly firm against the tide, and that movement hardly exists outside of the United States." https://brownstone.org/articles/seven-theories-of-why-the-lockdowns-happened/.

Recently in the *London Telegraph* Lord Sumption, who served on the UK Supreme Court (2012-2018), wrote an article entitled, "Europe's latest wave of Covid authoritarianism has set a dangerous new precedent".[12] In it he states:

> *Across Europe, basic norms of civilised society are giving way to panic. The unvaccinated are being excluded from an ever-wider range of basic rights. Austria has criminalised them. Italy has stopped them doing their jobs. The Dutch police have fired on anti-lockdown demonstrators, seriously injuring some of them. We are witnessing the ultimate folly of frightened politicians who cannot accept that they are impotent in the face of some natural phenomena.*
>
> *...The Netherlands and Belgium are among the most thoroughly vaccinated countries in Europe, at 74 per cent, but have seen some of the steepest rises in infection. Meanwhile, the moral dimension is forgotten. The basic problem is an approach to the pandemic which treats it as a purely technical issue of public health management, when it is a complex economic, social and political issue as well.... The absence of moral scruple in pursuit of what is thought to be a public good, is the first symptom of totalitarianism. The reduction of human beings to mere instruments of state policy is the next.*
>
> *...Social interaction with other people is not an optional leisure activity but a basic need of humankind. A minimum of respect for the personal autonomy of our fellows is essential if we are to live together in any kind of harmony. These things are what make us a community. Governments which ignore them cross an important moral line, and inevitably find themselves engaged in a sustained assault on the humanity of their people.*

---

[12] 22 Nov. 2021. See also: https://edition.cnn.com/2021/11/30/europe/covid-vaccine-mandates-austria-europe-cmd-intl/index.html

Not to be outdone by secular Europe, Canada's tyrants have now outlawed any Bible teaching on sexuality, declaring it "myth" and establishing the world's most comprehensive laws against "conversion therapy". In a recent news interview, faithful Canadian pastors James Coates and Tim Stephens (both jailed in 2021 for holding church) spoke out:

> *I believe our government is capitalizing on a politically expedient segment of its constituency in an effort to further dismantle Western civilization as we know it. To do this, it must outlaw its very foundation, which is rooted in a Judeo-Christian worldview. Bill C-4 is another brick laid in this effort and is evidence that our government is under the judgment of God.*
>
> *...As governments seek totalitarian authority over every aspect of society, it's inevitable that they will persecute any and all who refuse to declare allegiance to the state. As such, unless the tide of totalitarianism is stemmed, Christians can expect persecution to increase.*
>
> *We've seen that the new prevailing worldview is totalitarian, seeking to define marriage, sexuality, and control health choices. It is absolutely intolerant to opposing beliefs. All socialistic and communistic movements hate the authority and law of God that Christianity promotes. Much of the church in Canada believes that compliance and compromise will promote peace and freedom, but this attitude only feeds the beast and will increase persecution and eliminate freedom.*
>
> *...Social engineering is reaching new levels here in Canada...[our politicians] are less subtle with intolerance to nonconformity than their American counterparts. Whether COVID protocols, religious liberty, compelled speech — they are imposing a new social order devoid of our legal, religious or cultural heritage. A regime and agenda based on lies has to be coercive in order to maintain its power. It can't rely on persuasion, truth, or beauty. So I anticipate*

> *further exile and punishment for non-conformists and those who will still stand and preach truth and reality in our time.*[13]

This is the increasingly inhumane age into which God has called Christians to stand up for their Lord, for His Word, and for human dignity. In a time when even trusted, reformed evangelical leaders are wavering, may our faithful Lord use these essays to help you navigate troubled waters by the sure compass of His Word.

Tim Cantrell
Honeydew, Johannesburg
February 2022

FURTHER ENDNOTES

(1) Regarding South African President Ramaphosa's recent speech, these were helpful insights:[14]

We caution that the government may attempt to lift the state of disaster only to try entrenching those powers as part of ordinary, permanent state powers. ...The country must not be permanently at the mercy of a government that can act without limit. ...this is not just about vaccinations. [We must beware of] a 'permanent bodily surveillance' system...in which healthy people constantly need to prove they are 'certified healthy enough' to move around and conduct their affairs, is an onerous system that in various ways can and will constitute tyranny...

It acclimatises people to state-managed movement control and surveillance and the co-option of the private sector for implementation. ...with forced vaccinations and forced booster shots, perhaps indefinitely – we are risking

---

[13] https://www.foxnews.com/world/thousands-churches-raise-alarm-scope-new-canadian-conversion-therapy-ban
[14] 28 November, 2021

a permanently medicalised and monitored society. It will also lead to unprecedented government corruption.[15]

On the positive side here in South Africa, it is good to see some religious leaders speaking up: https://joynews.co.za/meshoe-calls-on-sa-citizens-to-stand-together-against-covid-tyranny/

(2) To illustrate how vaccine mandates are dividing churches, read what Redeemer Presbyterian Church, founded by Tim Keller (a flagship church for The Gospel Coalition), states on their website:

Individuals who are fully vaccinated (two weeks have elapsed since your final dose or single-shot dose) will be allowed to sit on the first floor of the auditorium without social distancing and masks will be optional.[16]

(3) See also James White's apt response to John Piper:

...It is undeniable that the vaccines are not a solo issue. They are coming to us after mask mandates and church closures and pastoral imprisonments and before the next onerous demands from governments drunk on the power that inevitably comes from the rise of secularism. The secular state is far worse than the ancient pagan context of Rome (which was bad enough), for by its very definition it must be ultimate in all things as there is no Creator.

Why Piper does not see the role the vaccines play in the overall demands of the newly empowered totalitarianism I cannot say.... What Piper has missed, badly, is the role these vaccinations play in a much bigger, much

---

[15] (https://sakeliga.co.za/en/sakeliga-regards-president-cyril-ramaphosas-covid-19-statement-on-sunday-evening-significant-in-both-helpful-and-harmful-ways/). See also this excellent, South African response: https://chriswaldburger.substack.com/p/a-sincere-plea-to-the-pro-vax-mandaters.

[16] https://churchleaders.com/news/408495-redeemer-presbyterian-vaccination.html; https://www.dailywire.com/news/neither-vaccinated-nor-unvaccinated-how-churches-imposing-vaccine-mandates-are-dividing-christians-with-a-different-gospel; see also in Canadian churches: https://www.lifesitenews.com/news/breaking-quebec-announces-new-covid-restrictions-vaccine-passports-for-churches-week-before-christmas/

more basic movement into a technologically based, chemically and medically controlled secular totalitarianism.[17]

(4) Jewish columnist, Dennis Prager, sums up the failure of religious leaders over the past two years of blind compliance and capitulation:

...Most religious institutions and leaders have become largely indistinguishable from their secular counterparts. With the exception of attending church or synagogue, most Christians and Jews think and act like most secular Americans. ...The tragedy of American religious life is that religious people who lack courage are concentrated in leadership positions.

After speaking of leading an open, unrestricted worship service in synagogue, Prager continues: *Other synagogues could have done the same thing -- but nearly all rabbis and synagogue boards were too scared and too obedient to do so. And of course, the same holds true for most churches, whether Catholic, Protestant or Mormon. Too scared. And too obedient to irrational dictates.*

They will pay a price as people will gradually come to understand how weak their religious leaders were. And they will pay another price: by keeping their churches and synagogues closed for so long (for no good reason), many of their congregants may just not return. If my clergy didn't think it was important that I attend for nearly two years, maybe it just isn't that important.[18]

(5) In light of the long-awaited end of mandates and restrictions in some places, this author gives a timely warning:[19]

---

[17] https://www.aomin.org/aoblog/personal/freedom-is-the-primary-casualty-of-the-experimental-mandated-vaccines/.

[18] https://townhall.com/columnists/dennisprager/2022/02/15/covid19-and-the-failure-of-americas-major-religions-n2603293; see also: https://brownstone.org/articles/in-praise-of-disobedience/

...In March of 2020, in violation of the principles embedded in our constitutions, governments around the world convinced citizens to give their leaders and public institutions the authority to overrule individual rights in order to "flatten the curve." That impulse went unchallenged under the false assumption that human rights violations could be justified as long as the benefits to the majority outweighed the costs to the minority. By accepting this excuse for overriding unconditional rights, we transformed ourselves into an authoritarian police state where "might makes right." That is the moment when all the checks and balances in our scientific and democratic institutions stopped functioning.

Liberal democracy was built around the principle that individual rights must be unconditional. *In other words, they are meant to supersede the authority of government. Consequently, individual rights (such as bodily autonomy) were meant to serve as checks and balances on government power***.** *They were meant to provide a hard limit to what our government can do to us without our individual consent.*

...Withdrawing mandates because "the Omicron variant is mild" or because "the costs of continuing the measures outweigh the benefits" does not undo what has been normalized and legitimized. <u>If the legitimacy of mandates is not overturned, you will not be going back to your normal life. It may superficially look similar to your life before Covid, but in reality you will be living in a Brave New World where governments temporarily grant privileges to those who conform with the government's vision of how we should live.</u>

You will no longer be celebrating your differences, cultivating your individuality, or making your own free choices. Only conformity will enable you to exist. You will be living under a regime in which any new "crisis" can serve as justification to impose restrictions on those who don't "get with the program" as long as mobs and technocrats think the restrictions are "reasonable." You will no longer be the master of your own life. A golden cage is still a cage if someone else controls the lock on the door."

...If the legal and ethical fallacies that were used to justify mandates are not called out as inexcusable violations of our constitutional rights, we will have inadvertently normalized the illiberal idea that, as long as someone in a lab coat says it's okay, this can be done to us again, at any time, whether to fight the next wave of Covid, to take away freedoms to fight "climate change", to seize assets to solve a government debt crisis, or simply to socially engineer outcomes according to whatever our leaders define as a "fairer and more equitable world".

How we navigate the end of mandates determines whether we win our freedom or whether we allow our leaders to normalize a Brave New World with conditional rights that can be turned off again during the next "emergency." (https://brownstone.org/articles/ending-mandates-does-not-strip-government-of-the-ability-to-do-this-again/)

(6) Here is a vital R.C. Sproul story I have relayed to others often over the past two years:

About thirty years ago, I shared a taxi cab in St. Louis with Francis Schaeffer. I had known Dr. Schaeffer for many years, and he had been instrumental in helping us begin our ministry in Ligonier, Pennsylvania, in 1971. Since our time together in St. Louis was during the twilight of Schaeffer's career, I posed this question to him: "Dr. Schaeffer, what is your biggest concern for the future of the church in America?"

Without hesitation, Dr. Schaeffer turned to me and spoke one word: "Statism." Schaeffer's biggest concern at that point in his life was that the citizens of the United States were beginning to invest their country with supreme authority, such that the free nation of America would become one that would be dominated by a philosophy of the supremacy of the state.[20]

---

[20] https://www.ligonier.org/learn/articles/statism

1
LIVE NOT BY COVID LIES!
(December 2021)

By Pastor Mark Christopher[21]
Cape Town, South Africa

The famed Soviet dissident Alexander Solzhenitsyn wrote a profound essay "Live Not By Lies" in 1974 just prior to his exile to the West. The crux of this essay compared the Marxist ideology of Russia to "lies". His premise was simple — the whole Marxist framework of communist Russia was predicated on a foundation of lies. Thus, all that flowed from the ideology wreaked of dishonesty. The solution Solzhenitsyn offered was to admonish those caught in the trap of totalitarianism to passively resist the lies and thus bring an end to the edifice built on these lies.

Early in his essay, Solzhenitsyn describes a situation that has much in common with the situation much of the world finds itself in due to government overreach and draconian regulations due to the current Covid-19 crisis:

> *We are approaching the brink; already a universal spiritual demise is upon us; a physical one is about to flare up and engulf us and our*

[21]Mark is a 1994 graduate of The Master's Seminary and, along with his wife, Debbie, has served as a Grace Church missionary in Cape Town, South Africa for 27 years.

> *children, while we continue to smile sheepishly and babble: 'But what can we do to stop it? We haven't the strength.'*
>
> *We have so hopelessly ceded our humanity that for the modest handouts of today we are ready to surrender up all principles, our soul, all the labours of our ancestors, all the prospects of our descendants — anything to avoid disrupting our meager existence ... We hope only not to stray from the herd, not to set out on our own, and risk suddenly having to make do without the white bread, the hot water heater, a Moscow residency permit.*[22]

Later in the same manuscript, Solzhenitsyn identifies the heart of the matter by admonishing his fellow Russians, "Our way must be: Never knowingly support lies!" Of course, this not a novel or new idea. The Bible is replete with numerous warnings and admonishments related to the scourge of lies and deceptions.

The Apostle Paul's graphic portrayal of total depravity includes the unflattering characteristic of sin evidenced by the vessels of speech: "'Their throat is an open grave, with their tongues they keep deceiving,' 'The poison of asps is under their lips'; 'Whose mouth is full of cursing and bitterness'" (Romans 3:13-14). In other words, the default position of sinful man is that of a liar and deceiver obsessed with protecting his or her own self-interest.

Truth Stumbling in the Streets

So, it should not surprise us that one of the hallmarks of an apostate society is that truth stumbles in the street: "Justice is turned back, and righteousness stands far away; for truth has stumbled in the street, and uprightness cannot enter. Yes, truth is lacking; and he who turns aside from evil makes himself a prey. Now the LORD saw, and it was displeasing in His sight that there was no justice" (Isaiah 59:14-15). The present-day examples of this are far too numerous to mention here. Suffice it to say that one should look no further

---

[22] https://www.solzhenitsyncenter.org/live-not-by-lies

than today's headlines to find glaring demonstrations of truth flailing in the streets. Especially as it relates to the issues of the day, like Covid-19.

Early in the pandemic it quickly become obvious that the truth was being intentionally distorted and would ultimately stumble in the street and be exchanged for expediency. And while Covid is very real and to be taken seriously, it also became clear from day one that this public health crisis was going to be exploited for political and economic gain. Politicians, ideologues, and medical bureaucrats wasted no time and squandered no opportunity to use this crisis to further their own self-interest. This only cheapens the suffering and misery that has been inflicted on so many by this pandemic.

The following examples of truth stumbling in the streets on this issue are merely representative of hundreds of examples that could have been included to illustrate the point that we need to be wise and discerning about what is happening:

ELEVEN COVID LIES

1. Botched Response: Back in January of 2020 the World Health Organization (WHO) said that Covid-19 was not something that people needed to be too concerned about outside of China itself.[23] By the end of that same month, the realities of what was happening forced them to think differently and issue a warning. Had they issued their warning a few weeks earlier it may have led to very different outcomes for the world at large and saved many lives and economies.

2. Only Three Weeks: When the first lockdown was announced in late March 2020 in South Africa, we were all told it would only take three weeks to flatten the curve and prepare field hospitals for the casualties they expected. That was twenty months ago, and the only thing flattened was the

[23] https://www.foxnews.com/opinion/gordon-g-chang-trump-right-to-stop-funding-world-health-organization-over-its-botched-coronavirus-response .

economy and livelihoods while we still live under the spectre of elevated lockdowns and failed attempts to eradicate what is now an endemic virus.

3. Panic Modelling: In the dawning days of global lockdowns, mortality modelers in the UK and the US predicted mass casualties from the virus.[24] One UK model prognosticated that the US would have as many as 2.2 million causalities in the first 6 months, while the UK would see 500,000 deaths during that same period. Almost two years on now, the US has just recorded over 773,000 Covid-related deaths. And the UK has just over 144,000 deaths. Some of the models were not just wrong, they were astronomically wrong. All of this is important because based on these aberrant models, draconian lockdowns and overreaching regulations were justified.

4. Deadly Lockdowns: We were told to stop the virus from spreading, harsh lockdowns were required. In the end, the lockdowns destroyed economies, jobs, businesses, and supply chains while only prolonging the inevitable spread of the virus.[25] It was not simply a matter of "Lives for money", it has proven to be a matter "Lives for lives", as lockdowns silently kill untold numbers of people. Many had to forego medical treatments that could have prevented major illness, while countless others faced depression, suicide, alcohol and drug abuse, all as a direct result of locking people up and destroying their livelihoods.[26] A more strategic and focused response would have been much better. Sweden serves as good example of a more focused strategy that sought to protect the most vulnerable while allowing life to

---

[24] https://www.dailysignal.com/2020/05/16/the-failures-of-an-influential-covid-19-model-used-to-justify-lockdowns/ and https://www.heritage.org/public-health/commentary/failures-influential-covid-19-model-used-justify-lockdowns

[25] https://www.biznews.com/thought-leaders/2020/11/05/jay-bhattacharya-lockdowns; "The great body of evidence shows that COVID-19 lockdowns, shelter-in-place policies, masks, school closures, and mask mandates have failed in their purpose of curbing transmission or reducing deaths. These restrictive policies were ineffective and devastating failures, causing immense harm especially to the poorer and vulnerable within societies." https://brownstone.org/articles/more-than-400-studies-on-the-failure-of-compulsory-covid-interventions

[26] https://off-guardian.org/2020/04/01/could-the-covid19-response-be-more-deadly-than-the-virus/

continue with minimal disruptions.[27] This is in keeping with the biblical example of quarantine, whereby those affected by the disease are isolated from the healthy (cf. Leviticus 13-15) as opposed to punishing and accusing the healthy. A massive study has since been released with devastating evidence against any significant benefit from lockdowns, while none can debate the untold harm.[28]

5. Surface Transmission: In the beginning of the pandemic, we were repeatedly told we could catch Covid from surfaces and that the virus could last on inanimate objects up to seven days. Many were wearing surgical gloves and power-washing their groceries every time they returned from the store. We now know that the primary means of transmission is through respiratory droplets. Even the Center for Disease Control (CDC) acknowledges that the chance of surface transmission is very low.[29] After all, a virus needs a living host. Yet how many people "followed the science" on this dictum?

6. Mask Masquerade: Throughout the Covid pandemic, the debate regarding wearing masks has raged on and has been nothing short of thermo-nuclear war at times. Yet a landmark study from Denmark with 4,860 participants, half masked and half unmasked, concluded that 1.8% or 42 of the masked subjects contracted Covid while 2.1% or 53 of the unmasked subjects caught Covid during the same time period.[30] Not a significant difference. This follows closely what Dr. Fauci himself said in the beginning

---

[27] https://www.westernjournal.com/graphs-sweden-never-shut-masked-libs-will-hate-results/ and https://www.outkick.com/locked-down-four-vaxd-israel-still-getting-crushed-by-covid-while-wide-open-sweden-soars/

[28] https://brownstone.org/articles/lockdowns-did-not-save-lives-concludes-meta-analysis/

[29] https://nypost.com/2021/04/05/low-risk-of-catching-covid-from-surfaces-new-cdc-guidelines/

[30] https://fee.org/articles/new-danish-study-finds-masks-don-t-protect-wearers-from-covid-infection/. As an interesting sidenote, in 2008 Dr. Fauci, along with three other colleagues, wrote a medical journal article comparing mitigative protocol approaches taken in the 1918 Spanish Flu pandemic with the Avian Flu outbreak of 2007. One of the conclusions drawn in the paper was that a high percentage of those who perished did so because of a secondary bacterial infection promoted by the wearing of cloth masks. All of which is reason to question the ongoing use of masks in this current pandemic https://journals.sagepub.com/doi/pdf/10.1177/003335490912400105.

of the pandemic: "When you're in the middle of an outbreak, wearing a mask might make people feel a little bit better, and it might even block a droplet. But it is not providing the perfect protection that people think that it is, and often there are unintended consequences; people keep fiddling with the mask and touching their face."[31] *The New England Journal of Medicine* concluded that unless one is wearing an N-95 mask properly fitted, then the value of wearing a cloth mask is primarily psychological.[32]

7. Super-Spreader Events: When the CDC was asked about whether one could contract Covid outside, their response was that there is a "less than 10% chance". The actual chance of catching Covid outside is less than 1%.[33] There is quite a disparity between 10% and less than 1%. The deception of the CDC can readily be seen here in their response. The sight of a person wearing a mask when all alone outside, or driving in their car, has become the icon of our insanity, a symbol of the kind of fear-driven, irrational society that lies produce. Recent US college football games lend credence to the less-than-1% statistic as they were thought to be super-spreader events because thousands of fans filled stadiums around the US on Fall Saturday afternoons. But the fears of filled stadiums serving as super-spreader events proved unfounded.[34]

8. False Positives: By now many, if not most, have had a PCR test to detect the presence of Covid-19. It is now widely known that the PCR test produces a high number of false positive results. The test essentially amplifies the presence of trace microscopic particles. Because this test works on the principle of cycle threshold, it is easy to process the culture at too high a cycle threshold and detect particles that are not infectious. The inventor of the PCR

---

[31] https://www.newswars.com/video-dr-fauci-admits-face-masks-ineffective-against-coronavirus/

[32] https://www.nejm.org/doi/pdf/10.1056/NEJMp2006372?articleTools=true; see also: https://brownstone.org/articles/facemasks-are-not-a-mere-inconvenience/; https://brownstone.org/articles/a-partial-list-of-the-myriad-abuses-that-facemasks-inflict-on-our-children/

[33] https://jonathanturley.org/2021/05/11/cdc-admits-that-it-miscalculated-the-risk-of-outdoor-covid-transmission/

[34] https://www.boston25news.com/news/health/new-study-shows-outdoor-football-games-dont-pose-superspreader-risk-covid-19/FZOYRV6NFRHYNMOKYGN346YXLQ/

test, Kary Mullis, who died prior to the pandemic, said in an interview in 1993 that the PCR test "is just a process that allows you to make a whole lot of something out of something. It doesn't tell you that you are sick, or that the thing that you ended up with was going to hurt you or anything like that."[35] All of which explains why Elon Musk was tested 4 times in one day which resulted in two positive results and two negatives.[36] Think of how this brings all the stats and data we have into question![37]

9. Asymptomatic Myth: The myth of asymptomatic spread as a driver of the pandemic has been disproven, even though it was one of the main pillars of the panic, lockdowns, and all manner of economic and social ruin.[38] Plus, the utopian lie of attaining a zero-Covid world has also come unravelled by now, even though it was heralded for over a year as the goal of all the severe regulations and restrictions.[39]

10. Vexing Vaccines: A whole book could be written on the vaccines that were created to combat Covid-19. What we now know 11 months into the current global vaccination program is that the efficacy of these vaccines can reduce the severity of the symptoms, but they do not confer immunity, nor do they prevent transmission.[40] According to the *British Medical Journal* the

---

[35] https://off-guardian.org/2020/10/05/pcr-inventor-it-doesnt-tell-you-that-you-are-sick/

[36] https://www.dailywire.com/news/elon-musk-i-got-a-covid-test-four-times-in-one-day-two-came-back-negative-two-came-back-positive

[37] The PCR test is unable to determine the variant one might have. The variant has to be genotyped in order to identify it: https://www.citizensjournal.us/bombshell-pcr-tests-cant-identify-delta-variant-its-all-fiction/?utm_source=rss&utm_medium=rss&utm_campaign=bombshell-pcr-tests-cant-identify-delta-variant-its-all-fiction

[38] https://www.pandata.org/are-asymptomatics-sick-until-proven-healthy/; https://www.pandata.org/a-critical-analysis-of-the-covid-response/; https://www.cnbc.com/2020/06/08/asymptomatic-coronavirus-patients-arent-spreading-new-infections-who-says.html

[39] https://www.pandata.org/elephants-in-the-room/; https://time.com/6104303/china-zero-covid/; https://timesofmalta.com/articles/view/the-zero-covid-myth-jean-karl-soler.890320

[40] Yet only a year ago, the experts boldly assured us otherwise: Bill Gates (30 July 2020 on "Influencers with Andy Serwer"): "During 2021 we should be able to manufacture a lot of vaccines, and that vaccine's key goal is to stop the transmission, to get the immunity levels up so that you can get almost no infection going on whatsoever." Gates again (28 Jan. 2021 on MSNBC): "Everyone who takes the vaccine is not just protecting themselves but reducing their

clinical trials of these vaccines were not designed to determine if they even limit transmission.[41]

Because these vaccines were rushed to market, there is no way to evaluate their medium to long-term effects or safety until sufficient time has elapsed. That has not stopped those promoting the vaccine from assuring everyone that these vaccines are "safe".[42] But if the data from the CDC's Vaccine Adverse Effects Reporting System (VAERS) and the European Medicines Agency Data (EMAD) is anything to go by, one would be justified in asking whether these vaccines are safe or not: Based on current VAERS data some 18,853 deaths are attributed to the vaccine in the US since the vaccine rollout.[43] And according to the EMAD, some 30,551 fatalities have been recorded in Europe.[44] This does not include serious life-altering injuries and less severe effects.[45]

---

transmission to other people and allowing society to get back to normal." Dr. Rochelle Walensky (Head of CDC, on 29 Mar. 2021 on MSNBC): "We can kind of almost see the end. Our data from the CDC today suggests that vaccinated people do not carry the virus, don't get sick…." Rachel Maddow (on 29 Mar. 2021 on her show on MSNBC): "Now we know that the vaccines work well enough, that the virus stops with every vaccinated person. The vaccinated person gets exposed to the virus, the virus does not infect them, the virus cannot then use that person to go anywhere else. …It cannot use a vaccinated person as a host to go get more people. That means the vaccines will get us to the end of this." Dr. Monica Gandhi (UCSF Infectious Disease Expert, on 30 Mar. 2021 on on NBC Bay Area), "Essentially, vaccines block you from getting and giving the virus." President Biden (13 May 2021 at the White House on C-SPAN): "Fully vaccinated people are at a very, very low risk of getting Covid-19. Therefore, if you've been fully vaccinated, you no longer need to wear a mask." Dr. Fauci (17 May 2021 on MSNBC): "When people are fully vaccinated, they can feel safe that they are not going to get infected." (https://youtu.be/K8n9GpftejE, Dave Rubin Report).

[41] https://www.bmj.com/content/371/bmj.m4037

[42] A recent whistleblower who worked for one of the labs contracted by Pfizer for their clinical trials alleges that the lab in question is guilty of data tampering affecting the integrity of the data: https://science.thewire.in/the-sciences/company-that-managed-pfizer-vaccine-trial-sites-falsified-data-whistleblower/

[43] https://childrenshealthdefense.org/defender/vaers-cdc-injuries-covid-vaccines-fda-pfizer-moderna-bosters/
https://thepulse.one/2021/11/25/pfizer-was-aware-of-over-50k-serious-covid-vaccine-reactions-with-months-of-distribution/

[44] https://www.thegatewaypundit.com/2021/11/european-medicines-agency-data-shows-1163356-adverse-drug-reactions-30551-fatalities-covid-19-vaccinations/

[45] In the 1976 Swine Flu epidemic, a vaccine was rushed to market and some 45 million people in the US were vaccinated before the vaccine effort was halted because 25 people died and there 500 cases of Guillain-Barre syndrome diagnosed. My how things have changed:

From a Christian perspective, the decision to vaccinate or not to vaccinate is a personal soul liberty issue predicated on an informed conscience (cf. Romans 14:5). No one has ever asked me if I have had the flu shot, or any other shot for that matter. Yet I have lost count of how many times I have been asked in the last year whether I have had the Covid vaccine. This should be an individual decision one makes between their doctor and God. If the vaccine is as effective as some pretend, it would not matter whether someone else has been vaccinated or not, because immunity would prevail for those who have been vaxxed.[46] But this is not the case with the Covid vaccine.[47]

11. Natural Immunity: One missing element in the current Covid discussions by the media and so-called "experts" has been the issue of natural immunity for those who have already had Covid.[48] The headlines regarding this are conspicuous by their absence. The one-size-fits-all approach of the vaccine has conveniently omitted the efficacy of natural immunity from the discussion. This underscores that it is not always what is said that counts, but what is left unsaid. And the silence on natural immunity has been deafening. There are number of studies out on this now. The Israeli study is probably the most quoted.[49] The Israeli study indicates that natural immunity is at least 13 times more effective than the vaccine. But the gatekeepers of all things Covid ignore, evade, dismiss, deflect, and otherwise deny this. Why?

---

https://www.latimes.com/archives/la-xpm-2009-apr-27-sci-swine-history27-story.html; https://www.biznews.com/thought-leaders/2021/09/15/vaccine-deaths/amp; https://www.pandata.org/wp-content/uploads/EP-Petition-25_01_2021.pdf

[46] At this writing, 4th wave cases of COVID are surging across Europe even though Europe has a very high percentage of fully vaccinated people: https://www.zerohedge.com/covid-19/despite-vaccine-passport-schemes-covid-cases-surging-across-europe; https://www.biznews.com/thought-leaders/2021/09/13/mandatory-vaccination-panda (proving there is no rational basis for vaccine mandates)

[47] "Covid-19 injections are experimental therapies being deployed under emergency use authorisation (EUA). They are not fully approved by any regulatory body and have not undergone the complete review process required for full approval. All individuals have certain inalienable rights: informed consent and bodily autonomy being two of them." https://www.pandata.org/wp-content/uploads/PANDA_Informed-Consent.pdf; see also: https://www.aier.org/article/on-skepticism-of-covid-19-vaccines/

[48] The CDC is not even keeping any records of natural immunity: https://redstate.com/bonchie/2021/11/11/the-cdc-gives-the-entire-game-away-on-covid-19-natural-immunity-n474019?fr=operanews

[49] https://www.citizensjournal.us/this-ends-the-debate-israeli-study-shows-natural-immunity-13x-more-effective-than-vaccines-at-stopping-delta/

All of this is enough to justify a fair degree of scepticism where Covid and the regulations and protocols surrounding Covid are concerned. Science by its very nature is meant to engender scepticism and vigorous debate to move forward. But as things stand now, no debate or questioning is allowed.[50] This makes it difficult to "follow the science" because science is being denied and replaced with scientism (a worldview that infuses science with politics).[51] Instead, lies, deceptions, cherry-picked data, and hyperbole have been the order of day.[52] All of which is enough to convince many of us that there is something sinister going on with globalists exploiting a public health crisis for their own agenda.[53][54]

Omicron Arrives

As this is being written, a new variant has just been discovered here in South Africa. The media are making much out of this and already using it to promote more vaccination while talks have already begun to consider escalating lockdown levels over Christmas.[55] Given the lies and half-truths we have already observed, why should we believe them now? It is like the boy who cried wolf. This new variant may prove to be more transmissible but not necessarily more lethal. Yet, it will not be portrayed that way. It is not even known if the current vaccine, based on last year's virus, will have any

---

[50] https://www.pandata.org/wp-content/uploads/PANDA-COVID-and-the-Clash-of-Ideologies-withnotes.pdf

[51] Science is meant to be a method, not a dogma. Sadly, much that is labeled "science" is political science dressed up as science. https://fee.org/articles/the-author-who-warned-us-against-blindly-trusting-the-science/

[52] This article helpfully categorizes and lists various articles and studies related to many of the key Covid issues that are obfuscated and conveniently omitted from the prevailing narrative: https://www.zerohedge.com/covid-19/30-facts-you-need-know-covid-cribsheet

[53] On May 11, Fauci testified before a Senate Committee that "the NIH (National Institute of Health) has not ever and does not now fund gain-of-function research in the Wuhan Institute of Virology." On October 20, NIH wrote they funded an experiment at the Wuhan lab testing if "spike proteins from naturally occurring bat coronaviruses circulating in China were capable of binding to the human ACE2 receptor in a mouse model." That is gain-of-function research.

[54] "This really has nothing to do with vaccines or vaccine safety, or vaccine mis/disinformation. It certainly has nothing to do with a commitment to truth. This is about money and power. Or money as an aspect of power. And it certainly has everything to do with totalitarianism and mass formation psychosis."
https://rwmalonemd.substack.com/p/regarding-the-defense-medical-epidemiological

[55] https://www.bbc.com/news/world-59438723

impact on the new variant dubbed Omicron.[56] This will not stop authorities from using this to promote more vaccination though, or the escalation of lockdown levels replete with travel restrictions.[57]

It was Nietzsche who once said, "I am not upset because you lied to me, I am upset because now I can't believe you." This is precisely what many think where Covid is concerned. It is hard to believe anything one hears in the mainline press or governmental panels on Covid or the vaccine because they are now too invested in the lies and deception.[58]

Recently, esteemed South African journalist and author, Brian Pottinger, concluded:

> *Virtually all the scientific certainties initially established with papal infallibility by the architects of the panicked health response to Covid-19 have been challenged, repudiated or ridiculed by subsequent measured and evidence-based science.*[59]

Christians of all people should be those leading the way and seeking to recover the truth that has "stumbled in the streets", not falling for the lies and closing their church doors. We should be thinking critically and discerning the times as the Day of Christ dawns, while living out our salvation in both

---

[56] Very little is known about this variant at this stage, but this has not stopped those eager to weaponize this variant to promote more fear and uncertainty. See: https://brownstone.org/articles/are-we-overreacting-to-omicron/amp/

[57] https://dailyfriend.co.za/2021/11/28/disgraceful-travel-bans-achieve-nothing-but-poverty-and-despair/?fbclid=IwAR0e4UTzOP2TUf73tLmD_Jls8dQI6X3cyOowUuMSFHbD-z3VVSro3yO-gT8; https://businesstech.co.za/news/business/542186/the-areas-services-and-businesses-that-could-require-mandatory-vaccines-in-south-africa/ https://malone.substack.com/p/overton-window

[58] See also: *The Great Covid Panic: What Happened, Why, and What To Do Next,* by Paul Frijters, Gigi Foster, and Michael Baker, which brings rigorous scholarship to all the issues central to the pandemic and the disastrous policy response, a book both comprehensive and intellectually devastating to the mainstream narrative; see also: https://www.pandata.org/who-decides-africas-health-learning-from-the-covid-19-disaster/

[59] https://www.biznews.com/thought-leaders/2022/02/01/trc-covid-19-narrative; https://www.smashwords.com/books/view/1063995; see also: https://thecitizenmedia.com/2021/01/04/perspectives-on-covid19-from-a-christian-epidemiologist/https://off-guardian.org2022/01/18/the-last-days-of-the-covidian-cult/; https://off-guardian.org/2021/09/22/30-facts-you-need-to-know-your-covid-cribsheet/

fear and trembling (Php. 2:12-13). Just as Solzhenitsyn admonished, "Our way must be: Never knowingly support lies!"[60] So let us expose the lies while living for Christ. In a Romans 1, truth-suppressing world, we are unashamed of the only gospel that saves! (Rom. 1:16-18)

UPDATE (February 2022)

One of the challenges of writing a chapter or book like this one, is that by the time one finishes the chapter, the information already needs updated. It has been a couple of months since the ink dried on this chapter. True to form, the evolving dynamics of COVID-19 have morphed as more information is now available.

A few weeks ago, the Omicron variant was just making its debut, and little was known about it. As this chapter originally intimated, Omicron did prove to be far more transmissive but significantly less lethal. The following bullet points serve as a partial update to the Omicron variant as well as other COVID aspects mentioned in this chapter:

- Omicron has proven to be significantly milder than other strains of COVID. There are studies out of the UK indicating that the likelihood of hospitalization with Omicron is reduced by up to 70% over the Delta variant.[61]

- One would think this would be cause for a bit of good cheer, but the South African doctor, Angelique Coetzee, who discovered the variant in late November 2021, was reportedly pressured by European politicians not to publicize that Omicron was much milder than the previous Delta variant. *Evidence once again of political science trying to subvert empirical science.* [62]

---

[60] See further wise pastoral application here from David Debruyn: https://churcheswithoutchests.net/2021/11/16/living-with-an-endemic-3/

[61] https://www.bbc.com/news/health-59769969

[62] https://www.zerohedge.com/markets/they-will-not-silence-me-doctor-who-discovered-omicron-was-pressured-not-reveal-its-mild; see also https://www.aier.org/article/science-kardashians-vs-the-great-barrington-declaration/

- There has been a daily deluge of data and stats from the mainstream media related to hospitalizations and COVID mortality. What has not been widely reported is that a high percentage of hospitalizations are those who were hospitalized for some reason other than COVID and tested positive while in the hospital. These are then counted as "COVID hospitalizations". In the US, in the state of New York, recent data claims that some 43% of "COVID" patients were admitted for something other than COVID.[63]

- In London, 60% of all COVID admissions are classified as incidental, meaning they were not admitted for COVID.[64] Neither the media nor the politicians who take center stage on all things COVID are ever forthcoming about these distinctions. Once again, truth stumbles in the street. For this reason, some have warned about overinterpreting the data for the sake of a narrative.[65]

- As Omicron rapidly spread around the world, the issue of vaccination efficacy was discussed in the news *ad nauseum*. It now appears that vaccination status was not much of a deterrent for Omicron, as both vaccinated and unvaccinated alike as well as those previously infected with COVID, succumbed to the highly infectious Omicron variant. A recent article catalogues some of the worldwide stats of Omicron cases by percentages between the vaccinated and unvaccinated: In Canada 81% of all recent cases were fully vaccinated; In Germany 95% of all Omicron cases were fully vaccinated; In Israel — one of the highest vaccination rates in the world — 61% of the Omicron cases were boosted while another 18% were double jabbed; and in Denmark 89% of the cases were fully vaccinated.[66] While the vast majority of these cases were mild, it

---

[63] https://news.yahoo.com/data-york-differentiates-between-patients-213613061.html
[64] https://www.dailymail.co.uk/news/article-10422117/Up-60-Covid-patients-Londons-hospitals-not-primarily-treated-virus.html
[65] https://www.zerohedge.com/covid-19/uk-expert-warns-against-overinterpreting-covid-19-data.
[66] https://tennesseestar.com/2022/01/03/data-from-around-the-world-including-antarctica-show-omicron-favoring-the-fully-vaccinated/?fr=operanews

does not square with what Dr. Fauci said in the beginning of the vaccination process, "If you're vaccinated you won't get infected" and the vaccines "work well against all variants."[67] Is it any wonder that many are vaccine hesitant?[68]

- A recent meta-analysis study out of Johns Hopkins details the deleterious effects of the lockdown approach which has been one of the pillars of COVID protocols.[69] Their conclusion is that the carte blanche approach to lockdowns only reduced mortality by .2%, but the damage done by this one-size-fits-all protocol will reverberate throughout society for years to come resulting in untold health and mortality consequences. From day one of the pandemic, there were those, like Dr. Jay Bhattacharya from Stanford, who warned of the dangers of a wholesale-lockdown approach while advocating a more focused approach like that of Sweden.[70] It is little surprise though that the mainline media has completely ignored this landmark study.[71]

- When it comes to natural immunity, the media and the experts have completely ignored it, despite study after study strongly indicating the superiority of natural immunity when compared to the artificial immunity of the double-jabbed person. Until recently, the CDC did not have any data concerning this invisible elephant in the room. At long last though, the CDC's own medical journal concluded that natural immunity is six time better than being fully vaccinated and slightly less effective than someone who is boosted — understanding

---

[67] Ibid

[68] It is acknowledged that in a highly vaccinated country the majority of COVID cases will be breakthrough cases. Yet, the message only a year ago was that the vaccinated would not get infected nor would they be able transmit the virus.

[69] https://www.foxnews.com/us/lockdowns-reduced-covid-19-mortality-by-2-study-finds-lockdowns-should-be-rejected-out-of-hand?fbclid=IwAR2IEWLMZBxq00ZFksz858-3JjkAiEtyTA_E-dE6jpS7MeBNTAyYSD4rIds

[70] https://www.dailywire.com/news/what-happened-after-sweden-took-a-hands-off-approach-to-covid-19?fr=operanews

[71] https://www.dailymail.co.uk/news/article-10471265/Johns-Hopkins-professor-blasts-college-media-downplaying-study-COVID-lockdowns.html

that the boosted person's artificial immunity will quickly wane. Truly, natural immunity is the proverbial canary in the coal mine.[72]

- The media has been pejoratively mentioned several times in this chapter, but there is one positive to report. A Danish newspaper, *Ekstra Bladet,* publicly apologized to the Danish people for not questioning the government's hardline COVID stance. While this is a step in the right direction, I, for one, will not hold my breath waiting for the likes of major media outlets and Big Tech to cry *mea culpa*. Rather, we will see a gradual backing away from the narrative of the last two years while politicians and medical bureaucrats collectively pat themselves on the back celebrating the fact that they finally beat the dreaded pandemic.[73]

- Thanks to Omicron, the world is now much closer to herd immunity as this pandemic follows the historical pattern of past pandemics by transitioning to an endemic virus after two to three years. As this happens, those who are guilty of exaggerating and cherry picking the data and evidence will gradually alter their message to fit reality. Aspects of COVID that were deemed "misinformation" and "conspiratorial" only a few months ago, will now be heralded as fact and part and parcel of "following the science".[74]

---

[72] https://www.theepochtimes.com/natural-immunity-superior-to-vaccination-against-delta-virus-variant-study_4223936.html

[73] https://www.spectator.co.uk/article/-we-failed-denmark-s-media-is-finally-waking-up-to-its-pandemic-failings

[74] https://www.zerohedge.com/markets/natural-immunity-and-other-conspiracy-theories-have-magically-become-fact-checked

The False Narrative Behind the Fear: A deadly novel virus is sweeping the planet. It's spread by droplets and fomites. Nobody is immune and there is no treatment. Asymptomatic people are major drivers of disease. PCR tests diagnose COVID. So we have to lock down and wear masks until everyone is vaccinated. Variants will haunt us forever. Long COVID and reinfections are of concern. Those who challenges this narrative are a danger.

The Reality: A virus that presents high risk to few and negligible risk to most hit some regions. It's airborne, spreads by minute particles. Few are susceptible to severe disease. There are several available treatments. Asymptomatics are not major drivers of disease. Lockdowns and mask mandates, never recommended before, were tried. They haven't worked and caused great harm. Variants are not of concern. PCR test doesn't diagnose. Immunity is long lasting. The vulnerable were hurt instead of helped.[75]

[75] https://www.pandata.org/wp-content/uploads/PANDA-COVID-and-the-Clash-of-Ideologies-withnotes.pdf (from June 2021)

DR. ROBERT MALONE ON MASS PSYCHOSIS[76]

...What is the thing that bothers me the most? It's the lack of transparency and data manipulation apparently in the service of the idea that it's acceptable to minimize disclosure of risks associated with the vaccine product in order to minimize vaccine hesitancy. That concept of the noble lie, of the willingness of the government and government officials, to mislead the public by withholding information, has been weaponized using modern technology, media, censorship - really, let's call it what it is: thought control - in a way that was never possible before.

There is a whole cascade of actions here that just don't make sense if the primary driver is public health and saving lives. In dictatorships, obedience comes from a basic fear of the dictator. But, with totalitarianism, the people are hypnotized into obedience.

In psychological terms, this mass hypnosis is known as mass formation. And totalitarianism always starts with a mass formation inside the population. A mass formation requires 4 conditions to take root:

1. *The masses must feel alone and isolated.*
2. *Their lives must feel pointless and meaningless.*
3. *The masses must experience constant free-floating anxiety.*
4. *They must experience free floating frustration and aggression. These conditions were met in 2020 with the Covid lockdowns and the BLM riots.*

---

[76] https://malone.substack.com/p/the-noble-lie; https://malone.substack.com/p/mass-formation-psychosis

2
GIVE ME LIBERTY OR GIVE ME DEATH!
A Theology of Human Freedom (and a Biblical Case Against Coercion)
(November 2021)

Freedom At What Price?

I am willing to go to jail for not complying with the vaccine mandates, just as I also have stood against the mask mandates and bans on church services. How about you? What price do you put on human liberty for the glory of God and good of your neighbour? I pray this essay may help you in forming your own biblical convictions in these trying times, days of great opportunity to stand up for our Lord and in His strength alone.

The most blessed, prosperous, and generous nation history has ever known was birthed through the bravery of Christian men like Patrick Henry. It was 23 March, 1775, when this godly patriot and statesman closed his stirring speech to the Continental Congress with these words: "Is life so dear, or peace so sweet, as to be purchased at the price of chains and slavery? Forbid it, Almighty God! I know not what course others may take; but as for me, give me liberty or give me death!"[77]

---

[77] https://www.colonialwilliamsburg.org/learn/deep-dives/give-me-liberty-or-give-me-death/

Yet our society today asks: 'Is freedom really worth dying for? Why all the fuss about tyranny and coercion? This too shall pass.' Even Christians say, 'This all sounds so American. Shouldn't the Church just focus on the gospel, and not worry about our freedoms? Has the pulpit now become politicised?'[78]

Pastors ask, 'Is there even such a thing as a religious exemption from vaccine mandates? What legitimate grounds could there possibly be for a Christian to be a conscientious objector?' Sincere believers ask, 'Pastor, is it worth losing my job, or being kicked out of my school? How will I provide for my family?'

Statues of Liberty

It was France that gave to the USA the now 92-metre tall (30-story), 220-ton Statue of Liberty in gratitude for the global reach of freedom, with the famous plaque from poet Emma Lazarus (a Jew) that reads:

> *Give me your tired, your poor,*
> *Your huddled masses yearning to breathe free,*
> *The wretched refuse of your teeming shore.*
> *Send these, the homeless, tempest-tossed to me,*
> *I lift my lamp beside the golden door!*

Yet right here in South Africa, we have a smaller monument that makes a bigger, clearer statement about freedom than even Lady Liberty: the Huguenot monument in Franschoek, one of my favourite spots to visit (see cover of this book). It was built to commemorate those stalwart French Protestants who fled persecution and tyranny. This nation would not be what it is today without their contributions.

---

[78] See here for an excellent rebuttal to The Gospel Coalition Canada for not standing with the few Canadian pastors who've stood against tyranny and gone to jail for their faith, their flocks and for their country's freedom: https://trinitybiblechapel.ca/we-found-billy-a-blessing-of-persecution/

At the centre of this monument is a large marble statue of a woman atop a globe of the world. She wears no crown, for she is neither a queen or a goddess; she represents all humanity. In her right hand, she carries a broken chain, depicting freedom from bondage. In her left hand, she holds a Bible, the source of all freedom.

Behind her stand three very tall, white arches symbolising the triune God of our Christian faith, crowned at the top with a cross, symbolising the greatest liberation ever at Calvary. What a privilege for us to stand with this unnamed brave woman, with our Huguenot forefathers in the faith, and in a long line of godly defenders of human dignity and liberty.

Rightly do we sing here in our South African national anthem, originally a Xhosa Christian revival hymn:

> *Sound the call to come together*
> *And united we shall stand.*
> *Let us live and strive for freedom*
> *In South Africa our land!*

But do we mean those words, or is it just for a good feeling before the kick-off of a soccer or rugby match? Should Christians also (or especially) sing those words; and if so, why?

Vanishing Freedoms & Voice of the Church

Here we are watching our freedoms vanish almost by the day. In this era of Covid lockdowns, we've all been eyewitnesses to more attacks on freedom than the world has seen since Hitler and the Nazi Holocaust 80 years ago.[79] I agree with Dr. MacArthur and the pastoral staff at Grace Community Church who recently stated:

---

[79] Here are but three of hundreds of credible, empirical sources exposing and proving the Covid lies, propaganda and tyranny of the past two years: https://brownstone.org/articles/the-six-major-fails-of-anthony-fauci/; https://www.amazon.com/gp/product/0982456069; https://www.pandata.org/

> *We are convinced that governmental encroachment on basic human freedoms constitutes a more intimidating threat to individuals, a greater impediment to the work of the church, and a larger calamity for all of society than any pestilence or other natural disaster. These are difficult times, calling for a thoughtful, biblical, and wise response from church leaders and their congregations.*[80]

Part of a pastor's biblical duty is to "equip the saints" for serving Christ, which includes teaching them how to "love their neighbour", how to be "salt", "light", and "leaven" in society, "zealous for good works" (Matt. 5:13-16; 7:12; 13:33; 22:39; Tit. 2:14; 3:14). If the local church is to be "the pillar and support of the truth", centred on gospel proclamation, that includes *gospel application* to ethics and daily life (1 Tim. 3:15).

Preaching "the whole counsel of God" means not shrinking back from wherever God's Word must be applied to the issues of the day, proving the authority and sufficiency of Scripture for "training in righteousness", equipping believers to stand up for what is right in every realm of life (Acts 20:27; 2 Tim. 3:16-17). Whenever the church has shone the brightest, she has always had a prophetic voice into society, calling the "kings of the earth" to take heed and hear the word of the Lord (Ps. 2; Jer. 22:29, etc.)

Yet I am baffled and dismayed at how my generation of Christians and church leaders, in the name of being 'gospel-centred', has embraced worldly, secular, leftist attitudes that are more Marxist than Christian, that are anti-freedom, anti-patriotism, anti-human-dignity, and unethical altogether. We've become like a spoiled kid, fat and lazy from enjoying our blood-bought freedoms for so long; yet unwilling to pay a price to preserve them for future generations. Yet we're more than happy to emigrate to free countries to enjoy all those freedoms achieved and defended by others?

---

[80] https://www.gracechurch.org/news/posts/2254

Mission of the Church

Dear reader, please understand: This is a call for responsible Christian citizenship, not for political revolutionaries (What political party would we even align with in these tumultuous times in South Africa?!). Defending civil freedoms or humanitarian concerns *has never been and cannot become* the mission of a biblical church, or the message of our gospel, as we remain fixed on preaching "Christ and Him crucified" (1 Cor. 2:2; Col. 1:28-29; Rom. 1:16-17).

But upholding human dignity and freedom has always been *the fruit of the church and the result of the gospel's spread.* As the message of the cross powerfully saves souls, it transforms lives, homes and society, so that believers have proven to be the best of citizens, finest of neighbours, and most honest and hard-working employees, as we pray for our rulers "that we may lead a tranquil and quiet life in all godliness and dignity" (1 Tim. 2:1-4; "seeking the good of the city" in a pagan land, Jer. 29:4-7).

Aim of this Essay

Each church and believer may have different applications in how they stand up for human freedom; but if these principles are biblical, we cannot ignore them. What follows are *four battle cries for Christians to be champions of liberty in the face of tyranny*:

1. Freedom is from God
2. Freedom is Defined by God's Word
3. Freedom is a Treasure
4. Freedom is Fragile

Vaccine Disclaimer

This essay says almost nothing directly about vaccine mandates; yet it has a ton of indirect applications (and see this endnote for more).[81] My short, pastoral answer for those asking about vaccine mandates is: 'Yes, there is definitely a religious case for vaccine exemptions (see sample church letters in Appendices C&D). Inform your conscience biblically about the three spheres of authority, and the limitations of government authority, and the vital Christian doctrine of the liberty of conscience.' As my fellow pastor, Robin Brown, often says, "It is one thing to get vaxxed for medical reasons; it's a very different thing to get vaxxed to purchase your freedom. Be sure you know the difference."

In our church, we're thankfully aware of no conflicts among our people over vaccines (and we have people on both sides of the issue). In 2020 we already made clear to our people that we see vaccines in the same category as masks – an area of personal Christian liberty in the family sphere, outside of both church and government authority.[82]

Taking Thoughts Captive

The aim, however, of this essay, is not to give a short answer or a shallow response, but to lay some biblical and historic foundations. We are living

---

[81] https://founders.org/2021/08/13/vaccine-mandates-and-the-christians-liberty-of-conscience-from-2021-to-1721-and-back-again/; https://warrentondeclaration.com/; https://doctorsandscientistsdeclaration.org/; https://brownstone.org/articles/20-essential-studies-that-raise-grave-doubts-about-covid-19-vaccine-mandates/; https://brownstone.org/articles/this-is-not-a-pandemic-of-the-unvaccinated/?s=09; https://www.aier.org/article/resisting-tyranny-depends-on-the-courage-to-not-conform/; "If human nature and history teach anything, it is that civil liberties face grave risks when governments proclaim indefinite states of emergency." Quote taken from: https://www.standingforfreedom.com/2021/12/louisiana-judge-puts-nationwide-hold-on-healthcare-worker-vaccine-mandate-citing-grave-risks-to-civil-liberties. See also excellent sermon here, "The Church, the State and a Biblical Response to Vaccine Mandates": https://youtu.be/OVAiWOHQ4ac.

[82] See upcoming Essay #2 in this book. (Note: the government actually *does* have a God-given coercive "power of the sword" against evil; the problem comes when that power is misplaced and abused outside of their lawful realm.)

through a time of massive cultural upheaval and an onslaught of godless worldviews and deadly ideologies. If we do not recognise and refute these lies, "destroying" and "taking them captive to the obedience of Christ", they will keep shaping our instincts and our imaginations (2 Cor. 10:5).

We must "understand the times", renew our minds lest we conform, and plant our roots deep in a biblical worldview (1 Chron. 12:32; Eph. 4:14-16; Rom. 12:2). For example, the last 20 months have exposed our world's bondage to statism (state as god) and (safety is god).[83] Ideas have consequences, so we must win the battle at the level of beliefs, not just behaviour (Col. 2:8).

(1) FREEDOM IS FROM GOD.

Made in His Image

Historian Dean Curry notes, "The roots of tyranny are found in man's denial of God's transcendence."[84] If freedom is not from God, it must come from dictators, the state, or whomever claims to be all-powerful. Yet Scripture says otherwise. Listen to Genesis 1:26-28:

> *Then God said, "Let us make man in our image, after our likeness. And let them have dominion over the fish of the sea and over the birds of the heavens and over the livestock and over all the earth and over every creeping thing that creeps on the earth." So God created man in his own image, in the image of God he created him; male and female he created them. And God blessed them. And God said to them, "Be fruitful and multiply and fill the earth and subdue it, and have dominion over the fish of the sea and over the birds of the heavens and over every living thing that moves on the earth."*

---

[83] "Cowardice asks the question 'Is it safe?' Expediency asks the question 'Is it popular?' But conscience asks the question, 'Is it right?'" (Martin Luther-King Jr.)
[84] p. 143, *A World Without Tyranny*

To be human is to reflect God. That is why we speak of God's communicable attributes, those traits of His that are share-able, translatable to us. For example, "Be holy as I am holy" (Lev. 19). God is loving, He is good, He is just, He is wise, and so must we be. And God is also free, as are we, made in His likeness.

God's Freedom

Theologians for centuries have taught that freedom is one of God's attributes, that God does whatever He pleases according to His holy will. God is unconstrained and unrestrained by anything outside Himself. He is the most liberated and only being in the universe who is totally free: Psalm 115:3 (unlike the dead, enslaved idols), "Our God is in the heavens; He does whatever He pleases." Psalm 135:6, "Whatever the LORD pleases, He does, in heaven and in earth, in the seas and in all deeps." Daniel 4, "He does according to His will in the host of heaven, and among the inhabitants of earth; and no one can ward off His hand or say to Him, 'What have you done?'" (cf. Job. 42:2; Isa. 43:13; 45:9; Ps. 33:11; Prov. 21:1; Rom. 9)

God's freedom is infinite and inherent, as independent Creator. Our freedom, as dependent creatures, is finite, derived, relative and limited. Since the Fall, our freedom is depraved, corrupted, and badly damaged. But it is not erased. Fallen man is still made in God's image (Gen. 9:6). And we are still called to "rule, subdue" and cultivate the earth, as His vice-regents, with a subordinate authority under Him. That means God has entrusted humans with moral agency, the power and duty to bring about results on this earth and in our vocations to which He calls us.

Inalienable Rights[85]

Let's be clear: No human government bestows on people their rights or liberties. If rulers want to be blessed, they should recognise what God has already given mankind – inalienable, inherent, fixed rights as His sacred, unique image-bearers. If civil authorities want to be cursed, they will deny man those created, inalienable rights. Psalm 8 declares the royal, God-given dignity of humanity: "What is man that You are mindful of him? Yet you have made him a little lower than the angels, and crowned him with glory and honour, and made him ruler over creation…." There is no more dignified creature in the universe.

Not even the most beautiful plants or most adorable pets, not the most brilliant horse, dolphin or monkey – none of them can escape their plant/animal nature and instincts, to which they are held captive. They have no soul or conscience, which only mankind has been given as image-bearers of the Almighty. To bear God's likeness means volition and will, a freedom to choose.

Curry again points out it is no accident that the first freedom in America's Bill of Rights is the freedom of religion:

> *The Framers of American democracy realized that freedom of religion was basic to all other freedoms and therefore was the bedrock of democracy. …The right to freedom of conscience is premised not upon science, nor upon utility, nor upon pride of species. Rather it is premised upon the inviolable (God-given)*

---

[85] As the Declaration of Independence begins: "We hold these truths to be self-evident, that all men are created equal, that they are endowed by their Creator with certain unalienable Rights, that among these are Life, Liberty and the pursuit of Happiness. That to secure these rights, Governments are instituted among Men…." (July 4th, 1776). Is this more John Locke than Bible? Historian Glenn Sunshine answers that question and shows where we biblically can and cannot agree with Locke, plus the extent of his influence upon America's founding fathers, in this excellent book: https://www.amazon.com/Slaying-Leviathan-Government-Resistance-Christian/dp/195241072X/

> *dignity of the human person. It is the foundation of, and is integrally related to, all other rights and freedoms.*
>
> *...The inviolability of the conscience is the foundational right from which all others flow. ...Religious belief is an ever-present threat to the tyrant. ...continually reminding mankind that human power is less than ultimate.*[86]

Biblical Cultures

Vishal Mangalwadi is perhaps India's foremost Christian intellectual. He wrote, *The Book That Made Your World*, in which he describes how Israel's Exodus set them apart from all other nations, ancient peoples, and pagan worldviews:

> *[The Exodus] revealed that God was free. He was not limited by either the political or military might of Egypt, however oppressive or brutal. Nor was God limited by historical factors, oppressive armies, or insurmountable natural obstacles, such as the Red Sea. God was not part of the cosmic machine. He was free, and He wanted His children to be free like Him. Oppression and slavery were evils to be routed. They were evil because they were contrary to all that God had intended for the human beings made in His own image. ... Biblical cultures highly value freedom as the essence of God and of His image – humanity* (p. 337).

Or as Wayne Grudem states:

> *When human beings are deprived of their ability to make free choices by evil governments or by other circumstances, a significant part of their God-likeness is suppressed. It is not surprising that they will pay almost any price to regain their freedom. American revolutionary*

---

[86] pp. 150-51, *A World Without Tyranny*

> *Patrick Henry's cry, 'Give me liberty or give me death!' finds an echo deep within every soul created in the image of God.*[87]

Even secular voices see this sometimes. Jeffrey Tucker has been a reliable voice for decades in history and economics, and in the last two years an outspoken critic of Covid lockdowns and tyranny. Recently he wrote:

> *...Human beings will not be forced [forever] to live in cages and think only what our masters tell us to think. We are wired to be free, creative, and truth telling, and cannot abide by systems that attempt to stamp out all those instincts and instead treat us all like lab rats.... No, never.*
>
> *The crazy rules and practices governments and corporations adopted and imposed over the last 20 months will in time look ridiculous and embarrassing to nearly everyone. That we went along with such preposterous practices is a sad commentary on the human condition and its primitive ways.*[88]

Forgetting God, Forfeiting Freedom

Yet such observers are still limited by their secular, naturalistic worldview. What they fail to see is the spiritual root problem beneath all these bad fruits. "The fool says in his heart, 'There is no God.'", declares Psalm 14. Folly is always self-destructive, as Proverbs often describes (e.g., Prov. 13:20; 15:32; 18:7,9). *Once you deny who God is, you deny who man is* as His image-bearer.

Why then fight for human freedom if there's nothing unique about being human? If there's nothing sacred about human life, why should we not all be miserable slaves? *Everything starts with our view of God.* Psalm 36, "In Your light we see light". "God is light, in Him there is no darkness at all" (1

---

[87] pp. 217-18, *Systematic Theology*

[88] https://brownstone.org/articles/the-war-weve-lived-and-the-birth-of-the-new/

Jn. 1:5). But outside of God we find darkness – spiritually, morally and in every way.

Aleksandr Solzhenitsyn was perhaps the greatest defender of freedom in the 20th century, exposing the West to the evils of Soviet Communism (where he spent 8 years in their Gulag prison camps). Solzhenitsyn said:

> *More than half a century ago, while I was still a child, I recall hearing a number of older people offer the following explanation for the great disasters that had befallen Russia: Men have forgotten God; that's why all this has happened.*
>
> *Since then I have spent well-nigh fifty years working on the history of our Revolution; in the process I have read hundreds of books, collected hundreds of personal testimonies, and have already contributed eight volumes of my own toward the effort of clearing away the rubble left by that upheaval. But if I were asked today to formulate as concisely as possible the main cause of the ruinous Revolution that swallowed up some sixty million of our people, I could not put it more accurately than to repeat: Men have forgotten God; that's why all this has happened.*
>
> *What is more, the events of the Russian Revolution can only be understood now, at the end of the century, against the background of what has since occurred in the rest of the world. What emerges here is a process of universal significance. And if I were called upon to identify briefly the principal trait of the* entire *twentieth century, here too, I would be unable to find anything more precise and pithy than to repeat once again: Men have forgotten God.*[89]

[89] https://www.pravoslavie.ru/47643.html

Tyranny Down Under

Nations that remember God are free; nations that forget God are shackled and bound. "Only those who face up toward God can face down tyrants".[90] Look at what is happening today in some of the world's most secular nations (where many South Africans have emigrated): Australia and New Zealand, with their seemingly endless lockdowns and Covid regulations, and statism.

Purely because of supposed violations of 'public health' martial law, mothers are being pulled away from their own children, protestors shot at, employers threatened, and civilians tackled in the streets. Unvaccinated parliamentarians lose their voting rights. 'No jab, no job; no shot, no shopping' is now the slogan of the day. For not complying, individuals are fined $21,000 for each incident; businesses/churches are fined $110,000! What do you call people who need state permission to eat, travel, shop, worship, get haircut, go to gym, and live life? You call them slaves.

There's more tyranny in Australia: Once you are vaxxed, you must always check in with your QR code. All businesses are being recruited to join the state's total digital surveillance apparatus. Soon, all must use the EQR code for every purchase, for all trading, in order for the government to track all spending automatically, as further steps toward an Australian Digital ID system. This will provide an easy path toward Chinese-style social credits, tracking your carbon footprint to test your loyalty to the climate change cult.

After a mere two-day's notice, the Victoria state Premier has now been given permanent emergency powers. Children caught without a mask are fined $181.74 per offense; unmasked teens or adults are fined $726.97! Every business must have 'covid marshalls' to report any breach of the restrictions to a special hotline (Nazi-style snitchers).

Yet most Australians seem to comply, like sheep led to slaughter. Solzhenitsyn's words ring out once more: "men have forgotten God".

---

[90] https://dougwils.com/books-and-culture/s7-engaging-the-culture/aphorisms-on-liberty.html

Fascism and dictatorships always seem far-fetched at first, until you're in the middle of it, and then it's too late. It's called incrementalism, the 'frog in the kettle' syndrome, slowly and imperceptibly raising the temperature.[91]

As de Tocqueville warned Americans nearly 200 years ago, "Despotism may be able to do without faith, but freedom cannot. …When a people's religion is destroyed…then not only will they let their freedom be taken from them, but often they actually *hand it over themselves*."[92] By design, we are made to be worshippers; if we don't worship God, the state will replace Him as the next most powerful alternative.

(2) FREEDOM IS DEFINED BY GOD'S WORD.

Curry again states, "There is a direct relationship between biblical faith and democratic government, between Judeo-Christianity and human liberty."[93]

Obedient Freedom

Look back at Genesis, as Moses now zooms in on God's creation and command of man on Day 6:

> *The LORD God took the man and put him in the garden of Eden to work it and keep it. And the LORD God commanded the man, saying, "You may surely eat of every tree of the garden, but of the tree of the knowledge of good and evil you shall not eat, for in the day that you eat of it you shall surely die." ...And the man and his wife were both naked and were not ashamed* (vv. 15-17, 25).

---

[91] See also France: "[President] Macron does not get to decide that a person's medical decisions are irresponsible and that somehow a person's irresponsible decision means he can revoke their citizenship. No leader can unilaterally take away a person's citizenship — unless they are a dictator. ...authoritarianism, even in pursuit of some greater good, will always lead to increasing levels of force. And once the beast of dehumanization is unleashed, it cannot be constrained nor its course predicted." https://www.standingforfreedom.com/2022/01/liberte-egalite-fraterniteor-budding-reign-of-terror-frances-president-macron-says-the-unvaccinated-are-no-longer-citizens/

[92] https://xroads.virginia.edu/~Hyper/DETOC/1_ch17.htm

[93] p. 147, *A World Without Tyranny*

Adam and Eve were perfectly and joyfully free – emancipated to live all of life in obedience to their King, following His good and wise commands. Even before the Fall, human freedom was found in God's Word alone.[94] Inside God's revealed, stated boundaries, mankind was free, blessed and prosperous. Outside of God's Law was only cursing, bondage and death. That was the great lie of Satan: "you shall be like God", finding freedom outside of obedience to His Word (Gen. 3:1-7).

No wonder the entire Psalter begins as it does, 'How blessed is the man who does not walk…stand…sit with sinners. But his delight is in the law of the LORD…, whatever he does prospers. Not so the wicked...the way of the wicked will perish' (Psalm 1). Twice in the Book of James, God's Word is called, "the law of liberty", because *this Book liberates like no other book!* It is God's truth that spiritually transforms and unshackles you from sin's bondage. Who then in society should be bigger champions of human liberty, if not us, the people of the Book, whose entire faith is built upon this "royal" and "perfect law of liberty"?

Freed to Obey

Watch for this theme throughout Scripture, throughout history, and throughout your life: Obedience liberates; disobedience enslaves. Walking God's way brings freedom; walking any other way brings bondage. "I shall run the way of Your commandments, For You will enlarge my heart" (Ps. 119:32).

Why did God tell Moses to lead His people out of bondage in Egypt? "Tell Pharoah, 'Let My people go, *so that* they may serve Me" (Exod. 8:1; 9:1). On what basis did God give Israel His Ten Commandments? "I am the LORD your God, who brought you out of the land of Egypt, out of the house of slavery. You shall (x10)…." (Exod. 20). In other words, the Lord was

---

[94] "If we take the cultural mandate seriously, we understand that it necessitates liberty: economic liberty, political liberty, and religious liberty." https://pandrewsandlin.substack.com/p/creational-economics

saying, 'I am your King because I am your Redeemer. I freed you so that you will obey Me. You are redeemed for holiness, liberated for the sake of godliness.'

Otherwise, the Israelites would've just gone right back to their old ways as slaves for 400 years in Egypt; they'd just replace Egyptian tyrants with Hebrew ones. *'You can take the slave out of Egypt easier than you can take Egypt out of the slave.'*

A God-Centred Freedom

Want proof of how central God's Law was to defining human freedom? Those two tablets with His Ten Commandments (the summary of His entire Law) were written by "His own finger" (Exod. 31:18; Deut. 9:10). They were placed in the Ark of the Covenant and kept inside the tabernacle, inside the very Holy of Holies, under the mercy seat – all this at the centre of their nation wherever they went. God gave His people this constant, visual reminder that durable, lasting freedom is possibly only under the rule of God and the rule of His Law.

In the first place, why did Pharoah even care if the Jews just went away for a few days for a brief worship getaway in the desert? Because Pharoah knew what freedom meant; this pagan king knew more than some pastors today: "*Pharaoh instinctively knew that if Israel was set free to worship God, they would never be slaves again. True worship of the living God sets the captives free.*"[95] Everything starts with worship. "The fear of the LORD is the beginning of wisdom" and "of understanding" (Prov. 1:7; 9:10). Preserving freedom starts with religious liberty – the freedom to gather and worship the Source and Author of all freedom, the one true and living God.

---

[95] Toby Sumpter (https://www.christkirk.com/sermon/christian-basis-for-freedom/)

An Ordered Liberty

In the New Testament, God's Word continues to define freedom further: "having been freed from sin, you became slaves of righteousness. ...For the law of the Spirit of life in Christ Jesus has set you free from the law of sin and death", so that we might obey God's Law and walk in His Spirit, not in the flesh (Rom. 6:17; 8:2-4). Fact is that everyone is a slave; the only question is *whose slave are you*? Do you belong to sin's cruel mastery, or are you subject to Christ's gracious lordship, under His easy yoke (Matt. 11:28-30)?

America's founding fathers, in separating from the tyranny of King George III in England, made clear that this hard-won freedom was not a freedom for selfishness; it was an "ordered liberty", a lawful freedom under the authority of the Creator, King and Judge, the One to Whom we will answer for how we've stewarded these freedoms entrusted to us.

Paul further declares freedom's purpose in Galatians 5, "It was for freedom that Christ set us free; therefore keep standing firm and do not be subject again to a yoke of slavery... For you were called to freedom brethren; only do not turn your freedom into an opportunity for the flesh, but through love serve one another" (vv. 1,13). Or as Peter succinctly states, "Act as free men, and do not use your freedom as a covering for evil, but us it as bondslaves of God" (1 Pet. 2:17).

Free Indeed

"Freedom" is a battle cry for the Christian. Yet we must all beware, especially in these days of rising tyranny: If "freedom!" becomes our only watchword (our one-string guitar, the only drum we beat), detached from faith, love and obedience, or cut off from Christ and His cross, then we will be the next casualty in a long line of antinomian, lawless believers. Paul repeatedly warns us against selfishly abusing our liberties at the expense of others (1 Cor. 8-10; Rom. 14).

Jesus Himself put it most boldly, in light of the worst bondage of all, the captivity behind all other captivities: "Truly, truly I say to you, everyone who commits sin is a slave to sin. …If the Son makes you free, you will be free indeed" (Jn. 8:34,36). As Charles Wesley testified of his own conversion:

> *Long my imprisoned spirit lay*
> *Fast bound in sin and nature's night;*
> *Thine eye diffused a quickening ray,*
> *I woke, the dungeon flamed with light;*
> *My chains fell off, my heart was free,*
> *I rose, went forth, and followed Thee.*

It is imperative that we define freedom correctly. Our society uses the same word but smuggles in a new definition. God says "freedom" is about obeying Him; our world says, "freedom" is about satisfying self, as long as you don't 'harm anyone else'. These are polar opposite definitions. Scripture does not teach a freedom that exalts *personal autonomy* as the highest good; it says *personal virtue* and duty are the highest good. *Liberty is not to do as I please, but to do as God pleases.*

False Freedoms

We live in culture drowning in false freedom, thanks especially to Hollywood. For example, consider the demonic, false doctrines of Disney: "No right, no wrong, no rules for me I'm free. Let it go, let it go!" (from the movie, *Frozen*). The culture says freedom means: 'freedom of choice' to murder unborn babies; 'freedom of expression' to pursue every form of pornographic perversion and sexual immorality; 'freedom to marry' the same gender; 'freedom of identity' to indoctrinate children with LGBTQ lies, to restrict free speech, to cancel all dissent. Yet all these abuses of freedom should not silence Christians; it should make us all the more vocal in defending true human freedom.

John Adams (2nd president of USA), once warned: "Our Constitution was made only for a moral and religious people. It is wholly inadequate to the government of any other."[96] Or as another historian warned in 1805:

> *If this (bondage) should ever become the deplorable situation of the United States, let some unborn historian in a far distant day, detail the lapse, and hold up the contrast between a simple, virtuous, and free people, and a degenerate, servile race of beings, corrupted by wealth, effeminated by luxury, impoverished by licentiousness, and become the automatons of intoxicated ambition.*[97]

(3) FREEDOM IS A TREASURE.

Miguel de Cervantes (author of *Don Quixote*) famously said:

> *Liberty is one of the choicest gifts that Heaven hath bestowed upon man and exceeds in volume all the treasures which the earth contains within its bosom.... Liberty, as well as honor, man ought to preserve at the hazard of his life, for without it, life is insupportable.*[98]

Benjamin Franklin rightly warned, "Those who would give up essential liberty to purchase a little temporary safety, deserve neither liberty nor safety."[99] From painful experience and careful study, he knew what few today seem to recognise – freedom's inestimable value.

How God Views Bondage

Why did God appear at the burning bush and send Moses to rescue the Israelites? Yes, it was supremely for His glory and His great redemption

---

96 https://founders.archives.gov/documents/Adams/99-02-02-3102
97 https://theimaginativeconservative.org/2021/10/essence-freedom-bradley-birzer.html
98 https://www.gutenberg.org/cache/epub/996/pg996-images.html
99 https://oll.libertyfund.org/quote/benjamin-franklin-on-the-trade-off-between-essential-liberty-and-temporary-safety-1775

plan; but He also makes clear it was His compassion for His captive people in their misery: "I have surely seen the affliction of My people who are in Egypt, and have given heed to their cry because of their taskmasters, for I am aware of their sufferings" (Exod. 3:7). There was nothing desirable about human bondage.

In the Bible, slavery to tyrants is always a curse, never a blessing. Oppression signifies God's judgment, never His favour. The whole Book of Judges tells the story of repeated cycles of God's discipline upon His wayward people, handing them over to tyrants. Idolatry always brings bondage. Yet God hears the cries of the oppressed and delivers.

What is one of the most beloved Old Testament images for prizing human freedom? It is the glad prospect of "every man under his own vine and under his own fig tree" (1 Kgs 4:25; 2 Kgs 18:31; Isa. 36:16; Micah 4:4). The vine and the fig tree are means of sustenance, objects of ownership and work, signifying peace, prosperity – the blessings of liberty.

Human Responsibility

Personhood for us, as God's image-bearers, means choosing between right and wrong. "I have set before you life and death, blessing and curse. Therefore choose life!" (Deut. 30:19). "Choose you this day whom you will serve!" (Josh 24:15). Often our Lord Jesus invited people, 'Come to Me, Take and eat, Follow Me, Listen to Me!' (Matt. 11:28; Rev. 22:17, etc.). Our biblical convictions about the bondage of the will should underline human responsibility and dignity, not negate it.[100]

The Jubilee

Why did the prophets declare that Messiah would come? Isaiah makes clear (the first text Jesus' read aloud in the synagogue at outset of His public ministry): "The Spirit of the LORD is upon Me to…proclaim liberty/release

---

[100] https://www.gotquestions.org/free-will.html

to the captives…to set free those who are oppressed" (Isa. 61:1; Lk. 4:18). True, that promise is *not* about political, earthly freedom (we reject all forms of Liberation Theology). It is entirely about spiritual liberty of the heart from sin and guilt. Yet the obvious assumption is that liberty is good, slavery is bad.

When a desperate, impoverished Jew would sell themselves into slavery, what provision did our merciful God make? On both the 7th year and the 50th, they were liberated (Deut. 15:15; Lev. 25:42. For this reason, God called for the Jubilee declaration: "Proclaim liberty throughout all the land!" (Lev. 25:10). Those are the biblical words engraved on America's famous Liberty Bell in Philadelphia.

Defending Tyranny?

God outlawed all forms of slavery: "He who kidnaps a man, whether he sells him or he is found in his possession, shall surely be put to death" (Exod. 21:16). That meant stealing another person's autonomy/freedom through forcible enslavement was prohibited. The New Testament teaches the same, that it is against God's law to be a "slave-trader, man-stealer, kidnapper" (1 Tim. 1:10). Likewise, Paul wrote to converted slaves, "If you are able to become free, do that. You were bought with a price [Christ's own blood]; do not become slaves of men" (1 Cor. 7:21ff). God's Word never romanticises or minimises human slavery. *How then, in the name of being 'gospel-centred', did it become a virtue to speak out against human freedom and in defense of tyranny?*

Giving Up Which Freedoms?

We hear Christian leaders saying, 'Lockdowns, church bans, mask and vaccine mandates, these are all great opportunities to love our neighbour by *giving up our freedoms,* sacrificing our liberties for the greater good.' But no matter how nice and spiritual that sounds at first, it is a half-truth and a twisting of Scripture. Paul speaks about giving up personal opinions and religious preferences for the sake of the weaker brother, lest he violate his own conscience and injure his faith (1 Cor. 8-10; Rom. 14).

But that is not the same as giving up hard-won civic freedoms and the public good of my neighbour and of all society to become a doormat to dictators. There is nothing Christian about throwing away the cherished liberties we enjoy in the West that were birthed out of a biblical worldview.

Unlike in Bible times, we're reaping the rich fruits of centuries of Christian influence, for which we should be profoundly thankful, not cavalier and dismissive. For the love of God and country, my grandfather and my father bravely fought and risked their lives for freedom and against tyranny. I'm grateful for holidays that remind us of this, like Memorial Day and Veteran's Day, "lest we forget". I gladly sing patriotic hymns rooted in biblical truth, such as:

My country, 'tis of thee,
Sweet land of liberty,
Of thee I sing;
Land where my fathers died,
Land of the pilgrims' pride,
From ev'ry mountainside
Let freedom ring!

...Our fathers' God to Thee,
Author of liberty,
To Thee we sing.
Long may our land be bright,
With freedom's holy light,
Protect us by Thy might,
Great God our King.
(Samuel F. Smith, 1831)

True Neighbour-Love

In our church, we have numerous men who bravely served in our South African military service during the Border War of the 1970s and 80s against communism, securing freedoms we still enjoy today because of their sacrifice. Even if the enemy was mislabelled 'die swaart gevaar' ('the black danger') by a racist, apartheid government, 'die rooi gevaar' ('the red danger' of communism) was a true enemy and is today a greater threat to our world perhaps than ever before. I thank God for these valiant men who defended our treasured liberties.[101]

It is also an unbiblical redefining of love to suggest that we give up human rights in the name of Christian love. As one pastor well stated:

> *If we turn our heads or act with indifference when our neighbours are covered with the weight of tyranny or injustice, we are in fact hating our neighbours. If I am not jealous for their liberty, their freedom and protection, I hate my neighbour. Love for neighbour demands that we resist tyranny as an act of obedience to God* (Jeff Durbin).[102]

We praise God for faithful churches that have stood against tyranny and for true love of neighbour, such as Grace Life church in Edmonton, Canada. Their pastor, James Coates, went to jail for 35 days, because of this conviction:

> *We are gravely concerned that COVID-19 is being used to fundamentally alter society and strip us all of our civil liberties. By the time the so-called "pandemic" is over, if it is ever permitted to be over, Albertans will be utterly reliant on government, instead of*

[101] "These are the times that try men's souls; the summer soldier and the sunshine patriot will, in this crisis, shrink from the service of his country; but he that stands it now, deserves the love and thanks of man and woman." (Thomas Paine, 1776)

[102] Or D. Curry states, "The biblical injunction that we love our neighbor means that we cannot ignore modern tyranny." (p. 143, *A World Without Tyranny*)

> *free, prosperous, and independent. As such, we believe love for our neighbor demands that we exercise our civil liberties* (from their church website).

Upholding Human Freedom

The 8th Commandment is yet another biblical proof of God's commitment to human freedom: "You shall not steal" (Exod. 20:15; Deut. 5:19). Unlike Karl Marx (and socialists and communists), God believes in private property rights – in your freedom to earn, acquire and own. God and His prophets rebuke state thieves who trample on human freedom – such as King David taking another man's wife, or King Ahab stealing Naboth's vineyard (2 Sam. 11-12; 1 Kgs 21).

Grudem concludes:

> *Throughout the Bible, from the beginning of Genesis to the last chapter of Revelation, God honors and protects human freedom and human choice. Liberty is an essential component of our humanity. Any government that significantly denies people's liberty exerts a terribly dehumanizing influence on its people.*[103]

Hear the cry of the unvaccinated captives: "Hi, I'm a Canadian citizen. I haven't broken any laws, but I can't work, can't go to a restaurant/movie theatre, can't ski, can't take my kid to swimming or soccer; cannot leave my country, or fly within it, nor board a train or a ship. SOS!"[104]

This writer captures well freedom's priceless value:

---

[103] p. 92, *Politics According to the Bible.* Grudem also updates, develops and applies these arguments further in his superb book, *The Poverty of Nations: A Sustainable Solution* (2013, Crossway). Based on biblical principle and specific examples, Grudem spells out 21 different freedoms government should protect for a nation to prosper (pp. 259-307).

[104] https://twitter.com/truthwins_/status/1452477298414800904

> *Freedom matters—even in a pandemic. Without freedom, elderly people may spend their remaining time on earth isolated from their loved ones, and we know that social isolation kills. Without freedom, people may lose not only their livelihoods but the momentum and opportunity to build careers as flight attendants, orchestra musicians, chefs, or scientists working on viruses. Without freedom, children may lose important and irretrievable experiences and milestones. Without freedom, life becomes a shadow of itself.*[105]

Inner & Outer Freedom

Dear friends, there is a badly forgotten, much-needed truth in our day: *Inner freedom leads to outer freedom*. Spiritual liberation cannot stay there; it spills over into all of life. This is the story of the past 2,000 years, wherever the Bible has gone. This treasure of liberty has been Christianity's gift to the world!

British historian, Paul Johnson, wrote:

> *[Spiritual freedom in Christ] is the father of all other freedoms. For conscience is the enemy of tyranny and the compulsory society [that coerces].... The notions of political and economic freedom both spring from the Christian conscience as a historic force.*[106]

Puritan Thomas Brooks wrote, "What goes from a people when the gospel goes? Answer: peace, prosperity, safety, civil liberty, true glory, and soul-happiness, the presence of God (2 Chron. 13: 9; 15: 3, 5, 6; 1 Sam. 4: 22; Jer. 2: 11-13)".[107]

Curry reminds us:

---

[105] https://brownstone.org/articles/the-freedumb-fallacy/

[106] p. 516, *A History of Christianity*

[107] p. 9, *Smooth Stones From Ancient Brooks*

> *Throughout the long centuries of history, the twin tyrannies of oppression and poverty have been a normal part of the human experience. Just 300 years ago famines ravaged the world every generation, plagues were a regular occurrence, life expectancy in many countries was below thirty, there were no effective medicines, most people were illiterate, infant mortality rates exceeded 50 percent, and the average person spent most, if not all, that he had to provide food and shelter for himself and his family.*
>
> *Moreover, nearly all individuals lived their lives unprotected from the capricious acts of despotic rulers. Respect for the dignity and inviolability of human beings was – with the exception of England, and there only partially – institutionalized nowhere. The rule of law was arbitrary and often nonexistent. The concept of human rights was virtually unknown.*[108]

19th-century poet, James Russel Lowell, stated:

> *I challenge any skeptic to find a 10-square mile spot on this planet where they can live their lives in peace and safety and decency, where womanhood is honoured, where infancy and old age are revered, where they can educate their children, where the Gospel of Jesus Christ has not gone first to prepare the way. If they find such a place, then I would encourage them to emigrate [there] and proclaim their unbelief.*[109]

Freedom as Fruit of the Gospel

Mangalwadi writes of William Carey's missionary legacy, "India's freedom was a fruit of the gospel. ...Without the Bible's political ideas, Muslim emperors, Hindu militia, or European merchants would still be ruling

[108] pp. 143-44, *A World Without Tyranny*
[109] p. 330 in D. Noebel, *Understanding the Times*

India".[110] He contrasts this to the unbiblical, bloody freedoms trumpeted by the French Revolution:

> *Without the Bible, democracy became what Plato had condemned as the worst of all political systems. ...America, not France, became the beacon of liberty, precisely because it allowed the Bible to shape its cultural ethos. ...Only cultures founded on the Bible have viewed freedom as a virtue worth dying for.* ...[As another historian observes] *It is impossible to enslave mentally or socially a Bible-reading people.*[111]

As de Tocqueville famously stated in his classic, *Democracy in America*, "Despotism may be able to do without faith, but freedom cannot."

The Best Friend of Slaves

Here in South Africa, when was slavery finally abolished? In 1833, because of that heroic defender of freedom in England, Christian politician William Wilberforce. And 150 years later, what brought the end of the evils of Apartheid here in this land? Once again, significant Christian influence and prayer played a vital role.[112] During the American Civil War, it was an abolitionist hymnwriter, in defending the civil rights of black slaves and upholding human liberty and equality, who wrote "The Battle Hymn of the Republic":

> *As Christ died to make men holy,*
> *Let us die to make men free.*

---

[110] p. 351, *The Book That Made Your World*
[111] P. 337, ibid
[112] https://www.jubilee-centre.org/cambridge-papers/peacebuilding-ending-apartheid-jeremy-ive; https://www.amazon.com/Footprints-African-Sand-Life-Times-ebook/dp/B07NP6TDY5 (Michael Cassidy's autobiography); https://www.christianitytoday.com/ct/1994/august15/4t9019.html; https://www.amazon.com/Story-Church-South-Africa/dp/1839731583/ (Kevin Roy's excellent history of Christianity in S.Africa)

This divine gift of human freedom cannot be kept to ourselves. At the University of Stellenbosch in the 1990s, Wynoma Michaels was a PhD student and the first black woman to be student president. She said, 'although the Bible was abused, nothing else gave her people a greater sense of their own worth and meaning than the Good Book. It was the one book the slave-owner and slave shared in common; they both knew they stood under its authority as equals. …A great number of my people took the trouble to become literate for one supreme reason – to read the Bible.' And so Mangalwadi concludes: "Today the Bible is the chief factor in the opening of the African mind, just as it was the key to opening the Western mind."[113] Who can put a price on this treasure of freedom which God's Word brought to the modern world?[114]

(4) FREEDOM IS FRAGILE.

One defender of freedom wrote:

> *It is the common fate of the indolent to see their rights become a prey to the active. The condition upon which God hath given liberty to man is eternal vigilance; which condition if he break, servitude is at once the consequence of his crime and the punishment of his guilt.*[115]

Ronald Reagan stated:

> *Freedom is never more than one generation away from extinction. We didn't pass it to our children in the bloodstream. It must be fought for, protected, and handed on for them to do the same, or one day we will*

---

[113] p. 354, ibid

[114] "If liberty is to be preserved against the materialistic paternalism of the modern state, there must be something more than courts and legal guarantees; freedom must be written not merely in the constitution but in the people's heart. And it can be written in the heart, we believe, only as a result of the redeeming work of Christ." (J. Gresham Machen, *Selected Shorter Writings*)

[115] https://pacificlegal.org/eternal-vigilance-the-price-of-freedom/

spend our sunset years telling our children and our children's children what it was once like...where men were free.[116]

As Mohler points out on our immediate horizon:

...We're looking at a re-definition of the world order. That's what Vladimir Putin is pushing for. That's what Xi Jinping is pushing for as the dictator of China. ...Western elites, having separated themselves so much from the biblical understanding of sin, vastly over-estimate human goodness. They also vastly over-calculate just how committed other nations are to a certain kind of political agreement.

...John Quincy Adam's famously said that Americans "do not go abroad seeking monsters to destroy"; but we do need to understand we live in a world that increasingly is demonstrating the challenge of monsters who would destroy us and would destroy ordered liberty, constitutional government.[117]

Stewarding Freedom

These leaders are stating what the Bible said long ago, from our Lord Himself: "To whom much is given, much will be required" (Luke 12:48). As with all of God's gifts, if we don't steward them wisely, He will take them away. We live in a Romans 1 world of ingratitude and idolatry, "suppressing the truth in unrighteousness", being handed over by God Himself to all kinds of bondage (Rom. 1:18-32).

It is because of freedom's fragility that God's Word designates the separate spheres of authority, lest any sphere encroach upon the jurisdiction of

[116] https://www.reaganlibrary.gov/archives/speech/january-5-1967-inaugural-address-public-ceremony. Thomas Jefferson wrote, "Was the government to prescribe to us our medicine and diet, our bodies would be in such keeping as our souls are now (under tyranny)." (1785, *Notes on the State of Virginia*)

[117] https://albertmohler.com/2022/02/15/briefing-2-15-22

another.[118] History is replete with examples of the harm that comes from family dynasty's ruling church or state, or church empires ruling family and state, or today's iron-fisted state trampling over the rights of families and churches.[119]

Historian Dean Curry writes:

> *A biblically faithful, responsible Christian approach to international politics must start with a sensitivity to the evils of tyranny and an appreciation of the achievements of democratic government. God, through His grace, has given mankind the gift of freedom. It is our Christian responsibility to act as stewards of this gift.*[120]

As another historian rightly sobers us with the ongoing evils of North Korea, as testified by insiders who have escaped:

> *When [we] behave like devotees to bureaucrats and politicians, much can go wrong. North Koreans worship authority. ...to avoid further forfeiture of our liberties, we can recognize the warning signs of where the worship of authority mindset can lead us.*
>
> *...Today, many [people], including healthcare professionals, stifle their questions because to ask means they can 'no longer exist in their system.' Inquiry is being crushed and freedom is eroding. [This] 'soft' crushing of inquiry is far removed from North Korea's brutal totalitarian dystopia. Yet, lessons from North Korea are warning signs. Why would we go further down the path to hell on*

---

[118] See B. Laird, *Family, Government & Church: Relating Three Jurisdictions of Divinely Delegated Authority* (2021, Shepherd Press)

[119] "We must resist authoritarian impulses and exercises by various officials seeking to consolidate power and impose their will over the constitutional processes and guarantees we enjoy. Our Constitution was designed and ratified for exactly such challenges and it has endured 231 years through a myriad of challenges far more grave than a virus." https://www.gatestoneinstitute.org/17984/vaccines-and-power

[120] p. 152, *A World Without Tyranny*

earth when North Korea is a living example of the mindset that generates such a hell?[121]

Don't Kid Yourself

Solzhenitsyn often warned the apathetic, complacent free world in the West (looking on at the evils of communism): "There always is this fallacious belief: 'It would not be the same here; here such things are impossible.' Alas, all the evil of the twentieth century is possible everywhere on earth." It is not a virtue to be naïve; the Bible calls us to live soberly and temperately, unsurprised by any extent of human evil and depravity in this fallen world.

Hear this urgent and specific call to preserve our freedoms:

> *At the heart of any free society are institutions that support freedom and protect us from government tendencies toward tyranny. ... "We the People" are responsible for seeing that the government does not begin to serve itself instead of the people who have elected it. So, the people in a free society have a serious obligation to "keep the republic," to paraphrase Ben Franklin. We are responsible for living out our freedoms — and for exercising them.*
>
> *But usually, we do that best through institutions, like universities. ...To the extent universities have surrendered to corrosive* [anti-freedom] *forces and are increasingly unable to countenance ideas or voices or opinions that might push against the increasingly propagandistic shouting of the secular left, we should expect the same fruit as we have seen grow every time this has happened before.*
>
> *If ideas they consider "conservative" or "faith-based" are categorically and cavalierly demonized as "racist" or "bigoted"*

---

[121] https://www.aier.org/article/worshiping-authority-leads-to-tyranny-five-lessons-from-north-korea/

> *and disallowed, truth has already left the building, and murder and general tragedy cannot help but follow. If those of us in universities especially — but everywhere in our culture — do not fight heroically against the culturally Marxist stormtroopers around us, we will certainly not have the opportunity to fight tomorrow.*[122]

As society today moves increasingly leftward, inequality is now seen as the greatest threat, not tyranny. Good and evil are replaced by the new 'moral' categories of rich and poor (privileged and under-privileged) as the greater injustice. Thus, the highest goal for society is no longer, "liberty and justice for all", and creation of wealth from which all benefit. Instead, the chief aim is material equality and redistribution of wealth. This is the product of Marxist thinking, which has led to tyranny and poverty every single time.[123]

Protecting Individuals from the Herd

One historian gives this sobering description of how our liberties are under assault today:

> *...The great horrors of the 20th century, like Stalin's Holodomor, the Holocaust, and the Khmer Rouge's Cambodian genocide, were all rationalized by their perpetrators as necessary to achieve some alleged greater good. When the inalienable individual rights of the minority conflicted with an alleged greater good for the majority, inalienable rights were swept aside. The end justified the means.*
>
> *...Once society allowed the philosophy of utilitarianism to erode the ironclad protection of individual rights and freedoms, it was just a matter of time until some critical emergency would justify sweeping away individual human rights to achieve some alleged greater good.*

---

[122] https://www.standingforfreedom.com/2022/01/indoctrination-the-paved-road-to-deceit-and-death/

[123] See Dennis Prager, *Still the Best Hope* (2013, Broadside Books)

> *...Life, liberty, the pursuit of happiness, property rights, freedom of speech, limits on the power of government, universal human rights, etc., are principles designed to protect the individual from the herd.*
>
> *...Pop culture increasingly mirrors and reinforces this shift. Even the current batch of superhero movies reflect this. Most no longer follow the theme of "one against many" but have shifted instead to a team approach to solving problems. The lone warrior has been replaced by the team player. And it is not the individual that requires protection, but rather the entire herd or team because safety lies at the center of the collective, which must pull together for the greater good. We're all supposed to be in this together, so responsibility to protect the individual has been replaced by responsibility to protect the herd.*
>
> *...Even censorship, propaganda, and radical social engineering all begin to take on a moral veneer when they are justified as being for the good of the herd. The woke culture wars of today and the lockdown/COVID-Zero crowd have the same philosophical impulses as the ambitious social-engineers of the past, like Robespierre, Marx, Engels, Stalin, Hilter, Mao, and Castro, who also had no qualms about sacrificing truth, liberty, and even lives for the alleged good of the herd.*[124]

Conclusion

The more we are convinced of a biblical view of individual, inalienable human rights granted by God, and the more we appreciate our rich and costly heritage of freedom, the more we will hate tyranny and oppose it wherever we can. Even if your resistance looks different than mine. But if we don't treasure God's gift of freedom, there will be little or no resistance at all; it won't be worth the sacrifice.

---

[124] https://www.juliusruechel.com/2021/03/preparing-ground-for-mass-hysteria-what.html

[February 2022 update #1] Here's a recent, fine example of a Christian defence of civic freedom, from Lafayette, Indiana in the United States. Their City Council is proposing to ban all efforts at helping people to live out their God-given gender, something that the Christian gospel is all about - transformed lives (1 Cor. 6:9-11; 2 Cor. 5:17)! Faith Church is leading an effort among churches to protest this attack on religious freedom, which effectively outlaws biblical Christianity altogether. They declare, "The principles of religious freedom and the separation of church and state are cherished ideals which must never be surrendered."[125] And they have since won this battle![126]

[February 2022 update #2] Christians should also rejoice at God's common grace (and the fruit of Christian history) in how brave Canadian truckers have led the "Freedom Convoy", one of history's largest ever peaceful human rights protests, which is bearing fruit globally and bringing an end to unjust, divisive and oppressive mandates.[127] At one of the rally's, Dr. Julie Ponesse rightly stated of the lockdowns:

> *...our true moral failure is that we did this to ourselves. We allowed it. And some of us embraced it. We forgot for a while that freedom needs to be lived every day and that, some days, we need to fight for it. We forgot that, as Premier Brian Peckford said, "Even in the best of times we are only a heartbeat away from tyranny." We took our freedom for granted and now we are in danger of losing it.*

---

[125] https://www.freedomlafayette.org/

[126] https://www.freedomlafayette.org/post/a-big-win-for-the-integrity-of-christian-ministry-and-christian-families. Here's another positive initiative out of the UK: "Together, we represent more than 200 organisations, business groups, campaigners and professionals who have come together because we are gravely concerned about where the introduction of vaccine passports could lead. In the UK, we enjoy many hard-won liberties and rights, all fought for and defended by our ancestors. These rights are not only fundamental to our understanding of democracy, they are rights we believe all humans should have." (https://togetherdeclaration.org/)

[127] https://www.allisrael.com/freedom-convoy-expected-tomorrow-in-israeli-capital-in-support-and-inspiration-of-canadian-truckers; https://brownstone.org/articles/ending-mandates-does-not-strip-government-of-the-ability-to-do-this-again/; https://maybury.ca/the-reformed-physicist/2022/02/03/a-night-with-the-untouchables/; https://brownstone.org/articles/the-power-of-protest/

> *...The last two years will be remembered by our children as the most catastrophic moral failure of our generation. But I believe they will also be remembered as the time that woke a sleeping giant. And that giant is truth. The thing about the truth is, it's buoyant, it is lighter than lies and deception. It always rises to the top.*[128]

Not Escapists

As Christians, we know that Jesus said the world will get worse in these last days before His return (Matt. 24). Countless believers across history and around the world today have been imprisoned and martyred for the sake of Christ, with no earthly hope of preserving their freedoms. Yet they gladly suffered for their Lord, and so must we. During the great 7-year tribulation, by God's own design, Antichrist will brutally trample on every vestige of human rights and freedoms (Rev. 12-13). The world will at last unite under one ruler, and he will be the most evil tyrant history has ever known.

Yet Christ will then come and crush all His foes and usher in His kingdom of perfect righteousness, peace, and freedom. None of these prospects make us escapists in the present age or cancel our duty to love our neighbour and defend human rights wherever we can. We labour this day in light of that day to be found faithful when the King returns.

To answer the vital question of, 'What is the biblical role of government in protecting our freedoms (instead of trampling over them)?', see Essay #3 upcoming, and Appendix A. In the last two years no biblical text has been more misquoted and abused than Romans 13. Instead of being the standard Christian text for lawful submission to authority, it has become the favourite prooftext for capitulating to all forms of tyranny and evil.[129]

---

[128] https://brownstone.org/articles/five-freedoms-julie-ponesses-speech-to-the-trucker-convoy/
[129] I've also done a sermon on when and how Christians ought to resist evil: https://www.antiochbiblechurch.org.za/multimedia-archive/when-to-resist-evil-matt-539/; https://youtu.be/_9TyCkoMEUM

We need to remember a battle cry and biblical conviction of our Protestant forefathers, "Resistant to tyrants is obedience to God", as illustrated by the Hebrew midwives, Elijah, John the Baptist and our Lord Himself and the apostles (Exod. 1:17; 1 Kgs 18:17; Mk 6:18-29; Matt. 22:21; 26:64). But obedience to tyrants is disobedience to God (Acts 4:19-20; 5:29).[130]

Power of One

Don't underestimate the power of one brave voice willing to swim upstream, willing to live by conviction instead of coercion, one 'Athanasius Contra Mundum' with a Christlike face like flint (Isa. 50:7), willing to stand alone, like Luther against the entire Diet of Worms. All that it takes for evil to triumph is for good men to do nothing.

Choose now to refuse to live any longer by lies, but to live by truth and stand for freedom. Abraham Kuyper, Christian theologian and Prime Minister of the Netherlands (1901-05) said: "In any successful attack on freedom, the state can only be an accomplice. The chief culprit is the citizen who forgets his duty."[131]

Sophie Scholl was a 21-year-old Christian university student executed for leading a peaceful protest against Hitler. These were her last recorded words:

> *How can we expect righteousness to prevail when there is hardly anyone willing to give himself up individually to a righteous cause? Such a fine, sunny day, and I have to go, but what does my death matter, if through us, thousands of people are awakened and stirred to action?*[132]

[130] https://www.gracechurch.org/news/posts/2254

[131] https://www.cpjustice.org/public/page/content/2017_kuyper_lecture_remarks; another fine example of standing up for freedom at the local level, a small Christian university taking on the White House: https://adfmedia.org/case/college-ozarks-v-biden

[132] https://historicalsnaps.com/2018/02/11/the-last-words-of-sophie-scholl/; https://www.thegospelcoalition.org/article/75-years-ago-hans-sophie-scholl/

How would slavery or apartheid have ever ended if all the Christians, in the name of being 'gospel-centred', just stayed in hiding or submitted to unlawful and evil regulations? Can you not see how the last 20 months of mask mandates and now vax mandates fuel hatred, segregation, and discrimination? How could a Christian have anything to do with such evils?[133] Beware of the complicity of silence and indifference:

> *...You don't have to be any of those abominable scoundrels to be an enabler of tyranny. You simply need to hold your tongue. You simply need to look the other way. You simply need to turn a deaf ear. You simply need to stifle your gut feeling that something is profoundly, irrevocably wrong about every venomous lie, absurd policy, and malignant mandate that has bombarded the public since spring 2020.*
>
> *You simply need to live in fear. You simply need to cling to your ignorance. You simply need to follow the leader. You simply need to surrender to cowardice. Every act of collusion, every stain on your conscience, every bureaucratic compromise of your values etches an ineradicable scar into your soul.*[134]

---

[133] https://brownstone.org/articles/vaccine-passports-institutionalized-segregation/; https://slowtowrite.com/unvaccinated-people-are-not-the-virus/; "Vaccine passports will not be about health, vaccine passports are part of a financial transaction control grid that will absolutely end human liberty in the West." (https://twitter.com/WeAreTheNewz/status/1459795966094192644?s=09);

[134] https://off-guardian.org/2021/11/12/letter-to-a-colluder-stop-enabling-tyranny/. For a sobering, first-hand testimony of where Europe and the world are headed with medical apartheid and vaccine segregation, listen to this desperate Lithuanian citizen: "Covid Pass restrictions are being imposed throughout Europe. By my count, at least 14 European countries now have different types of domestic restrictions based on the Covid Pass. And every country has travel restrictions within Europe based on the Covid Pass. There hasn't been much reporting in English-language media about what has happened. ...Our freedom has become conditional on vaccination or daily testing. ...We're not unusual among the European countries in the apathy and lack of protest of the broad population. In the last 18 months, it's been rare in most of Europe to see massive, broad-based opposition to Covid measures. That's surprised me very much. It's staggering to me that large numbers of people, in my country and throughout Europe, don't seem to care much about individual rights and liberty. The contrast with recent history is stark. In my country, we were occupied for decades by the Soviet Union. We fought for - and won - a revolution of independence 30 years ago. Hundreds of thousands of people

As Martin Niemoller, one of the few brave pastors who confronted Nazi Germany (and was imprisoned), warned:

> *First they came for the socialists, and I did not speak out—because I was not a socialist. Then they came for the trade unionists, and I did not speak out— because I was not a trade unionist. Then they came for the Jews, and I did not speak out—because I was not a Jew. Then they came for me—and there was no one left to speak for me.*[135]

Without the influence of the Bible and Christianity, there would've been no William Wallace and no free Scotland. As the movie Braveheart portrays in that final battle:

> *I am William Wallace, and I see a whole army of my countrymen here in defiance of tyranny! You have come to fight as free men, and free men you are. What would you do with that freedom? Will you fight?*
>
> A voice cries out: '*Fight? Against that? No, we will run, and we will live.*' Wallace replies: *Aye, fight and you may die. Run and you'll live, at least a while. And dying in your beds many years from now, would you be willing to trade all the days from this day to that for one chance, just one chance to come back here and tell our enemies that they may take our lives, but they'll never take our freedom!*

---

took real risks to oppose the oppressive communist regime. In the most famous incident, in August 1989, 30% of the entire population of the Baltic states of Lithuania, Latvia, and Estonia joined hands to form a human chain of 675 kilometers in support of freedom and independence from the authoritarian Soviet occupation.

But now, three decades later, our current population is apathetic about losing freedoms which the previous generation fought for. Covid restrictions are introducing a more authoritarian form of government in Europe. …We love where we live. It's our home, our culture, our language, our nature. We're not important people, but we have deep roots in the area: both my family and my wife's family have lived here for hundreds of years. We're part of this place. We want to continue to raise our children here. We don't want to leave. So what will we do?..."("How recent vaccine mandate laws have upended my family's life" https://txti.es/covid-pass/images?fbclid=IwAR1fBxODjK1gS-Hofv0Y1x2EoaZmBk0aAAVOO76PiWbi-xtZh9OVfO5l0Po, complete with pictures also)

[135] https://encyclopedia.ushmm.org/content/en/article/martin-niemoeller-first-they-came-for-the-socialists

3
WHEN TO DISOBEY
A Theology of Resistance for Reluctant Protestants (Romans 13, Sphere-Sovereignty & the Lesser Magistrate)
(February 2021)

Hitler's Loyal Churches

In July 1933, during Hitler's first summer in power, a young German pastor named Joachim Hossenfelder preached a sermon in the towering Kaiser Wilhelm Memorial Church, Berlin's most important church. He used the words of Romans 13 to remind worshippers of the importance of obedience to those in authority. The church was all decked out with Nazi banners, its pews packed with the Nazi faithful and soldiers in uniform.

Earlier that same year, Friedrich Dibelius, a German bishop and one of the highest Protestant officials in the country, had also preached on Romans 13 to justify all the Nazi seizures of power and brutal policies, and misquoting Martin Luther himself about the supposed paramount powers of state authority.[136] Three days after this sermon, the German parliament dissolved, and Hitler took over. Within a few years, six million Jews had been slaughtered and the world devastated by World War Two.

---

[136] The dean of the Magdeburg Cathedral (of all places!) exulted in the Nazi flags prominently displayed in his church. "Whoever reviles this symbol of ours is reviling our Germany," he declared. "The swastika flags around the altar radiate hope—hope that the day is at last about to dawn." When German churches located near the railways would hear the cries of Jews being hauled off to the gas chambers, they were told to sing louder to drown out the distraction to their worship service. (https://www.christianitytoday.com/history/issues/issue-32/radical-resistance.html)

In the 1980s in Zimbabwe, notorious dictator Robert Mugabe smugly quoted Romans 13, making him untouchable in a 'Christian' country.[137] Speaking of the bloody Idi Amin era in Uganda, one African Christian author notes:

> *My own feeling is that the Ugandan Church, for all the magnificence of its courageous testimony once Amin's wrath was let loose on it, left its prophetic words of challenge and warning until too late. The same was true of Rwanda before the 1994 genocide. The Rwandan Church delayed its strong prophetic witness until it was too late.*[138]

Apartheid's Submissive Saints

Likewise, Romans 13 was a favourite text of presidents John Vorster and PW Botha here in South Africa to defend the evils of apartheid. Said Botha on Easter 1985 when addressing the Zion Christian Church masses of worshippers at their 'Mt. Moriah', quoting from Romans 13:

> *The Bible ... has a message for the governments and the governed of the world. Thus we read in Romans 13 that every person be subject to the governing authorities. There is no authority except from God. Rulers are not a terror to good conduct, but to bad conduct. Do what is good and you will receive the approval of the ruler. He is God's servant for your good.*

Rex Lex?

Recall that before the biblical clarity and bravery of our Protestant Reformers, for centuries the Dark Ages revolved around the great lie of the "divine right of kings" (i.e., 'Rex Lex', 'The King is Law'). Most of Europe at the time believed that if you were from the royal dynasty, God must have put you on that throne, and everyone obeys you, always and unconditionally.

---

[137] https://rumble.com/vsgqhk-the-failure-of-christians.html

[138] https://forsa.org.za/church-state-and-freedom-of-religion/

Because of this one deadly myth, the divine right of kings was used to justify the slaughter of countless innocent people and many of our Christian forefathers. Yes, God was sovereign. Yes, Christ was exalted through these faithful martyrs. But realise that many of these brutal kings and tyrannical monarchs eagerly quoted Romans 13 to justify a pagan, godless ideology.

Twisting Romans 13

One New Testament scholar writes that the misuse of Romans 13 has "caused more unhappiness and misery…than any other seven verses in the New Testament by the license they have given to tyrants…used to justify a host of horrendous abuses of individual human rights."[139]

But you say, 'Hitler's Holocaust and racist Apartheid have nothing to do with responding to a global pandemic!' To which the verdict of history answers: Both the Jews in Germany and blacks in South Africa were viewed as a threat to public health and national security (the "Swart Gevaar", the "black danger")[140]. 'Trust us,' said government tearfully, 'we truly have your best interests at heart. All we want to do is help, to keep you safe. Nothing more, we promise.'

Friends, do you realise? By legalising abortion, world governments kill more unborn babies in *one year* than all the lives Covid-19 would kill in 100 years at the current rate (always in the name of "women's *health*" and "reproductive *health*")! Already, by mid-January 2021, over *two million* babies have been murdered by these wonderful, loving governments that are so concerned about human safety and public health. Not to mention countries like here in South Africa, where violent crime is still rampant and out of control; yet suddenly our authorities have great zeal for protecting you and me?

[139] https://scholarship.law.stjohns.edu/cgi/viewcontent.cgi?article=5576&context=lawreview
[140] Jesus was no stranger to conflicts over hygiene protocols: Matt. 15:1-20. Listen to Jordan Peterson describes Hitler's obsession with hand-washing: https://youtu.be/XBu6xI1iUM0

Public Health & Safety?

William Pitt (famed Prime Minister of UK, friend of William Wilberforce) once wrote, "Necessity (i.e., 'public health, common good', etc.) is the plea of every infringement of human freedom. It is the argument of tyrants. It is the creed of slaves."[141] Get people afraid, and they'll do whatever you want. A fearful society will always comply; panicking people will believe anything.

During the gruesome and bloody days of the French Revolution, when 40,000 innocent citizens lost their heads, simply because a neighbour snitched on them – *who* was it that operated the guillotine day and night? It was run by the *Committee for Public Safety.* As Thomas Paine famously said, "The greatest tyrannies are always perpetuated in the name of the noblest causes."

In applying this warning to our times, theologian Owen Strachan recently wrote:

> *We need church. Embodied congregational worship of Christ is essential--in all seasons. Should we be wise, and thoughtful, and even careful? Yes we should.*
>
> *Wisdom is not the enemy of divine commands, however. We modern Christians may have many "options" regarding whether we go to church or not, but outside of serious health concerns (and even possibly including them on a case-by-case basis), we do not have the "option" of skipping congregational worship.*
>
> *Our society says this is so, but our society is subsuming an entire ideology under the banner of "public health," one of the least-explored and most-exploited concepts on planet earth today. When you hear that term "public health," your brain should switch on, and*

---

[141] https://www.oxfordreference.com/view/10.1093/acref/9780191826719.001.0001/q-oro-ed4-00008337. Likewise, C.S. Lewis wrote, "Of all the tyrannies, a tyranny sincerely expressed for the good of its victims may be the most oppressive." (*God in the Dock*). Montesquieu said, "There is no crueller tyranny than that which is perpetuated under the shield of law and in the name of justice."

you should examine very critically what you hear from that point forward.

Discernment Not Optional

At present here in South Africa, we're under our second total ban (in less than a year) on all worship services of any size or location. Yet Scripture commands us not to forsake "our own assembling together, as is the habit of some, but encouraging one another; and all the more as you see the day drawing near" (Heb. 10:24-25).[142] What then must the Christian do?

Discernment is not optional for Christians (Prov. 15:14; 18:15). God defines spiritual maturity as having our "senses trained to discern good and evil" (Heb. 5:14). Church leaders especially must be vigilant in "pointing out these things", as shepherds spotting the wolves, as watchmen on the wall warning of approaching danger, lest they have blood on their hands (1 Tim. 4:6; Acts 20:28-31; Ezek. 33).

Kings are called to "search out a matter"; they cannot be mentally lazy or driven emotionally more than rationally (Prov. 25:2; Prov. 2:1-6). This is why an elder must be "temperate, prudent, sober-minded", not swayed by anecdotes more than arguments, not shaped by circumstances more than solid convictions (1 Tim. 3:1-7; Tit. 1:5-9; Eph. 4:14; Jam. 1:6-8; 1 Cor. 15:58).

Like the noble sons of Issachar, we must "understand the times" (1 Chron. 12:32).[143] As God's Word warns, we must not be "taken captive through philosophy and empty deception", and must not "be conformed to this world, but transformed by the renewing of our minds" (Col. 2:8; Rom. 12:2; 2 Cor.

[142] See my sermon here explaining this further, "Why We Gather": https://youtu.be/8u8e7Z0FNvQ

[143] Samuel Adams, one of America's founding fathers, said, "It is in the interest of tyrants to reduce the people to ignorance and vice. For tyrants cannot live in any country where knowledge and virtue prevail."

10:3-5).[144] After all, our Puritan heroes and forefathers were known as Non-conformists, willing to swim upstream.[145]

No matter the cost, we must determine to "live not by lies",[146] but to stand for truth in every realm. That's because we serve a "God of truth" and are followers of Truth incarnate, our Lord Jesus who speaks to us in His "word of truth", by His "Spirit of truth", calling churches to be the "pillar and support of the truth".[147] To participate in lies is to deny our faith.[148]

---

[144] Here are a few proven, tested resources (websites and published books) challenging the mainstream Covid narrative and the bigger agendas at stake: https://swprs.org/ ; https://gbdeclaration.org/ ; https://www.pandata.org/ ; https://www.aier.org/article/whats-up-with-the-great-reset/; https://malone.substack.com/p/the-great-reset
The Price of Panic: How the Tyranny of Experts Turned a Pandemic Into a Catastrophe (https://read.amazon.com/kp/embed?asin=B087CLDWFB&preview=newtab&linkCode=kpe&ref_=cm_sw_r_kb_dp_bhNeGbFRYQQVD)
Liberty or Lockdown, by Jeffrey Tucker (https://read.amazon.com/kp/embed?asin=B08K7QFNK4&preview=newtab&linkCode=kpe&ref_=cm_sw_r_kb_dp_1vNeGbW5RM02Y)
Unreported Truths About Covid-19 & Lockdowns, by Alex Berenson (https://read.amazon.com/kp/embed?asin=B08QND25GL&preview=newtab&linkCode=kpe&ref_=cm_sw_r_kb_dp_XwNeGbF4JHNPH).

[145] A virtue that shines all the brighter against today's obsession with political correctness, Woke-ness, cancel culture, intolerance of dissent, Big Tech (Big Brother) censorship and assault on free speech. Much bigger attacks on the Church are rising on the horizon; the sooner we develop this muscle of godly resistance, the better.

[146] A famous line from the great Alexander Solzhenitsyn (after his 8 years of hard labour in the Soviet Gulags), in his last essay to the Russian people before exile, calling for an obstinate refusal to participate in deception at any level, never to "remain consciously a servant of falsehood": https://journals.sagepub.com/doi/pdf/10.1080/03064220408537357

[147] Ps. 31:5; 25:5; 86:11; Ps. 19:7-9; 119:160; Jn. 14:6; 16:13; 17:17; Eph. 1:13; 4:21; Col. 1:5; Jm. 1:18; 1 Tim. 3:15. When a society is in the grip of mass hysteria and media fear-mongering, the saints want to separate from this worldliness, not spreading panic or condoning tyranny. Some may conclude, 'For me, wearing a mask is "bearing false witness", "bearing a false report…following the masses in doing evil" (Exod. 20:16; 23:1-2; Rom. 14).' See here for exposing the lies of today's doomsayers: https://www.aier.org/article/seven-times-superspreader-events-were-overblown/ ; https://www.aier.org/article/the-times-wants-you-consumed-by-fear-isolation-and-misery/

[148] "If the irrational and freedom-destroying mandates of the secular authorities in America (and the rest of the West) force serious Christians to confront the question of whether a Christian must always obey the government, that will be one of the few good things to come out of the COVID-19 era." https://townhall.com/columnists/dennisprager/2022/02/15/covid19-and-the-failure-of-americas-major-religions-n2603293

Aim of this Essay

In this essay, let's explore *two biblical reasons for disobeying lesser authorities out of obedience to our highest authority, the Lord Jesus Christ*:

(1) Civil disobedience in light of the three biblical spheres of authority
(2) Civil disobedience in light of the right use of Romans 13

(1) THREE BIBLICAL SPHERES OF AUTHORITY

This must be our fundamental starting point in this discussion; otherwise, nothing makes sense: *God alone has absolute authority, none other, regardless of what they may claim.* Only the triune LORD has inherent, intrinsic, and undelegated authority; unlimited dominion, unconditional and unqualified rule and reign over all His creation and all His creatures, including humanity. God requires permission from no one (Matt. 28:18; Romans 13:1). As Abraham Kuyper famously said, "There's not a square inch in the whole domain of our human existence over which Christ, who is Sovereign over all, does not cry, 'Mine!'"

Our local association of churches, Sola5, holds to a number of excellent, biblically-grounded, historically-rooted Core Values. Of these, the 3rd value is called, "Authority"[149] Under our Almighty God and King, He has established *three spheres of human government and earthly authority/sovereignty.*[150]

---

[149] http://sola5.org/core-value-3-authority/; also introduced in Wayne Grudem's, *Systematic Theology* (pp. 891-893)

[150] Abraham Kuyper helped formulate these 3 spheres in his classic, *Lectures on Calvinism*; see here for a brief introduction: https://blog.emergingscholars.org/2014/09/sphere-sovereignty/ In our day, Joe Boot has defended these scriptural categories in light of the current threats to the Church and society: https://www.ezrainstitute.ca/resource-library/articles/freedom-the-church-and-state-absolutism/. See more in excursus at end of this Essay #3.

(a) The FAMILY Sphere of Authority

Sola5 states that this 1st and most foundational sphere "is for the upbringing and education of children, as well as for the nurturing of orderly human relationships in honour, discipline and love. The family is the basic unit of society (Eph. 5:22–6:4; Deut. 6:4–9)." The family symbol of authority is the *rod of correction*, the very thing being outlawed by godless state governments (Prov. 13:24; 22:15; 23:13-14).

Think of God's design for the family as, 'The Ministry of Health, Education and Welfare', as responsible for the care of both soul and body. From food, clothing and shelter, to curfews, beliefs, and choosing a spouse and career – never in Scripture are these tasks assigned to the state, but always to the family (Gen. 18:19; Deut. 6:7-9; 1 Cor. 7:36-38; Eph. 5:22-6:4; 1 Tim. 5:8),. Nowhere does the Bible hold secular governments responsible for universal healthcare. Always that is listed as a family duty first, and then secondarily a church duty in caring for her widows and orphans (1 Tim. 5:1-16; Jam. 1:26-27).

South African pastor, David deBruyn, warns of what happens when the state transgresses into the family sphere:

> *Governments now get voted into power by promising to oversee housing, education, medicine, the economy, a good currency, a minimum income, food, water, land, and the list goes on. The government becomes a parent, and the citizens are dependents. The government in this role becomes a monstrous juggernaut of bureaucracy, devouring taxes and trying to regulate every detail of life.*

(b) The CHURCH Sphere of Authority

Our Sola5 statement goes on to say, "Church government is for the spiritual well-being and ministry of God's people (1 Cor. 12:12-27; 1 Thess. 5:12-15; Heb. 13:7,17). The local church's God-given symbol of authority are the *keys of the kingdom* – admitting and excluding members based on the gospel of Christ alone. Consider God's design for the church as, 'The Ministry of the Word and Sacrament'. Scripture calls the church's main focus to be, not the care of bodies, but souls (Heb. 13:17). Only King Jesus gets to complete this sentence, 'You may worship if....'[151]

Spiritual Authority Crisis

Right now in churches around the world, a crisis of spiritual authority is occurring that is testing believers' understanding and application of this 2nd biblical sphere. Members are watching to see how their leaders handle Covid and lockdowns, and should keep praying much for them. God's Word is clear: "...be subject to your elders"; "Obey your leaders and submit to them, for they keep watch *over your souls* as those who will give an account" (1 Pet. 5:5; Heb. 13:17).

It is a sad day when the body of Christ is paying more attention to Caesar's fallible regulations than to Christ's infallible Book and the loving counsel of their spiritual leaders who know and care for them. God forbid that the biblical authority of pastors/elders in the church be circumvented by 'Covid officers' functioning more as agents of the state.

Duly appointed church leaders are God's legitimate authorities over the spiritual health of their flock, and all of their biblical instructions must be obeyed, whether one agrees with them or not. Of course members can appeal, clarify, and engage with their leaders; but mutiny or divisiveness is not an option (1 Thess. 5:12; Rom. 16:17; Eph. 4:1-6; Tit. 3:10-11). More than ever, believers need to turn off the media and sit at the feet of their own godly, wise, proven shepherds (1 Tim. 3:2; 2 Tim. 2:24-4:5).

---

[151] Here are two recent and definitive biblical statements of this position, from churches in two different countries: https://trinitybiblechapel.ca/here-we-stand-the-church-must-meet/ https://www.gty.org/library/blog/B200723 (See Appendix A; Grace Community Church elder's statement clearly limits a church's civil disobedience in a worship service to three areas of Caesar's present overreach: attendance caps; prohibiting singing; mandating social distancing.)

The flock are being bombarded by today's popular narratives; they urgently need to hear the calming, clear voice of their Good Shepherd through His appointed under-shepherds expounding His Word (John 10:16; 1 Pet. 5:1-4). Members can rest in knowing that, in the end, their leaders are the ones who will answer to Christ for how they've led the flock (John 20:15-19; Acts 20:28; Jam. 3:1).

No Trespassing

In terms of how the church sphere relates to the government sphere, esteemed theologian John Murray wrote:

> *The sphere of the church is distinct from that of the civil magistrate ... What needs to be appreciated now is that its sphere is co-ordinate with that of the state. The church is not subordinate to the state, nor is the state subordinate to the church. They are both subordinate to God, and to Christ in his mediatorial dominion as head over all things to his body the church. Both church and state are under obligation to recognize this subordination, and the corresponding co-ordination of their respective spheres of operation in the divine institution.*
>
> *Each must maintain and assert its autonomy in reference to the other and preserve its freedom from intrusion on the part of the other. ...when the civil magistrate trespasses the limits of his authority, it is incumbent upon the church to expose and condemn such a violation of his authority.*[152]

Ecclesiastical Pacifism

R.B. Kuiper's classic text, *The Glorious Body of Christ*, rings out with a biblical rebuke to his age and to ours:

---

152 John Murray, *Collected Writings*, 1:253-54

> *Our age is one of ecclesiastical pacifism. ...When a church ceases to be militant it also ceases to be a church of Jesus Christ. ...A truly militant church stands opposed to the world both without its walls and within. ...Time and again in its history the church has found it necessary to assert its sovereignty over against usurpations by the state.*

Kuiper then gives biblical examples – like when King Saul or King Uzziah usurped the priesthood (1 Sam. 13; 2 Chron. 26), stating, "...In both cases, a representative of the state was severely punished for encroaching upon the sovereignty of the church."

Rising Statism

Lord Macauley of England summed up the Puritan reputation this way: "*He bowed himself in the dust before his Maker; but he set his foot on the neck of his king.*" As Kuiper continues:

> *...Ours is an age of state totalitarianism. All over the world statism is [rising].... In consequence, in many lands the church finds itself utterly at the mercy of the state whose mercy often proves cruelty, while in others the notion is rapidly gaining ground that the church exists and operates by the state's permission.*
>
> *Now, if ever, is the time for the church to assert its sovereignty over against encroachments by the state. The church is in sacred duty bound to rise up in majesty and proclaim to the world that it enjoys freedom of worship, not by the grace of the state, but as a God-given right; and that it preaches the Word of God, not by the grace of human governments, but solely at the command of the sovereign God and its sovereign King, seated at God's right hand.*
>
> *...It must be admitted to the church's shame that it has often cowered before the state. ...those power-hungry potentates who neither fear God nor regard man but take counsel together against the Lord and*

> *His Anointed, saying, 'Let us break their bands asunder and cast away their cords from us' (Ps. 2), must be told by the church that He that sits in the heavens will laugh, that the Lord will have them in derision, and that if they fail to kiss the Son, He will break them with a rod of iron and dash them in pieces like a potter's vessel. Let the church speak sovereignly for the sovereign God and the 'blessed and only Potentate, the King of kings and Lord of lords' (1 Tim. 6:15).*

To which our churches give a thunderous reply, "Amen and amen!" I love the way one of my fellow Sola5 pastors in South Africa, Martin Drysdale, recently applied this from the pulpit to our state's ban on public worship:

> *If the gathering (ekklesia) is not gathering, and the assembly is not assembling, then the church is not churching. And in these times let us not be fooled by any argument that suggests that a church can exist as a digital entity of like-minded YouTube subscribers. Away with that unholy, unhelpful, unwholesome, unbiblical thought!*

(c) The STATE sphere of authority

We see government first established by God after the flood to institute the death penalty on murderers and establish the value of human life (Genesis 9:6). In the Old Testament we get to see God governing a nation directly through theocratic laws, judges and kings. In the New Testament the apostle Paul makes it clear that even a godless state is a servant of God and is sanctioned for a particular purpose. The main function of the state is to punish evil (Gen. 9:6; Rom. 13:1-7).

Sola5's Core Value #3 says of this civic realm, it "is for the well-ordering and protection of society; this includes the appropriate punishment of criminals (Rom. 13:1–7)." The state's symbol of authority, as Romans 13 makes clear, is "the sword", clearly a tool for punishing criminals (v. 4). The focus of the state is not the care of souls (as in the church), or both souls and bodies (as in the family), but is focused on the protection of bodies, specifically of the human rights of its citizens.

Contrasting Functions

In Scripture, the entire *modus-operandi* of the church and state stand in stark contrast to one another. As Paul Hartwig writes: "The State has a coercive and forceful function; the Church has a non-coercive and persuasive one." People attend worship services freely and voluntarily; people pay their taxes by necessity, right? In the church 'you ought to' is the motive; but in the State it is 'you must'.

This is why any compelling 'must' commands issued by the State over church affairs are an alien intrusion into the nature of the Church and contrary to how she functions. If the armed response came to your door and insisted that you should let them in to nurse your children, you would say, "No entry. Please stay outside and guard the property."

Their presence in your home would be a threat, as much as it is a blessing outside. In the same way, the government as a "servant of God for our good" (Rom. 13:4) may warn churches about a possible threat and appeal to us temporarily to cease congregating; but the government must not bring its sword into the church mandating when and how we will worship.

Unconditional Submission?

The key parallel text to Romans 13 is 1 Peter 2:13-17:

> *Submit yourselves for the Lord's sake to every human institution, whether to a king as the one in authority, or to governors as sent by him for the punishment of evildoers and the praise of those who do right. For such is the will of God that by doing right you may silence the ignorance of foolish men. Act as free men, and do not use your freedom as a covering for evil, but use it as bond slaves of God. Honour all men; love the brotherhood, fear God, honour the king.*

This passage calls us to godly civil *obedience* based on Christ's sinless, selfless example of trusting God and submitting to wicked and unjust rulers

(1 Peter 2:21-25).[153] *Christians must submit to legitimate rulers giving lawful commands whether they agree or not, or like it or not.* Even if we don't agree with the amount of taxation, we pay our taxes. Even if we don't like the speed limits, we follow them.[154]

Yet *unqualified* Christian obedience to government cannot be taught from texts which explicitly limit the boundaries of government authority and the extent of our submission. God Himself clearly restricts the role of government, not giving it unlimited authority: it acts "for the punishment of evildoers and the praise of those who do right" (1 Pet. 2:14). *When rulers reverse that, as often happens, by praising evildoers and punishing those who do right, they violate their delegated, God-given authority and transgress their divinely established boundaries and assigned jurisdiction.*

When to Disobey?

With the present Covid lockdowns, when governments are trampling over human rights and replacing rule by constitutional, parliamentary law with rule by martial law (emergency regulations) under a dubious and indefinite 'state of disaster' (a known tool for tyrants historically), it must be admitted this creates a number of ethical dilemmas for citizens, especially God-fearing, law-abiding Christians. When one's religion, livelihood, education, or human dignity are at stake, believers need much wisdom and courage (and must show great grace in) knowing when, and when not, to obey harmful dictates and unjust laws (e.g., lockdowns that destroy income; forced masking/vaccines, forbidden facial hair, anal swabs, etc.).[155]

---

[153] See an excellent essay here, *No Cover For Tyrants: 1 Peter 2:13-17 Explained*: https://read.amazon.com/kp/embed?asin=B00CIDHCXK&preview=newtab&linkCode=kpe&ref_=cm_sw_r_kb_dp_j-MeGbB0QWYKA

[154] Last year in our church small groups we did an excellent study by R.C. Sproul (free on-line) on the overall biblical and historic doctrines of civil obedience and civil disobedience: https://www.ligonier.org/learn/series/church_and_state/ James Montgomery Boice also has a helpful, brief summary chapter entitled, "Church and State" (pp. 688-699, *Foundations of the Christian Faith*)

[155] See #8 below under "Further Resources" for one church's response to the mask controversy, respecting both sides of the debate. See also Essay #4 in this book. George Orwell famously

We obey our rulers, not for their own sake or just because they said so; no, we submit "for the Lord's sake" (v. 13), out of obedience to a much higher authority, King Jesus. God has clearly put a hierarchy in place, and we dare not circumvent or reverse that. When an earthly authority clashes with our highest, majestic and supreme heavenly authority, we must disobey Caesar and obey Christ, every time.

A Whole-Bible Approach

We must be whole-Bible Christians and learn from godly examples. The Hebrew midwives were honoured by God when they disobeyed Pharaoh's command to kill all of the baby boys (Exod. 1). We see Jonathan's nobility when he refuses to obey his father and kill David (1 Sam. 20). David refused to turn himself in, trusting God's promise (1 Sam. 19). Daniel kept praying, openly (Dan. 6). His three friends refused to bow (Dan. 3). Peter and John refused to stop preaching (Acts 5). If we can't obey government "in the Lord," we shouldn't obey. Passivity is not a virtue; protest is not always a vice. After all, we are *Protest-ants.*

This means we can make righteous appeals when we see authorities being unjust. We have record of the Apostle Paul twice appealing to his Roman citizenship, especially for the benefit of other believers and the churches he'd planted (Acts 16:37-38; 22:25-28).

Paul would be thrilled with the freedoms that Christians today enjoy in countries like South Africa. We are heirs of centuries of constitutional democracy built upon *Lex Rex* ('Law is King'), instead of the medieval idea

---

said in *1984*, his prophetic warning about the evils of statism/totalitarianism, "If you want a picture of the future, imagine a boot stamping on a human face – forever." Recall that our Protestant forefathers also disobeyed state authorities in matters not explicitly required/forbidden in Scripture – e.g., wearing of vestments, using the Book of Common Prayer, translating of Scripture, etc. Like Daniel praying three times a day before an open window (never commanded in Scripture; Dan. 6), our spiritual heroes resisted ungodly authority when it violated godly convictions that arose out of God's Word.
https://www.bloomberg.com/news/articles/2021-01-27/china-s-zero-tolerance-covid-approach-now-includes-anal-swabs

of the divine right of kings.[156] We are voting, involved citizens, not mere serfs and vassals. The highest human law of the land in South Africa is not a president, deputy minister, or disaster regulations; it is our Constitution, and to that we can rightly appeal.

Biting the Hand that Fed Us

It would be foolish and ungrateful for believers not to appreciate all the benefits we've received from these Judeo-Christian ideas and the price paid for these freedoms by our forefathers. Surely part of the Church being "salt and light" in society, and "loving our neighbour as ourselves", would be active participation in a democracy so that we are not responsible for allowing laws that punish good and reward evil to become entrenched (Matt. 5:12-14; 7:12).[157]

God is sovereign and Christ can build His Church under the worst of tyrants and fiercest of persecution; but that doesn't mean the consequences for the Church, missions and human dignity in those lands has not been devasting. Nor does it mean that we passively wait for South Africa to become the next North Korea or Venezuela, not doing all that we can to prevent it. It's been rightly said, "All that it takes for evil to triumph is for good men to do nothing."

Praise God for the brave Wilberforces of history whom God used in their vocation to overturn the global evil of slavery, and the faithful pastors like John Newton who equipped and encouraged Wilberforce to do so. Wilberforce's lifelong prayer was, "May I be the instrument of stopping such

---

[156] Written by the devout and renowned Scottish pastor, and saturated with biblical references defending the biblical view of limited government and rule of law: https://www.monergism.com/lex-rex-ebook. It was said that at the Westminster Assembly, that great original gathering of our Puritan forefathers and heroes, every single member had in hand of copy of Rutherford's *Lex Rex*.

[157] Wayne Grudem's fine work, *Politics According to the Bible*, grapples with many such questions.

a course of wickedness." As was rightly said about Wilberforce, "A private faith that does not act in the face of oppression is no faith at all."[158]

No Authority Outside Their Sphere

So we see from Romans 13 and 1 Peter 2 that God has given the government a specific sphere within which to function. It is ordained to punish evil and reward good. Christians are called to submit to the government only in the Lord. Obedience to these Scriptures protects us from both anarchy and tyranny.

In other words, outside of their own sphere, rulers have no authority. The state needs no permission from the church or family to perform its tasks (elect officials, go to war, punish crime, etc.). The family needs no permission from the church or state to do its God-given job of raising and caring for the bodies and souls of that household. Speeches from a head of state are not "family meetings"; they are speeches. Likewise, the church needs no permission from the family or state to fulfil its role.

No King But Caesar?

What happens when one sphere swells, expands, overreaches and trespasses into another God-ordained realm? Here's a sobering example, when the Jews declared to Pilate, "We have no king but Caesar!" (Jn. 19:15). That is statism – idolising the state, dethroning the Lord, and exchanging the true God for the false god of civil government.[159]

---

[158] p. xiii, introduction by C. Colson to Wilberforce's classic, *A Practical View of Christianity*
[159] Here's another outcome of statism: "...There are all kinds of problems with mask mandates, but this seems to me to be the most serious of all: it reduces us all to what can only be described as *amorality*. We act a certain way just because we have been told that it is right, and for no other reason than that. This can only serve to enervate and infantilise us, and to cause our moral muscles to atrophy. We increasingly turn not to our own moral compasses but come to behave as though those moral compasses do not exist at all, other than in the hearts and minds of those who rule us. As a consequence, we come to rely, unreflectingly, on the decisions of our rulers, exercised purportedly on our behalf – a kind of moral outsourcing that

It is the opposite of Jesus' famous answer when asked about paying taxes: "Render to Caesar the things that are Caesar's, and to God the things that are God's" (Mark 12:17). In one brilliant statement, our Lord both legitimizes and limits the role of the State. As Doug Wilson states, "If you were to summarize the essential feature of Christian political thought in one phrase, it would be *limited government*."[160]

Limited Government

Because man is fallen and finite, his authority must always be bounded and restricted, never absolute. Only our thrice-holy God is not corrupted by universal power. All human authority (in all three spheres) is limited both vertically and horizontally: limited upwards by the Law of God; limited outwards by the boundaries and jurisdiction of the other two respective spheres, which may not be trespassed.

Why do we, as reformed evangelicals, when it comes to our view of secular governments, suddenly get theological amnesia and forget our doctrine of human sinfulness and total depravity (Rom. 1:18-3:19,23; Eph. 2:1-3; 4:17-19)? Why are we offended at any hint of godly suspicion about a ruler's abuse of authority or overreach? Yes, we are called to submit to their just laws; no, we are not called to trust them. That's why there should always be checks and balances on fallen human authority, the reason for the different branches of civil government in a democracy[161]. God's Word makes clear

---

will in the long run cause us to lose our willingness or capacity to make moral choices in the first place.

"Whether masks work, or don't work, in 'stopping the spread' is thus really beside the point. Nor is it the appropriate question to ask whether one should or should not wear one; it seems to me that either position is legitimate, and I certainly cast no aspersions towards those who choose to mask up. The real question we ought to be asking is: what do we lose when a government decides on our behalf what is morally right, and then forces that decision on us all?" https://www.aier.org/article/the-real-problem-with-mask-mandates/

[160] https://dougwils.com/books-and-culture/s7-engaging-the-culture/on-the-lookout-for-a-sane-lesser-magistrate.html

[161] "If the separation of powers meant anything to the Constitutional framers, it meant that the three necessary ingredients to deprive a person of liberty or property – the power to make rules, to enforce them, and to judge their violations – could never fall into the same hands. ...If the

what we should expect from earthly rulers in their lust for power (1 Sam. 8:11-18, what God says to expect from a king, "to take, take, take").

South African Illustration

Paul Hartwig again helps us here in our local context:

> *The State in South Africa (SA) is increasingly encroaching upon the integrity and autonomy of both the family and the Church. Our State wants to regulate practices in nuclear families (such as child-discipline, sexual values, etc.) and coerce the family to comply with its ideologies. The temporary legal banning of Church gatherings is characteristic of this trend of the State to overreach into realms not under its authority. There is much to convince us that our Government considers itself sovereign in regulating the behaviour of its citizens; and there little to gainsay the conclusion that it is fast moving in the direction of state absolutism.*
>
> *Many statutory principles and laws of the SA government give Christians every reason to question its morality and integrity, including the science it bases its practices on. If we consider our government's policies on the beginning of human life, natural gender identity, the nature of marriage and its views on sexual ethics, the Christian in SA finds the values of its government opposed to the teachings of Jesus Christ. Biblical churches believe that our State's position on these basic and fundamental matters is destructive to human society, and reveals an ignorance in knowing what is actually good for its citizens. The position of our government on these matters*

---

executive branch is allowed to usurp the power of the legislative branch to make laws, two of the three powers conferred by our Constitution would be in the same hands. If human nature and history teach anything, it is that civil liberties face grave risks when governments proclaim indefinite states of emergency." (Louisiana Western District U.S. Judge Terry Doughty, in his ruling against Biden's vax mandates: https://www.dailywire.com/news/breaking-another-federal-judge-deals-blow-to-bidens-vaccine-mandate-issues-nationwide-injunction)

> *makes any form of State interference in ecclesiastical matters all the more alarming.*

But you say, 'The Apostle Paul wrote Romans 13 under wicked Nero, a vicious tyrant; yet Christians were still called to submit and obey.' Great question, which brings us to our 2nd biblical reason for civil disobedience:

(2) RIGHT USE OF ROMANS 13

Romans 13:1-7 reads:

> *Every person is to be subject to the governing authorities. For there is no authority except from God, and those which exist are established by God. Therefore, whoever resists authority has opposed the ordinance of God; and they who have opposed will receive condemnation upon themselves. For rulers are not a cause of fear for good behaviour, but for evil. Do you want to have no fear of authority? Do what is good and you will have praise from the same; for it is a servant of God to you for good. But if you do what is evil, be afraid; for it does not bear the sword for nothing; for it is a servant of God, an avenger who brings wrath on the one who practices evil. Therefore it is necessary to be in subjection, not only because of wrath, but also for the sake of conscience. For because of this you also pay taxes, for rulers are servants of God, devoting themselves to this very thing. Pay to all what is due them: tax to whom tax is due; custom to whom custom; respect to whom respect; honour to whom honour.*

Let's ask *six key questions of Romans 13*, allowing the text to speak for itself:[162]

---

[162] See here for an excellent treatment, *Resistance to Tyrants: Romans 13 and the Christian Duty to Oppose Wicked Rulers*: https://read.amazon.com/kp/embed?asin=B00925ZP4U&preview=newtab&linkCode=kpe&ref_=cm_sw_r_kb_dp_VqMeGbMKJBE0Q

(a) ***Who is writing this text?***

Clearly it was penned by the Apostle Paul (Rom. 1:1), the same man who says earlier in this same epistle that for the Lord "we are being put to death all day long...considered as sheep to be slaughtered", i.e., executed by the state. Romans 13 is written by the same Paul who was publicly charged as a treasonous, seditious troublemaker and threat to the empire. The same Paul who got arrested countless times and wrote many of his epistles from state prison, in chains for his Lord (Eph. 3:1; 4:1; Php. 1:7,13-17; 2 Tim. 1:8,12,16; 2:9, imprisoned "as a criminal"). Clearly then, Paul wasn't writing Romans 13 thinking of absolute, unconditional submission to government.

(b) ***When was Paul writing?***

Scholarly consensus is that this is early in Nero's reign, before his persecutions began.[163] Contrast this to the Apostle John's view of civil government in Revelation 13, writing during Domitian's fierce persecution (about AD 90). John describes the beastly, demonic, evil and murderous character of pagan government in persecuting Christians (just as Daniel depicts in Dan. 7-8).

A whole-Bible view of politics requires both Romans 13 and Revelation 13 (and the rest of Scripture). On the one hand, when government is in line with God's will and fulfilling its purpose of rewarding the right, punishing the wrong and not clashing with God's Law, it must be obeyed. But when government rewards evil, punishes the right and requires us to disobey God, it has become a beastly tool of Satan and must be resisted. *Since when did Christians start asking the Beast for permission to gather and worship the Lamb?*

---

[163] Nero's persecution began about AD 64; Paul probably penned Romans around AD 57 (Moo, p. 3). That doesn't mean Paul was naïve about evil rulers and tyrants, like those that crucified our Lord; but it does imply that Paul, while writing Romans 13, was neither ignoring or condoning Nero's evil, nor any other injustices.

(c) ***What is Paul's point?***

In the wider context of Romans 12-15, it should be clear that Romans 13:1-7 is not about training Christians to be doormats to tyrants, sponsors for dictators, or agents of the state. Paul just told us to "abhor what is evil" (Rom. 12:9). Rather, this text is showing us how, in light of God's marvellous saving mercies (Romans 1-11), we must renew our minds, resist worldliness, and live transformed lives through our ordinary submission in the God-ordained civic realm, just as we must be "living sacrifices" worshipping Christ in every other realm (12:1-2, the over-arching mandate that introduces and frames all of chps 12-15).

Often in Scripture we see ungodly submission to authority, an obedience that dishonours God: Doeg the Edomite obeys the king to murder 85 priests (1 Sam. 22); Bathsheba obeyed the king to commit adultery with him, and Joab obeyed to murder her husband (2 Sam. 11); soldiers obeyed wicked rulers by putting the innocent, righteous ones into prison (1 Kgs 22; Matt. 26:55-27:66); Aaron obeyed the voice of the people with the golden calf (Exod. 32).[164] This kind of submission cannot be what Paul has in mind.

(d) ***To whom will all rulers give an account?***

Look back at our text and count how many times "God" appears. Six times it is emphasized that HE is the one who establishes governments and uses them as His "servants, deacons, ministers". They will answer to no less than the very One who sent them, who delegated His authority temporarily to them. Every last king and cop will give an account to the Almighty. No human authorities are ever absolute, no matter how powerful or terrifying. Ask Nebuchadnezzar what happened when he forgot that and had to learn about God's supremacy the hard way (Dan. 4)! As the saying goes, 'Rulers who don't fear God will try to be God.'

---

[164] See many more examples here: https://www.sonofcarey.com/?p=2727

John Gill comments on Romans 13:2, which seems to forbid any resistance to government:

> *This is not to be understood, as if magistrates were above the laws, and had a lawless power to do as they will without opposition; for they are under the law, and liable to the penalty of it, in case of disobedience, as others; and when they make their own will a law, or exercise a lawless tyrannical power, in defiance of the laws of God, and of the land, to the endangering of the lives, liberties, and properties of subjects, they may be resisted (1 Sam. 14:45). But Romans 13 prohibits resisting magistrates in the right discharge of their office.*[165]

(e) *Why has God appointed them to govern?*

Notice again, just as we saw in 1 Peter 2:14, so also in Romans 13, the text itself contains clear limitation clauses showing the God-ordained boundaries around the government's sphere of authority: "For rulers are not a cause of fear for good behaviour; but for evil…a minister of God for your good…an avenger who brings wrath on the one who practices evil" (vv. 3-4; cf. Ps. 101:8; Prov. 20:8; 29:4). Yes, these are descriptive clauses, not conditional ones; but still they put boundaries upon government authority. (Answering to what extent we submit to abusive authorities is not an easy question, nor the purpose of Paul's teaching in Romans 13:1-7; but this essay seeks at least to establish some biblical principles as a starting point for the discussion.)

---

[165] https://www.biblestudytools.com/commentaries/gills-exposition-of-the-bible/romans-13/; Cf. D. Moo, "all our subordinate 'submissions' must always be measured in relationship to our all-embracing submission to Him. …Our own sad experience of situations like the Holocaust during WWII suggests that genuine Christian devotion to God must sometimes require *disobedience* of the government. …Clearly, a willingness to resist the demands of secular rulers, when those conflict with the demand of the God we serve, is part of the 'transformation of life' which Paul speaks about in Rom. 12-15. …we should refuse to give to government any absolute rights and should evaluate all its demands in the light of the gospel." (pp. 797, 806-10, *Romans*, NICNT) Cf. Schreiner on Rom. 13, "This text is misunderstood if it is taken out of context and used as an absolute word so that Christians uncritically comply with the state no matter what…." (p. 687, *Romans*, BECNT).

God calls government to a focused, limited role of mainly criminal justice and protection of human rights, not universal parenting in a nanny state. As a friend of mine recently said, "When law-abiding citizens are more afraid of the police than criminals are, government is outside of its God-given role."

As Francis Schaeffer said in applying Romans 13:

> *The State is to be an agent of justice, to restrain evil by punishing wrongdoers, and to protect the good in society. When the State does the reverse, it has no proper authority. It is then a usurped authority and as such it becomes lawless and is tyranny.*[166]

Or as an older writer stated:

> *It is blasphemy to call tyrants and oppressors, God's ministers. They are more properly the messengers of Satan to buffet us. No rulers are properly God's ministers, but such as are just, ruling in the fear of God. When once magistrates act contrary to their office ... they immediately cease to be the ordinance and ministers of God and no more deserve that glorious character than common pirates and highwaymen.*[167]

Not Regulating Pizza Intake

As pastor Tom Buck sums up well the biblical limitations of government's role:

> *...The government is not responsible to ensure that everyone avoids death as long as possible. The government does not have the right to outlaw pizza, because consuming too much pizza might clog your arteries and result in a heart attack. Or to regulate how much sugar*

[166] p. 90, *A Christian Manifesto*
[167] Jonathan Mayhew, Congregationalist Minister, 1750

a citizen eats to make sure no one dies from diabetes. Eating too much pizza or drinking too much soda do not infringe upon another person's rights, and so the government should not meddle in these types of actions.

The government only has the authority to make laws that incentivize obedience to God's commands and criminalize disobedience to God's commands within society. ...The government does not have the authority to close the church in the name of protecting life – that's not their job. Government has been established by God to protect rights, not to prevent all illness and death.[168]

Or as David deBruyn stated in a recent sermon:

...The most dangerous governments are those who think of themselves as pure and righteous, because they see their acts as for the greater good, and are blind to the pain they produce. To be more specific, the more the government takes on the role of omni-protector, the more freedoms will be crushed and extinguished. Modern governments are a far cry from what the Bible charges governments to do: which is simply maintain order by punishing crime or threats to life. That's the biblical role of government as seen in Romans 13.

(f) *Who defines "good" and "evil"?*

Look again at Romans 13:3-4: Three times Paul speaks of "the good", and three times he speaks of "the evil". But who defines and who decides what is "good" or "evil"? Secular society today defines morality by political correctness, the LGBTQ agenda and censorship of all 'hate speech', and by all that is pro-abortion and anti-marriage. In communist countries, "good" is

[168] https://www.aomin.org/aoblog/general-apologetics/revolution-or-obedience-a-response-to-jonathan-leemans-position-regarding-civil-disobedience/

atheism, racism, worship of the state, rejection of all private property, and resulting genocide; "evil" is any opposition to the state or political treason.

But that *cannot* be how God defines morality in Romans 13 or anywhere in His holy Word and His perfect Law. In the very next verses (vv. 8-10), Paul proceeds to show that God's absolute and objective Law defines our ethics, not any manmade subjective or situational standards. From the Garden of Eden, to Mount Sinai, to Jesus' Sermon on the Mount, God has made clear that His character and Law are the fixed, universal standard for "good" and "evil" (Exod. 20; Lev. 19; Micah 6:8; Matt. 5:17-20).

As James M. Willson warned long ago:

> *Convince men that any government that happens to exist, whatever its character, is to be obeyed, honoured and reverenced; we mean that the Bible enjoins this, and* <u>*you have struck a very heavy blow at the Bible itself.*</u> *Men - if they believe in God at all - cannot believe that He is the patron of iniquity and wrong.*[169]

No Absolute Power for Rulers

Therefore, rulers don't create morality; they must conform to it. Rulers don't define good and evil; their job is to reward the good and punish the evil, based on God's standards. As John Knox states, "Kings have not an absolute power in their regiment to do what pleases them; but their power is limited by God's Word. …Resistance to tyrants is obedience to God."[170]

But of course pagan governments often disregard the divine standard, though God's Law is still inscribed on their hearts and written on their consciences (Rom. 2:14-15). So we submit wherever possible and keep paying our taxes (Rom. 13:6-7); but we are watchful for any infringement on our first allegiance and highest duty of obedience to God's Law. As the famous

---

[169] *Civil Government: An Exposition of Romans XIII:1-7,* 1853
[170] p. 372 in M. Cassidy, *The Passing Summer*

Magdeburg Confession states, "divine laws necessarily trump human ones".[171]

Conditional Submission

The Bible does not teach that you must always obey the government. Wives are mandated to submit and "be subject to their husbands in everything", which sounds like absolute language (Eph. 5:22-24). Yet that cannot include obeying a husband who instructs his wife to break God's Law (e.g., be immoral, cheat on taxes, abort a baby, etc.). Children are commanded to "be obedient to your parents in all things", which sounds unconditional (Col. 3:20). Yet that cannot include submitting when dad asks his son to commit a crime or to sin, or when mom asks her daughter to steal or lie. What Scripture teaches is that we always obey government "in the rightful exercise of their authority".[172]

Whenever a human authority (in home, church or state) asks you to disobey God, at that point their authority is null and void. Likewise, Romans 13 presupposes an authority that is functioning justly, not requiring us to disobey the Word of God in any way. Writes John Calvin, "For earthly princes lay aside their power when they rise up against God, and are unworthy to be reckoned among the number of mankind."[173]

Conclusion

In closing, Scripture makes clear that submission to authority is not agreement. We submit "for the Lord's sake" to every human institution, no matter our opinion or preference. Any time a legitimate authority gives a lawful command, like it or not, we must trust God and submit, no matter how irrational or unreasonable it seems.

---

[171] https://defytyrants.com/magdeburg-book/

[172] p. 146, J. Murray, *Epistle to the Romans* (NICNT); he continues, "we are compelled to take account of exceptions to the absolute terms in which an obligation is affirmed (e.g., Acts 4-5)" (p. 149).

[173] Commentary on Daniel Lecture XXX, Daniel 6:32

But whenever we are commanded by an illegitimate authority (out of their biblical sphere) or an unlawful command (against the Law of God), we "must obey God rather than man" (Acts 5:29). *Biblical civil disobedience is required anytime we are commanded to do what God forbids (e.g., Exod. 1; Dan. 3, etc.), or forbidden to do what God requires (Dan 6; Acts 4-5), or whenever government usurps our God-given authority in the church or family sphere.*[174]

Unconditional & Maximum Obedience to Christ

The heart of a Christian is not for maximum obedience to the state and minimum obedience to Christ. Especially in the church sphere, our Lord has given us New Testament epistles packed with dozens of "one another" commands and principles for our church life[175], and our highest priority is to study and obey those divine regulations to please Christ our Lord and King, our Head, Shepherd and Ruler of His Church, whose glad slaves we are, who bought us with His own blood.

We dare not have a view of near-absolute submission to the State that effectively rules out any underground church, leaving only the registered churches that meet Caesar's approval and boast of their full compliance.[176] Church history is littered with the wreckage of professing Christians and churches who capitulated, with some version of that same fateful motto on their quivering lips: "We have no king but Caesar" (Jn. 19:15).
This preacher of old warns:

---

[174] See also here: https://www.gotquestions.org/civil-disobedience.html

[175] https://www.challies.com/articles/one-another-the-bible-community/ Compare this long biblical list to the very sparse texts (only in Proverbs) about corporal discipline of our children, now outlawed; yet we disobey Caesar (rightly) in this realm without hesitation. Is it because there is much less risk publicly and it is less costly, than if we obey Christ in gathering illegally?

[176] Read this powerful testimony from an imprisoned Chinese pastor: https://www.chinapartnership.org/blog/2018/12/my-declaration-of-faithful-disobedience

> *Though the partisans of arbitrary power will freely censure that preacher who speaks boldly for the liberties of the people, they will admire as an excellent divine the parson whose discourse is wholly in the opposite, and teaches that magistrates have a divine right for doing wrong, and are to be implicitly obeyed; men professing Christianity, as if the religion of the blessed Jesus bound them to bow their neck to any tyrant.* [177]

David deBruyn drives this home to our present situation here in South Africa:

> *...The difficulty we are going to face in the coming months, and maybe even years, is that as wave after wave of the virus comes our way, the government may keep banning religious gatherings.... We cannot live through another year where we are tossed to and fro by every announcement coming from Pretoria. At least one thing needs to remain certain in our lives, and that is our covenant with Christ and His people. We need the rock-solid pillar of the church, the pillar and ground of the truth (1 Tim. 3:15), not the shifting sands of whatever happens with Covid-19.*

FURTHER RESOURCES

1. The underground, Confessing Church in Nazi Germany in the 1930s (led by men like Dietrich Bonhoeffer, who was martyred) took a bold stand in their *Barmen Declaration*:

> *We reject the false doctrine that the Church could have permission to hand over the form of its message and of its order to whatever it itself might wish or to the vicissitudes of the prevailing ideological and political convictions of the day. ...We reject the false doctrine that...the Church could, and could have permission to give itself or allow itself to be given special leaders [Führer; political] vested*

[177] William Gordon, Sermon, 1794, qtd in *Caesar and the Church*, by A. Forsyth.

> *with ruling authority. ... We reject the false doctrine that beyond its special commission [biblical role] the State should and could become the sole and total order of human life and so fulfil the vocation of the Church as well.*[178]

2. To read about an unsung Christian hero of civil disobedience, get *One Woman Against the Reich: The True Story of a Mother's Struggle to Keep Her Family Faithful to God in a World Gone Mad*, by H.W. Ziefle (Kregel, 2003). A Christian movie, *The Printing*, also vividly shows the tempting comforts and security of the registered/state church in the former Soviet Union, compared to the price paid by the underground church: https://www.amazon.com/gp/video/detail/B01JNXOZIM/ref=atv_dp_share_cu_r

3. Common question and good answer from Phil Johnson (on behalf of the elders at Grace Community Church):

> *"Are the spheres of church and state as distinct as the statement implies? Doesn't the church submit to government fire codes and zoning restrictions? If so, why not likewise acquiesce to these public health restrictions?"*
>
> *Answer: While it is true that the church is subject to fire codes and zoning restrictions, those are routine civil, not spiritual, matters, so the state exercises legitimate authority enforcing them. But the government's authority in civil matters associated with the church does not give it authority in spiritual matters, which are the lifeblood of the church. Attendance caps, singing bans, and distancing requirements (especially those that are established arbitrarily and by executive fiat) have the effect of suppressing or eliminating the congregational worship that is an essential element of church life.*

---

[178] https://www.spucc.org/sites/default/files/BARMEN%20DECLARATION%20UCC.pdf

Therefore such orders fall outside the jurisdiction of civil authorities.[179]

4. On civil disobedience from Calvin's *Institutes*:

…But in that obedience which we hold to be due to the commands of rulers, we must always make the exception, nay, must be particularly careful that it is not incompatible with obedience to Him to whose will the wishes of all kings should be subject, to whose decrees their commands must yield, to whose majesty their sceptres must bow. And, indeed, how preposterous were it, in pleasing men, to incur the offence of Him for whose sake you obey men!

The Lord, therefore, is King of kings. When he opens his sacred mouth, he alone is to be heard, instead of all and above all. We are subject to the men who rule over us, but subject only in the Lord. If they command anything against Him let us not pay the least regard to it, nor be moved by all the dignity which they possess as magistrates—a dignity to which no injury is done when it is subordinated to the special and truly supreme power of God.[180]

5. The Scottish Covenanters were some of church history's finest examples of godly protest. One of their pioneers was saintly old Andrew Melville, who was jailed in the Tower of London for confronting King James with these words in 1611 (same year as the KJV was published):

There are two kings and two kingdoms in Scotland: There is King James, the head of the Commonwealth, and there is King Jesus, the Head of the Kirk, whose subject King James is, and of whose kingdom he is not the head, nor a lord, but a member.

---

[179] http://teampyro.blogspot.com/2020/08/questions-we-get-about-gcc-elders.html
[180] https://www.ccel.org/ccel/calvin/institutes.vi.xxi.html

> Later, in 1660 the Covenanters signed their National Covenant, some signing in their own blood. Historian S.M. Houghton tells of how they were determined to: *resist to the death the claims of the king and his minions to override the Crown Rights of the Redeemer in His Kirk (King Jesus). Their National Covenant gives high honour to the eternal God and His most holy Word; demands the faithful preaching of that Word, the due and right ministration of the sacraments....*
>
> *The subscribers further say that they fear neither 'the foul aspersions of rebellion, combination, or what else our adversaries from their craft and malice would put upon us, seeing what we do is so well warranted, and ariseth from an unfeigned desire to maintain the true worship of God, the majesty of our king, and the peace of the kingdom, for the common happiness of ourselves and our posterity'. They pledge themselves as in the sight of God to 'be good examples to others of all godliness, soberness, and righteousness, and of every duty we owe to God and man'.*

6. C.H. Spurgeon said this about Daniel's brave three friends who would not obey King Nebuchadnezzar (Daniel 3):

> *...They might have said, 'It is only for once, and not for long. Ten minutes or so, once in a lifetime, to please the king; such a trivial act cannot make any difference; at any rate, it is not enough to brave the fiery furnace for. ...It would be ridiculous to throw away our lives for such a trifle. ...In the supreme hour many fail, because the trial is seemingly so small.'*
>
> *They mean to stand for God; but this is scarcely the right time; they will wait, and choose a more worthy occasion, when something really heroic can be attempted. Were they to stand for such a little thing, the world would laugh with derision at such a straining out of a gnat.*

So Adam eats the apple; Esau the pottage; and the one temptation, unresisted, issues in life-long loss. Not even for a few minutes in a lifetime would these three brave men deny their God. May their stubborn faith be ours!

7. Theodore Dalrymple, English writer and social observer, warns:

Political correctness is communist propaganda writ small. In my study of communist societies, I came to the conclusion that the purpose of communist propaganda was not to persuade or convince, not to inform, but to humiliate; and therefore, the less it corresponded to reality the better. When people are forced to remain silent when they are being told the most obvious lies, or even worse when they are forced to repeat the lies themselves, they lose once and for all their sense of probity.

To assent to obvious lies is in some small way to become evil oneself. One's standing to resist anything is thus eroded, and even destroyed. A society of emasculated liars is easy to control. I think if you examine political correctness, it has the same effect and is intended to.[181]

8. Here is an "Elder's Statement On the Non-Enforcement of Masks" (our church's attempt biblically to guide the flock through this volatile issue, from November 2020):

We as elders have decided it is not our place to enforce the state's current mask-wearing regulations (when the church gathers), for the following biblical reasons:

(1) Our risen Lord is Head of the Church, not Caesar; Christ rules us through His Word (Acts 5:29; Mark 12:17). The New Testament has much to say about how we gather for corporate worship and about our communal life

[181] https://heidelblog.net/2015/02/the-purpose-of-political-correctness-is-to-humiliate/

together. Christ has not given us authority as church leaders to enforce masks, which goes "beyond what is written" (1 Cor. 4:6). Unlike other regulations, masks can be dehumanising, can inhibit our obedience to Christ in singing and fellowship, in recognising, greeting and caring for one another; masks can also hinder our welcoming of visitors, learning their names, and being able to hear them (1 Cor. 6:19-20; Eph. 5:19; Col. 3:16; Rom. 16; 1 Cor. 16:19-20; 2 Jn. 12; 3 Jn. 14; 1 Thess. 2:17; 3:10).

(2) In the three God-given spheres of authority, we see personal health decisions as the duty of the family sphere, not the church (Gen. 18:19; Eph. 6:4; 1 Tim. 5:8).

(3) Masks are what Romans 14 is all about – debatable matters of conscience, where Christian love and liberty must prevail. Listen to Core Value #22 in our Sola5 'Core Values', on Liberty of Conscience:

God in Christ has purchased the liberty of believers, freeing them from the guilt of sin, God's wrath, unbiblical traditions and regulations of men, Satan and the fear of death (Gal 5:1; Col 2:8–23; Heb 2:14–15):

- *Therefore we affirm that believers are bound in their consciences only to God and his Word, not to the impositions of men and of Satan (Rom 14:1–15:4). We further affirm that Christian liberty is nothing but freedom to serve God within the boundaries that God himself has set (Rom 6:8–22).*

- *We deny that Christian liberty gives licence to sin of any kind (Rom 6:1–7). We further deny that any church or its leaders have a right to expect obedience from members when they (as leaders) teach things that are contrary or additional to God's Word (Matt 15:1–9; Col 2:20–23).*

(4) Scripture requires us to believe the best about one another's motives, treating others the way we would want to be treated (1 Cor. 13:7; Matt. 7:12). Therefore:

a. When you see a brother/sister at church wearing a mask, you should assume: They are doing this "for the sake of conscience" before the Lord and out of Christian love (Rom. 14). (Perhaps out of medical or legal concerns for themselves or others, or for other good and godly reasons.)

b. When you see a brother/sister not wearing a mask, you should assume: They are doing this "for the sake of conscience" before the Lord and out of Christian love. (Perhaps out of personal or medical concerns, or other good and godly reasons.)

"Blessed is the one who does not condemn himself in what he approves," Rom. 14:22 (another beatitude). Both the masked and the unmasked can still be law-abiding citizens, trusting God, loving their neighbour, taking Covid seriously and caring for the vulnerable – just in different ways. Scripture, not society, defines those virtues for us.

This is why we as elders believe it is not our place to require masks but to defend your true Christian liberty to choose what you believe is best. Whenever you have any questions or concerns, please speak to us as elders (as you've been doing already). Let's keep praying and striving for our unity as one family and body in Christ, as a witness to a watching world.

SPHERE-SOVEREIGNTY & LESSER MAGISTRATES: ANSWERING OBJECTIONS[182]

Introducing a Key Component

A key component to the debate about the relation of the church to the state is the doctrine of sphere-sovereignty. Abraham Kuyper, the Dutch theologian of the 20th century, has best formulated this doctrine for the modern church, and he did so uniquely as both a theologian and a statesman. Not only was he a neo-Calvinist responsible for the establishment of the Reformed Churches in the Netherlands, but he had a long career as a politician including a term as Prime Minister of the Netherlands between 1901 and 1905. Thus, Kuyper can hardly be charged as an "anti-government rebel" in his remarks upon the God-ordained limits of the state's authority.

Kuyper's expression of the doctrine of sphere-sovereignty is often traced back to the six lectures that he gave on Calvinism at Princeton,[183] though he had developed his thoughts in his speech *Souvereiniteit in Eigen Kring.*[184] Within these lectures and his other works such as *On the Church*[185] and *Common Grace*,[186] Kuyper defends the view that the only absolute sovereign is God, and under Him all other authority is delegated by God.

---

[182] Most of this was researched and written by my friend, Warrick Jubber, a South African Master's Seminary graduate whom I enlisted because of his valuable insights; added in February 2022.

[183] Kuyper, Abraham. *Calvinism: Six Lectures Delivered in the Theological Seminary at Princeton*. New York; Chicago; Toronto: Fleming H. Revell Company, 1899.

[184] It is in this speech that Kuyper famously declared, "… there is not a square inch in the whole domain of our human existence over which Christ, who is Sovereign over all, does not cry: 'Mine!'" Abraham Kuyper, *Abraham Kuyper: A Centennial Reader*, ed. James D. Bratt (Grand Rapids, MI; Cambridge, U.K.; Carlisle: William B. Eerdmans Publishing Company; The Paternoster Press, 1998), 461.

[185] Kuyper, Abraham. *On the Church*. Edited by Jordan J. Ballor, Melvin Flikkema, John Halsey Wood Jr., and Andrew M. McGinnis. Translated by Harry Van Dyke, Nelson D. Kloosterman, Todd M. Rester, and Arjen Vreugdenhil. Abraham Kuyper Collected Works in Public Theology. Bellingham, WA: Lexham Press; Acton Institute, 2016.

[186] Kuyper, Abraham. *Common Grace: God's Gifts for a Fallen World: The Doctrinal Section*. Edited by Jordan J. Ballor, J. Daryl Charles, and Melvin Flikkema. Translated by Nelson D. Kloosterman and Ed M. van der Maas. Vol. 2. Abraham Kuyper Collected Works in Public Theology. Bellingham, WA: Lexham Press; Acton Institute, 2019.

Since all human authority is a delegated authority, it is also thereby limited. Kuyper gives much attention to how each sphere's limited authority relates to the others. He further argues that, under God, each sphere enjoys sovereignty over its God-delegated jurisdiction. As to the present debate on the church's relation to the state, Kuyper was clear to state that, "The sovereignty of the State and the sovereignty of the church exist side by side, and they mutually limit each other."[187]

Even in instances of alleged "overlap" between the spheres, which many seem to regard as the fatal flaw of the doctrine of sphere-sovereignty, Kuyper maintained that the distinction was clear:

> *Just as the church may never exercise any civil authority, the civil government may never exercise any ecclesiastical authority. These two spheres are completely distinct. There is a mixed arena where both authorities meet, since the member of the church is also citizen of the state. This can cause conflict if the church appropriates what belongs to Caesar, or if Caesar demands for himself what belongs to the church. And this does not negate the fact that these two spheres are strictly distinct. It merely shows that church and state sometimes fail to see this distinction clearly.*[188]

This is a brief biblical response to defend the doctrine of sphere-sovereignty as a key component to the church's relation to the state amidst COVID-19 restrictions. We echo the stand that Knox took during a debate in 1564 AD with William Maitland of Lethington, the Secretary of State for Mary, Queen of Scots. When Maitland sought to dismiss Knox for his defense of lesser magistrates opposing higher authorities, he declared, "I think ye shall not have many learned men of your opinion."

---

[187] Abraham Kuyper, *Calvinism: Six Lectures Delivered in the Theological Seminary at Princeton* (New York; Chicago; Toronto: Fleming H. Revell Company, 1899), 138.

[188] Abraham Kuyper, *On the Church*, ed. Jordan J. Ballor et al., trans. Harry Van Dyke et al., Abraham Kuyper Collected Works in Public Theology (Bellingham, WA: Lexham Press; Acton Institute, 2016), 137. Emphasis added.

To this Knox replied in characteristic boldness, "My lord, the truth ceases not to be the truth, howsoever it be that men either misknow it, or yet gainstand it. And yet, I praise my God, I lack not the consent of God's servants in that head."[189] Like Knox, we appeal to Scripture, and we praise the Lord that we're not alone in our defense of sphere sovereignty but have many learned men such as Kuyper who stand with us.

A simpler expression of Kuyper's doctrine of sphere-sovereignty is to speak of "spheres of authority." Bret Laird offers a helpful summary of this doctrine of spheres of authority in his excellent book *Family, Government and Church*:

> *The Bible is clear in its teaching that God is a God of order. In His love, in His kindness, and in His wisdom, He has established three primary jurisdictions of external authority in order to restrain evil, to reward good, and to facilitate the expansion of the gospel throughout the world. These three jurisdictions are: 1. The Family; 2. The Government; 3. The Church.*[190]

Allow me to answer five common objections we are hearing against those of us upholding the classic, Protestant position of sphere-sovereignty which we believe to be biblical: (1) Is it a recent invention?; (2) How does it apply in a democracy?; (3) Are we fostering anarchy?; (4) What about overlap between spheres?; (5) Are there only two grounds for civil disobedience?

(1) A Recent Invention?

Is sphere-sovereignty a recent invention, or a mere pragmatic excuse for civil rebellion? Pastors and theologians of the 16th century Protestant Reformation gave this matter great consideration and produced comprehensive works that defended their positions exegetically and applied their doctrine carefully. We

---

189 Matthew Trewhella, ed., *The Magdeburg Confession: 13th of April 1550 AD*, trans. Matthew Colvin (North Charleston, SC: Createspace Publishing, 2012), Kindle.

190 Bret M. Laird, *Family, Government and Church: Relating Three Jurisdictions of Divinely Delegated Authority* (Wapwallopen, PA: Shepherd Press, 2022), 69.

would do ourselves a great service to study the positions of Luther and Calvin, of Knox, the Scottish Covenanters, the Nonconformists and the Puritans.[191] None deserve our attention more than the pastors of Magdeburg, to whom even John Knox appealed when resisting Mary, Queen of Scots. Amidst widespread compromise, the courageous men of Magdeburg stood boldly for Christ and published their *Confession and Defense of the Pastors and Other Ministers of the Church of Magdeburg* in April 1550.

In their arguments, the pastors of Magdeburg declare the idea of unlimited deference to the State as "an invention of the devil."[192] As Trewhella summarizes in his foreword to this confession, "Their point is that no one in authority – whether in family, church, or civil government – holds his authority autonomously. Rather it is delegated to them from God. If the authority therefore makes a law which contravenes the Law of God, those subject to their authority can refuse obedience because, as the pastors state, '*divine laws necessarily trump human ones*.'"

Throughout their work, the 16th century theologians make their case that the God-given purpose of the civil authorities, as described in Romans 13 and 1 Peter 2, necessarily limits their authority. Thus, it falls upon "lesser magistrates" to hold those in higher positions accountable and to resist them insofar as they usurp their jurisdiction.[193]

(2) Relevant in a Democracy?

The doctrine of the lesser magistrates, is that which was developed in the Magdeburg confession (and furthered by Knox and Beza). It asserts that the God-ordained duty of lesser magistrates is to restrain the evil of greater authorities who do the opposite of their duty before the Lord in "punishing

---

[191] See, for instance, the monumental work of Samuel Rutherford, *Lex, Rex, or The Law and The Prince: A Dispute For The Just Prerogative of King and People*.

[192] Trewhella, *The Magdeburg Confession*, Kindle.

[193] "The Lesser Magistrate Doctrine declares that when the higher or superior authority makes an unjust or immoral law or decree, the lower or lesser magistrate has both a right and duty to refuse obedience to the superior authority. If need be, the lesser authorities even have the right and obligation to actively resist and oppose the superior authority." Ibid., Kindle.

evildoers and praising those who do good" (1 Pet. 2:14). The lesser magistrates honour the duty God has given them by resisting and restraining the evil of those greater authorities who punish the righteous and praise the wicked.[194]

If this is a biblical duty of lesser magistrates, then how might it apply in a constitutional democracy? Are not the voting citizens those who are responsible under God to hold their authorities accountable to act within the sphere of their God-given duties and limitations? This is made especially clear when the constitution of the land enshrines those biblical limitations of power. The Bill of Rights in the South African constitution guarantees these three pertinent rights to every resident of the country:

1. Freedom of religion[195]
2. Freedom of assembly and protest[196]
3. Freedom and security of the person, including medical autonomy[197]

Is it not therefore well within the rights of every lawful resident of the land to resist those mandates of the state which usurp the God-given authority of the family and church as well as infringe upon the constitutional rights of every lawful resident? It is not ungodly and rebellious to disobey and challenge unconstitutional regulations. It is a God-given duty of good citizens who are called to participate in democracy for the good of their neighbours.

---

[194] "The Magistrate is an ordinance of God for honor to good works, and a terror to evil works (Rom. 13). Therefore when he begins to be a terror to good works and honor to evil, there is no longer in him, because he does thus, the ordinance of God, but the ordinance of the devil. And he who resists such works, does not resist the ordinance of God, but the ordinance of the devil. But he who resists, it is necessary that he resist in his own station, as a matter of his calling. Next therefore it is the calling of another magistrate, either the superior or equal of him who inflicts the harm, or of the inferior who suffers the harm, who is himself the ordinance of God through the superior, to be an honor to good works and a terror to evil in his defense of his own citizens by the command of God." Ibid., Kindle.

[195] "Everyone has the right to freedom of conscience, religion, thought, belief and opinion."

[196] "Everyone has the right, peacefully and unarmed, to assemble, to demonstrate, to picket and to present petitions."

[197] "Everyone has the right to bodily and psychological integrity, which includes the right— to security in and control over their body."

(3) Fostering Anarchy?

We believe it is a straw man fallacy to say that those of us holding to sphere-sovereignty are saying that we can arbitrarily disobey evil authorities. As the authors of the Magdeburg Confession wrote,

> *Therefore when [a civic ruler] begins to be a terror to good works and honor to evil, there is no longer in him...the ordinance of God, but the ordinance of the devil. And he who resists such works, does not resist the ordinance of God, but the ordinance of the devil. ...By refusing obedience to superiors in those things which are contrary to God, they do not violate the majesty of their superiors, nor can they be judged obstinate or rebellious, as Daniel says, 'I have committed no crime against you, O king (Dan. 6:22).'*[198]

Neither the doctrine of sphere sovereignty, nor that of the lesser magistrates, assert that there may be a wholesale rejection of a person in authority simply because they are evil. Rather, we teach that *insofar as* the authority promotes sin or hinders obedience to God they may be justly disobeyed by a faithful Christian *in those matters, but that they should be obeyed in all other matters that are lawful under God.* To oversimplify this argument and then refute the straw man is both unfair and unfounded.

(4) Overlapping Spheres?

Kuyper was happy to concede areas of overlap but maintained that this "mixed arena" in no way negates the distinction between the spheres nor the jurisdiction of the respective authorities.[199] Laird likewise states:

---

[198] Trewhella, *The Magdeburg Confession*, Kindle.

[199] "Just as the church may never exercise any civil authority, the civil government may never exercise any ecclesiastical authority. These two spheres are completely distinct. There is a mixed arena where both authorities meet, since the member of the church is also citizen of the state. This can cause conflict if the church appropriates what belongs to Caesar, or if Caesar

> *The relationship between the three spheres is designed to be overlapping and symbiotic: (1) Churches influence families and the government through the preaching of God's Word; (2) Families influence the church and the state as active members and voting citizens;(3) Government influences both churches and families by upholding the rule of law without favoritism. The "circles" should overlap in mutually beneficial ways, but they are, nonetheless, separate jurisdictions."*[200]

What is helpful about Laird's argument is that it moves us away from thinking of overlap as a matter of authority, but rather a matter of service. Before that can be discussed, we must assert two points.

Firstly, the existence of the three spheres/realms/jurisdictions of authority are universally accepted by all theologians. Even those who critique sphere sovereignty will concede that Scripture clearly describes these three authorities. What is not universally accepted, however, is the jurisdiction of the respective spheres and their relationship to one another.

Secondly, Scripture gives no indication of a hierarchy between the spheres of authority. Therefore, the existence of three authorities without hierarchy in a "flat" position to one another, logically necessitates that the spheres are mutually limiting. If that is not the case, who then has the final say in matters where two or more spheres supposedly share authority?

Consider this diagram:

---

demands for himself what belongs to the church. And this does not negate the fact that these two spheres are strictly distinct. It merely shows that church and state sometimes fail to see this distinction clearly." Kuyper, *On the Church*, 137.

[200] Laird, *Family, Government and Church*, 110.

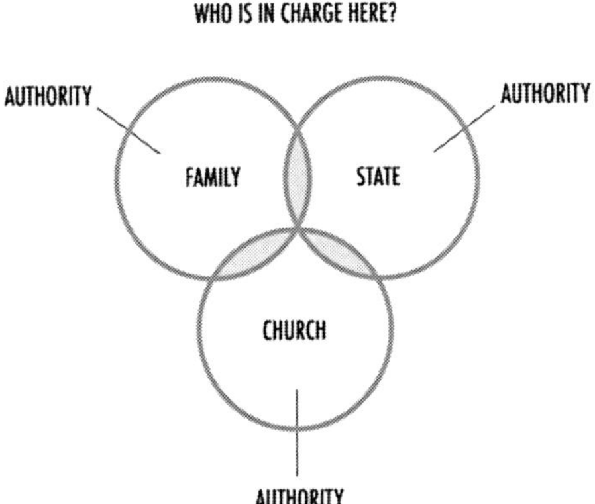

In the center of the overlap, which of the spheres has authority over the other? For example, all three spheres are concerned about the health and safety of their constituency. If there is a conflict regarding health and safety, who has the final say? In such a system, there must be a hierarchy in order to resolve the conflict. Many critics unwittingly endorse such a system where the state has authority over the church and family, as represented here:

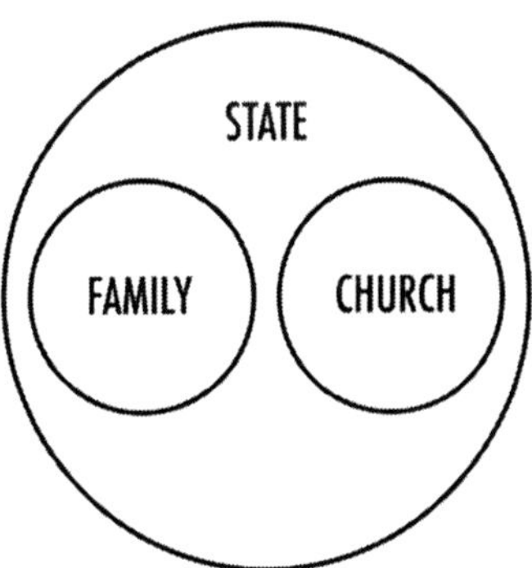

Here's another variation of such a hierarchy that gives the church precedence over the family, and the state precedence over both:

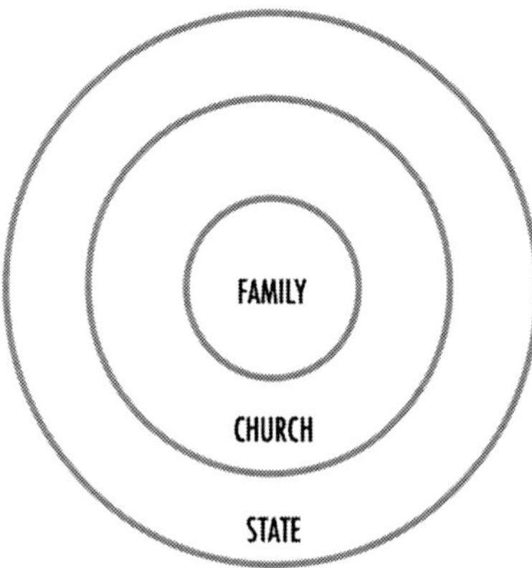

This unbiblical arrangement has terrible implications for the abuse of all three spheres, as Scripture and history often attest. As Kuyper said, the biblical distinction between the spheres must be maintained, since God has clearly given to each realm its own authority, without any indication that such governance is shared or subordinated to any authority other than His own.

None of this denies that there are areas of shared interest. For instance, do all three spheres of family, church, and state have an interest in seeing children raised in good homes where they are faithfully cared for and raised to walk in righteousness? Absolutely. However, <u>shared interest is not the same as shared authority</u>. In such areas the overlap should not be thought of as an overlap of authority, but rather an overlap of service. Consider this representation:

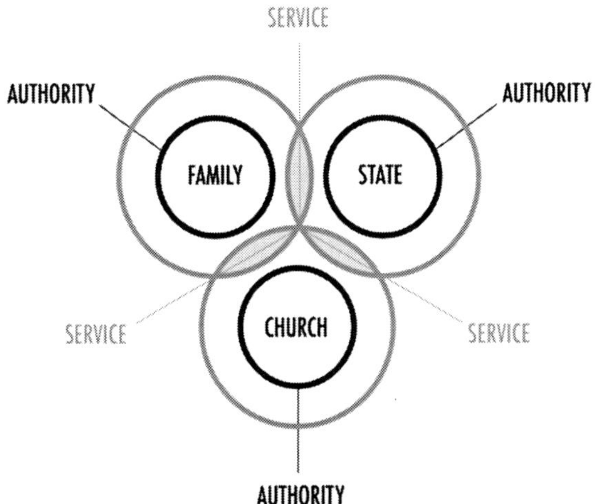

In the diagram above it is clear that each sphere retains its authority, or as Laird terms it, its "*exclusive domain,*" while at the same time serving the other spheres. We believe that this is a more accurate representation of what Scripture teaches.

For example, parents have the exclusive domain over raising their children, and any argument that God has delegated authority over these children to another sphere lacks biblical support. However, the church may serve the family by teaching Biblical principles of parenting and may counsel or even discipline parents who disobey God's Word. This, though, never gives the church authority over the children or the right to usurp the father as the head of the family.

Similarly, while matters of education and health are under the authority of the parents, the state may serve the family by providing public education and health services. Yet, again, this does not give the state the authority to mandate that the family use such services nor the right to usurp the father in the family.

How often have we heard in the past two years that fire and building codes are the great undoing of the doctrine of sphere sovereignty? Because we have allowed the state to serve us with these regulations in the past, some church leaders think that it is impossible to determine where the authority of the state stops. Yet when health and safety regulations are no longer serving the church but are rather ruling and regulating how the church gathers and worships, those services must be rejected by the proper authorities. Health decisions must be put back into the hands of the heads of households and the keys of the church must be put back into the hands of the congregation and her officers.

The spheres of authority are well established in Scripture and are critically important not only to this debate over the church and the state's mandates related to COVID-19, but to understanding how to faithfully navigate the many areas of shared interest. This will become even more important as the standards of the Christian family and the biblical church diverge from a society increasingly rebelling against God (Romans 1:18–32). As Laird wrote, "The concept of exclusive domain is important, because if one sphere of authority intrudes on the exclusive domain of another, disorder, suffering, and evil inevitably result."[201]

(5) Only Two Exceptions?

The standard Christian position on civil disobedience allows for only two exceptions: *We disobey government when they command what is forbidden, or forbid what is commanded by God.* But what if the government commands you to give yourself and your children up into slavery? There is no law in the Bible explicitly against that. Yet if we understand sphere sovereignty, we will understand that some commands can be disregarded simply because the law-maker is outside his jurisdiction. The pastors of Magdeburg wrote that, "No one is compelled by the command of God to submit to the usurpation of

[201] Laird, *Family, Government and Church*, 80.

his own right."[202] We propose then this expanded position on civil disobedience: *We disobey government when they command what is forbidden, forbid what is commanded by God, or exceed their delegated authority and intrude on the God-given jurisdictions of church or family.*

We can learn much from the Magdeburg example. They did not use the words "tyrants, tyranny" lightly or flippantly; they prayerfully examined each situation in light of Scripture, conscience, sound wisdom, and best response in light of Christian duty and witness before a watching world. Look how carefully they spelled out four levels of tyranny and how the godly should or could respond at each level:

> Level 1 – The Wicked Governor: bearable offenses, mostly injuring himself/his reputation, can be warned publicly but tolerated; resistance not necessary.
>
> Level 2 – The Lawless Tyrant: "atrocious and notorious injuries" to some; violates the laws of the land/constitution; resistance optional for lesser magistrate, *could* be opposed.
>
> Level 3 – The Coercive Tyrant: he forces his leaders/citizens to sin; his injustices extend to a greater degree, injuring society; he *should* be opposed by lesser magistrates – first by peaceable means, then by force if necessary.
>
> Level 4 – The Persecutor of God: forcing his subjects to perform evil and forsake the good; such a tyrant must be opposed at every level possible, by whatever means possible, out of obedience to God and His Law.[203]

---

[202] Trewhella, *The Magdeburg Confession*, Kindle.

[203] https://lcmside.org/wp-content/uploads/2016/05/4-Rev.-Michael-Kearney-Magdeburg-Confession-.pdf; https://www.intoyourhandsllc.com/component/content/article.html?id=84:4-levels-of-injustice-knowing-when-to-suffer-patiently-and-when-to-resist

This is exactly the kind of rigorous, whole-Bible analysis that must again be applied as we face 21st century tyranny in its many forms. Simplistic solutions will not suffice. It will require from us careful study of Scripture, history and current events, with great patience and Christian courage and integrity, striving for unity in the truth as believers.

Conclusion

This rejoinder is an all-too-brief response to five objections against sphere sovereignty as a biblical basis for civil disobedience. This debate is not taking place between enemies, but among brothers in Christ. Let us then continue to strive for faithfulness while clothing ourselves in humility and love towards one another and coming before the all-sufficient authority of God's Word. May we all be diligent to present ourselves approved to God as workmen who do not need to be ashamed, accurately handling the word of truth (2 Tim. 2:15) and may the Lord use us to serve one another to that end.

4
FACE-TO-FACE
Against Disembodied and Defaced Christianity
(A Theology of the Human Face)
(May 2021)

Greet One Another With a Holy Elbow?

Social habits that would've sounded bizarre and alien just one year ago have now become the norm – from bumping elbows in greeting, to wearing 1-3 masks or a face-shield, to vigilantism that rebukes unmasked strangers in public, to avoiding people altogether as a perpetual and miserable hermit. Likewise, religious habits once foreign are now the norm, as 'Zoom church' has taken the world by storm, and discipleship has gone entirely digital for many. If we allow them, the 'covid cult' will fundamentally reshape our lives and our faith – from how we greet, to how we gather, what we wear, and how we live and relate to one another.[204]

Recently I heard a powerful sermon from 1 Thessalonians 2-3 by a pastor-friend of mine, Brad Klassen. I was reminded afresh of the striking relevance

---

[204] "When a pandemic is believed to threaten widespread deaths in a culture that lacks the spiritual framework needed to deal with the fear of death, then respect for the fullness of life-before-death – love, family, community, culture – easily comes to be considered superfluous." https://brownstone.org/articles/seven-theories-of-why-the-lockdowns-happened/

of God's Word for every situation and every age. In a world that has willingly surrendered their faces to the State, we hear God reminding us that He cares about what we do with our faces. Allow me to share and adapt some of what I learned from that sermon and my own topical study on the importance of face-to-face fellowship.

Story of the Thessalonian Church

Acts 17 tells the story of how the Thessalonian church was birthed. The Apostle Paul was on his 2nd missionary journey, now with young Timothy by his side. Responding to the 'Macedonian Call' in a vision, they penetrated the European continent with the gospel for the very first time (Acts 16). Arriving at Thessalonica, they spent the next three Sabbaths in the synagogue, "reasoning with them from the Scriptures", explaining and defending the gospel of Christ. Jews and Greeks got saved, a church was planted.

Of course – enemies arose, wanting to shut the church down; so by night Paul and his associates escaped. The warrant for their arrest was that these preachers, "all act contrary to the decrees of Caesar, saying that there is *another king, Jesus*!" (Acts 17:7). Sound familiar? Not that different from preachers today being arrested in Canada and elsewhere for obeying Christ instead of complying with state health regulations and martial law.

Background to 1 Thessalonians

Weeks later, safely in Corinth, about AD 51, Paul sat down to write this beloved flock that were heavy on his heart, knowing that they too were facing persecution. It was guilt by association, because they had joined with the hated preacher, Paul, in this newfound faith. In coming to our text for this essay, two burdens seem to weigh most heavily upon the apostle: (a) new converts getting persecuted; (b) their leaders (Paul & co.) getting criticised, and being cut off from them. So Paul picks up pen and papyrus and gives us one of his most tender, affectionate statements anywhere in all of his writings (1 Thessalonians has been called an ancient "classic of friendship").

After using chapters 1-2 to speak of his ministry when present with them, Paul turns now to defend his absence from them in 2:17-3:20, which forms the literary centrepiece of this letter. The heart of the apostle shines forth at the heart of this epistle. "At this point, Paul's style becomes intensely emotional. The very words seem to tremble." (Hendriksen)

Our Screen-ified Society

Here we discover vital lessons about the superiority of personal presence (over all other forms of communication), about how God views the physical togetherness of His people, about how we should view face-to-face fellowship, and about how Satan views it and tries to stop it. What could be more relevant to the Church in these days of lockdowns, social distancing, and a digital delusion enveloping Christianity.

My fellow lecturer at Shepherds' Seminary and brother-pastor, David Debruyn, has written an excellent three-part blog series on "Disembodied Christianity"[205]. He states:

> *Media ecologists have been telling us for years that media shape us not only by their content, but by their form. For decades, we've been consuming media on screens: laptops, cellphones, flatscreens, tablets. They have become our primary form of information, education, communication, and entertainment. Screens have colonized us. And it appears that Christianity, at least in some parts of the world, has likewise been screenified.*
>
> *Put simply, the debate over the use or non-use of livestreaming, Zoom, online communion, and so on, is only secondarily a discussion of technology. It is primarily a debate over what a fully human Christianity is. It is the Christian view of the body that is*

---

[205] https://religiousaffections.org/articles/articles-on-church/let-us-break-bread-together-on-our-screens/ (Part 1); https://religiousaffections.org/articles/articles-on-church/disembodied-christianity/ (Part 2); https://religiousaffections.org/articles/articles-on-church/live-images-are-not-living-persons/ (Part 3)

> *behind these debates: do we need to be physically present to gather, do we need to be physically present to eat together, do we need to be physically in one another's presence to worship corporately or to be said to be assembling? And does 'virtual' presence still constitute a true, human presence?*

Aim of this Essay

In 1 Thessalonians 2:17-3:10, we find *four reasons for the believer to fight for face-to-face fellowship against all odds.* We should fight for face-to-face fellowship because of a godly desire; because of a satanic strategy; because of a glorious reward; and because of an unbearable risk.

(1) Fight for Face-to-face Fellowship Because of *A Godly Desire For Togetherness*:

"But we, brethren, having been taken away from you for a short while-- in person, not in spirit-- were all the more eager with great desire to see your face" (1 Thess. 2:17).

That great London preacher, Charles Spurgeon, once proclaimed:

> *Some Christians try to go to heaven alone, in solitude. But believers are not compared to bears or lions or other animals that wander alone. Those who belong to Christ are sheep in this respect, that they love to get together. Sheep go in flocks, and so do God's people.*

Paul the Orphan

In contrast to Paul's selfish and hostile opponents, we see in this passage the apostle's deep connection to the believers. When Paul describes how he was "torn away" from them, he employs a graphic image in the Greek: *orphanidzo*, "to be orphaned, forsaken, abandoned, kidnapped and stripped away from one's parents". Already in chapter 2, Paul had described their heartfelt ministry of spiritual mothering and fathering of these beloved offspring in the gospel (2:7-11).

Chrysostom describes 3:17 further: *Paul did not say 'separated from you,' nor 'torn from you,' nor 'left behind,' but 'orphaned from you.' He sought for a word that might sufficiently show the pain of his soul. Though standing in the relation of a father to them all, he yet uses the language of orphan children who have prematurely lost their parent.*

Malherbe's commentary states: *The image of an orphan describes Paul in the most poignant way possible as in need. One could have expected Paul to say that his separation had made him bereft of his Thessalonian children or that the Thessalonians had been orphaned by his absence, but Paul wrenches the metaphor to extract the most emotion possible from it* (p. 187).

The apostle Paul depicts himself as an orphan because he is robbed of togetherness with his flock. Paul must have in mind that scene in Acts 17 where the angry Jewish mob attacked the house of Jason, hunting for Paul and his companions. Only after Jason gave that "pledge/bond" was he released and the fury of the mob assuaged. After which, Paul and his men had to sneak out at night (17:10). Paul was thus orphaned from his beloved Thessalonians.

Yearning for Your Face

Note further in verse 17, Paul says they were orphaned, "in person, not in spirit", which literally reads, "with reference to face, not to heart". This is followed by yet a second reference to the face in the same verse: "we were all the more eager with great desire to see your face". Paul's language here is emphatic and emotional, proving to them his intense yearning for their physical presence, willing to brave all the dangers of ancient travel to be in-person with the saints.

Clearly this term, "face" is a dominant theme in this passage, because Paul uses it a third time in 3:10, "praying most earnestly that we may see your face", book-ending and framing this entire passage with a facial emphasis. In the Bible and according to God's design, your face is the sign of your physical presence, its most vivid demonstration. Just as we read elsewhere in Paul's writings:

> *For I want you to know how great a struggle I have in your behalf and for those who are at Laodicea, and for all those who have not personally seen my face, that their hearts may be encouraged, having been knit together in love* (Col. 2:1).

> *Though I have much to write to you, I would rather not use paper and ink. Instead, I hope to come to you and talk face-to-face, so that our joy may be complete* (2 John 12).

> *I had much to write to you, but I would rather not write with pen and ink. I hope to see you soon, and we will talk face-to-face* (3 John 13-14).

Your Face is You

Are you noticing a recurring biblical pattern in how God has designed us to communicate with one another? If your face is absent, you're not present, so to say. Your face is your unique identity, your special, God-given brand, your trademark and signature. That's how we know it's you and not someone else; your own fingerprint, your 'face-print' as it were. There's not another face identical to yours on the entire planet, amidst nearly eight billion distinctly different human faces. How great is our Creator![206]

There's a reason 'Facebook' and 'Facetime' have been so wildly popular across the globe. They didn't call it 'Elbow-book' or 'Knee-time'! Facial recognition technology has revolutionised our world in the past sixty years.

---

[206] E.L. House, *The Drama of the Face* (1901), "There is a story in every face. The face we have at fifteen is the one God has given. Our face at fifty is the one we have made for ourselves. The old man's face is a history; the young man's face is a prophecy. ...The old man's face is his autobiography; it is his life in miniature" (p. 11).

It began with the many landmarks on your face: the distance between your eyes; the shape of your eyes, your nose's height and width; the shape and position of your mouth; the size, location and style of your ears; your type of chin, jaw, forehead, hair-line, eyebrows, eyelashes, and so forth.

Technology then advanced to discern hair colour, lip thickness, etc. – an almost endless number of complex algorithms today applied to any CCTV camera. Facebook now uploads an average of 350 million new pictures every day and tags them, based only on facial recognition! They can even discern the difference between identical twins. In other words, the most detailed 'ID book' you possess is your face.

When firing squads or hangmen want to depersonalise those they must execute, they cover the faces of those condemned to die. When medical students must operate on cadavers, they cover the face.

Defacing of Society

So when Paul says here three times to the Thessalonian believers that he wants to "see your face", he is appealing to a powerful theological concept. The modern Church urgently needs to recover a biblical 'theology of the face'. Almost overnight, our society last year defaced itself, to the point now that almost no one hesitates about universal, permanent mask mandates. Now people are increasingly frightened even to see an unmasked human face. Some are admitting they prefer the 'incognito' fig-leaf security of wearing a mask.[207]

But are we surprised at this in a post-Christian, secularised, Darwinian society that rejected human uniqueness long ago? When you reject God, you reject man also, as His image-bearer. Hating God always leads to hating man; honouring God means honouring man. This era has rightly been dubbed, 'Covid-1984', because of all the uncanny parallels to the dystopian world

---

[207] https://www.refinery29.com/en-us/2021/04/10429659/how-long-face-mask-requirement-timeline

predicted by George Orwell nearly a century ago in his novel about the rise of tyranny (a book still banned in China today). He wrote, "If you want a vision of the future, imagine a boot stamping on a human face forever."

Defender of Human Dignity

For too long, our culture has already been disregarding the dignity of the human body – from aborting precious infants, to rampant sexual immorality, to gender reassignment, to widespread immodesty, to increasingly informal, worn-out and sloppy clothing, to obesity, cremation, skin graffiti and endless face and body piercings taking us back to pagan cultures. How ironic that humanism is so dehumanising! Yet wherever Christianity has gone, it has always elevated human dignity and rescued people from all kinds of degradation – from ending gladiatorial brutality and infant abandonment in ancient Rome, to ending widow-burning in India or female circumcision and slavery in Africa.

As a disclaimer, we have reiterated often in our church that both the masked and unmasked are most welcome in the name of the Lord (under Essay #3, see "Further Resources #8, our church's mask policy"). In today's climate, we expect there will be differing opinions on this matter for some time to come. The other day, dear Uncle Andy in our church came masked to church for the first time in a long time. As he greeted me at the door, he made sure to inform me, with his thick Polish accent, "Tim, I need to tell you the reason I'm wearing my mask this morning: I forgot my dentures!" Even behind his mask, his eyes sparkled with laughter, as I shared in the humour with him.

Masks are yet another superb opportunity for Christian love and godly tolerance to prevail in how we accept one another (Rom. 14). Yet that does not mean we cease striving to strengthen a weaker brother, and to grow in wisdom and unity in the body of Christ, seeking to be of "the same mind" and "the same judgment" (1 Cor. 1:10). Let's continue to allow Scripture, not culture, to shape our thoughts and emotions in every area of Christian liberty.

Our Open-Faced Faith

Pastor John MacArthur recently wrote these lines defending their church's policy of freedom with regard to mask wearing. It is also helpful in explaining why it is a godly desire and not a selfish desire to want to worship God and fellowship with other believers unhindered by masks.

> *Veils and face coverings have profound religious significance in many world religions. Indeed, much of the rhetoric surrounding COVID masks (even among evangelical Christians) describes them as symbols of personal piety. Serious questions about the usefulness, effectiveness, or medical necessity of masks are routinely dismissed or swept aside, and people are told to wear them simply because they are a tangible, visible means of showing love for one's neighbor. This rationale is pressed on people's consciences regardless of whether it can be proved statistically that masks really safeguard anyone from the virus, and irrespective of the fact that masks can cause other medical problems. But COVID masks have become, in effect, secularism's substitute for religious vestments. No one can reasonably deny that face coverings have become the chief symbol of popular culture's sanctimonious devotion to the secular credo.*
>
> *...Worship, in particular, is best seen as an open-face discipline. Covering the face is a symbol of disgrace or shame (Jeremiah 51:51; Job 40:4). Concealing one's mouth while praising God suppresses the visible expression of worship. The Psalms' calls to worship are filled with the words "tongue," "lips," and "mouth." "Sing aloud unto God our strength: make a joyful noise" (Psalm 81:1). " Wholehearted worship cannot be sung as intended—unrestrained and unmuted— from behind a state-mandated face covering. We see "the Light of the knowledge of the glory of God in the face of Christ" (4:6), and our faces were designed by him to reflect that glory back to heaven in uninhibited praise.*

> *...Yes, the language of [2 Cor. 3-4] is symbolic. We don't literally see the face of Christ physically. For now, we see Him as he is revealed on the pages of the New Testament. But the symbolism embodied in Paul's description of seeing Him with "unveiled face" is important, and the wearing of masks—especially government-mandated masks that serve as the vestments of secular religion—feels like a covert attempt to erase one of the core truths that makes Christianity unique.*
>
> *...we do not want to bind anyone's conscience with manmade restrictions. We especially do not want to shame the person who wears a mask purely because he or she genuinely believes the current secular orthodoxy about masks as a potentially effective shield against viral transmission. People in the church are free to wear masks if they choose. But people who share the above view are likewise free to worship, sing, pray, and proclaim God's Word without a face covering—even if that goes against the vacillating, sometimes arbitrary, and frequently heavy-handed dictates of government officials. It is simply not the church's duty to enforce executive orders based on a politician's whimsy—particularly when obeying those edicts impinge on our freedom of worship in our church.*[208]

The Biblical Story of the Face

Should Christians really care that much about the face? "Face" is used some 850x in the Old Testament, and 77x in the New Testament – nearly 1,000x in the Bible! God has a lot to say about our faces. He made them, He owns them, not the state, not the scientific elites, not the mob. Do not think it costs you nothing merely to cover your face; the Word of God clearly says otherwise. We must be aware of the trade-offs we are making whenever we mask up.

---

[208] https://justthenews.com/sites/default/files/2021-04/Rebuttal%20Decl.%20of%20Pastor%20MacArthur.pdf

In Genesis 1-2, man is the crown of God's creation, made in His likeness, with God intimately and uniquely breathing the breath of life into Adam's face. Unlike how God made all other creatures, He stoops down to make His image-bearer in the most personal, relational way possible – face-to-face.

The Face of God

For this reason, God has chosen to speak so often of His own face. Even though He is a spirit being without a body, yet He chooses the human "face" to say much about His own glory and how He relates to us. When Adam and Eve sinned, we read that they, "hid themselves from the face/presence of the LORD" (Gen. 3:8). Before Cain killed Abel, he was "very angry and his face/countenance fell", and the LORD said, "Cain, why has your face fallen? If you do well, will not your face be lifted up?" (Gen. 4:5-6). The sin of Sodom was great and came up before the "face of the LORD" (Gen. 19:13). Jacob wrestled with the angel of the LORD, and named the place 'Peniel', 'face of God'", because that is what He saw and who He met there (Gen. 32:30).

To know God is to seek His face and be satisfied with His likeness. Often in the Psalms we pray for God's face to shine upon us. When He hides His face, it is judgment. When He turns His face against us, it is terrifying. When He smiles on us, it is grace and peace. When He lifts up His countenance, there is hope. (See: Ps. 4:6; 31:16; 67:1; 27:8; 105:4, etc.)

With Unveiled Faces

What was most astonishing about Moses' rare friendship with God? It was that, unlike any other fallen man who ever lived, Moses enjoyed open, unhindered, unobstructed, face-to-face fellowship with God (Exod. 33:11; Num. 12:8; Deut. 5:4; 34:10). As a result, Moses had to wear a veil whenever he was in public, so that others were not blinded by the glow on his face, a sign of the Old Covenant. Yet now, under the New Covenant in Christ, wonder of wonders, we are told:

> *But we ALL* (not just Moses!), *with unveiled faces* (without fear!), *looking as in a mirror at the glory of the Lord, are being transformed into the same image from glory to glory, just as from the Lord, the Spirit. ...For God, who said, 'Light shall shine out of darkness', is the One who has shone in our hearts to give the light of the knowledge of the glory of God in the face of Christ* (2 Cor. 3-4).

What will be Heaven's highest joy and greatest privilege? "There will no longer be any curse; and the throne of God and of the Lamb will be in it, and His bond-servants will serve Him; they will see His face" (Rev. 22:3-4). "For now we see in a mirror dimly, but then face-to-face" (1 Cor. 13:12).

Listening to Faces

Not only is the Bible clear about the vertical, Godward implications of the face; it is also clear about the horizontal, manward implications too. Scripture often shows how the face displays all manner of inward joys and sorrows – from shame (Ps. 34:5; 44:15; Isa. 3:9), to dishonour (Ps. 69:7), to gladness (Ps. 104:14-15; Prov. 15:13), to defiance (Prov. 7:13; 21:29; Eccl. 8:1), to favour (Ps. 17:15), to wisdom (Prov. 17:24; Eccl. 8:1), to sadness (Eccl. 7:3), to love (Song of Songs 2:14). Often in the New Testament, the face is used to most warmly greet and express love for one another (the "holy kiss", Rom. 16:16; 1 Cor. 16:20; 1 Thess. 5:26). When we bid our last farewell to the body of a loved one, we kiss them a final time on their face.[209]

Look up a famous video called, "The Still Face Experiment", or try it yourself some time.[210] The mother sits down across from her six-month old baby and goes gravely silent, expressionless and emotionless. Her baby cannot bear this for even two minutes, before growing restless, disturbed, and visibly

---

[209] https://davidschrock.com/2020/10/31/a-biblical-theology-of-the-face-what-endless-mask-wearing-does-to-the-image-of-god-the-gospel-and-the-church/; https://dougwils.com/books-and-culture/s7-engaging-the-culture/they-dont-really-own-your-face-you-know.html; https://dougwils.com/books-and-culture/s7-engaging-the-culture/how-masks-became-the-flag-of-an-arrogant-ignorance.html

[210] https://www.youtube.com/watch?v=apzXGEbZht0

agitated and grieved. When the mother's face smiles and responds warmly to her baby, the baby is instantly relieved and at ease. Our God knew exactly what He was doing when He created us with faces and called us to face one another. Think again of Paul's words to the brethren at Thessalonica, "all the more eager with great desire to see your face. …as we night and day keep praying most earnestly that we may see your face".

A Defaced World

What an awful tragedy to see a whole society today turned into the miserable Phantom of the Opera, hiding their faces from each other; or like Muslim women, captive behind their veils. How inhumane our age has quickly become, where smiling is outlawed, and neighbours are weaponised against one another. Shop keepers now are required to treat customers like a threat to their health instead of a blessing to their business. How especially upsetting to see precious children's faces covered with masks as they do their school work isolated behind screens, or taking recess in their separate bubbles, learning to fear and avoid each other even though there is no proven medical benefit in these de-humanizing practices![211]

Famed economist, George Gilder, observed:

> *A nation without faces cannot be free or civilized. A nation without faces cannot even talk to one another. …We are consigned to C.S. Lewis's mythical nation of "Glome" in his novel* 'Till We Have Faces. *Glome is a barbaric, pre-Christian,* [defaced and dehumanised world].[212]

The desire for togetherness is a godly desire. It is a natural human desire that must be protected if civilization is to be protected. May our God raise up courageous voices and bold Christians in politics, business, law and

[211] https://www.pandata.org/children-and-young-people-declaration/; https://www.pandata.org/covid-kids-talk/
[212] https://www.aier.org/article/faceless-nation/

education to confront the evils of lockdowns and mask mandates, to stand against tyranny and to defend human dignity.

(2) Fight for Face-to-face Fellowship *Because of A Satanic Strategy For Isolation*:

"For we wanted to come to you--I, Paul, more than once--and yet Satan hindered us" (1 Thess. 2:18).

See the contrast? God calls us together (v. 17), the devil wants us apart, separated. Here in verse 18, Paul shows his active, deliberate efforts at face-to-face fellowship, through repeated attempts. Yet the adversary of our souls blocked him every time. No surprise for us who know our Bibles. Satan troubled the Jerusalem church (Acts 5); he harassed the Smyrna, Pergamum, Thyatira and Philadelphia churches (Rev. 2-3); and the devil is also mentioned showing up at the Ephesian and Corinthian churches (1 Tim. 3; 2 Cor. 2). We "wrestle not against flesh and blood", but are waging spiritual warfare with spiritual weapons (Eph. 6:10-18; 2 Cor. 10:3-5).

Satan's Top Target

Spurgeon warns and prepares us:

> *Satan always hates Christian fellowship; it is his policy to keep Christians apart. Anything which can divide saints from one another he delights in. He attaches far more importance to godly intercourse than we do. Since union is strength, he does his best to promote separation.*

Likewise, R.C. Sproul declares:

> *The church is the most important organization in the world. It is the target of every demonic, hostile attack in the universe. Jesus personally guaranteed that the gates of hell will never prevail*

> *against the church. He made no guarantee that the gates of hell would not be unleashed against it, however.*

In the end, it doesn't matter whether government hindrances to church life are targeted at us or not, whether they are persecution or not. One thing is clear, they are a tool of Satan to hinder God's people and harm our faith. Satan is more than happy to trouble night clubs and gyms also, as long as he can get to Christ's Church.

Pastoral Tenacity

No doubt, our sovereign God rules supreme over all of Satan's schemes, over every single tactic of the Tempter. Just look at how God used Paul's absence to produce this powerful epistle of 1 Thessalonians, so packed with encouragements! Yet God's perfect providence did not make Paul passive about gathering in-person with other believers. We see in Paul no indifference or ho-hum attitude of merely waiting around until Caesar says he can physically gather with the saints again. All over this passage we see Paul's pastoral tenacity and burning passion to be with the flock (2:17-18; 3:1,2,5,10).

Livestream vs. Living Persons

Listen as Pastor Debruyn further applies this to today's disembodied Christianity:

> *A Christianity that is still reeling from Enlightenment rationalism and from contemporary technopoly tends to see the faith in informational terms. Christianity becomes a set of ideas to be transmitted, and if one can see and hear what is being communicated, then worship is thought to be largely occurring. Everything can be reduced to sights and sounds: audio-visual information.*

> However: *A Christianity that is trying to shake off its modernistic and post-modernistic influences sees the faith in incarnational terms. Even loving God takes place when it is embodied in loving one another (1 John 4:12,20). The truth is embodied in persons, whom we must be with and share our lives with. Worship is not what happens "up front" where the pulpit and musicians sit. If that were the case, then we could point a camera at it, and replay that image to whomever, wherever.*
>
> *Instead, worship is* what we do when we gather. *When the believer is no longer solitary, but assembled together with other believers in the name of Jesus, there Christ is in a particular way (Matt 18:20). The context of Matthew 18 is church discipline, and Christ's presence there speaks of His authority behind the action of discipline, but this application does not alter the overall truth: the assembled people of God can expect the working of Christ through His Spirit in ways not available to a believer on his own.*
>
> *In short, the images and sounds might be "live" (i.e. their sending and receiving is roughly simultaneous). But they are not* living. *Humans are living, not their letters, phones, radios, or screens, nor the sounds and sights they produce. And worship is more than communication: it is the communion of living persons with one another.*

Let us not be "ignorant of Satan's schemes" (2 Cor. 2:11), but rather let the Church be the Church and gather boldly in His name! Let us "destroy arguments and every lofty opinion raised against the knowledge of God, and take every thought captive to obey Christ", that the world might know we are Christ's disciples by our "fervent" love for one another and zeal for face-to-face fellowship and mutual encouragement (2 Cor. 10:4-5; 1 Pet. 1:22-25; Jn. 13:35; Heb. 3:13; 10:24-25).

(3) Fight for Face-to-face Fellowship *Because of A Glorious Reward*:

"For who is our hope or joy or crown of exultation? Is it not even you, in the presence of our Lord Jesus at His coming? For you are our glory and joy" (1 Thess. 2:19-20).

Here is some of Paul's most affectionate language found anywhere in his writings. Here is the rationale behind Paul's yearning for face-to-face fellowship in verses 17-18. Paul's language here overflows in loftiest expression of his endearment to this church: "our hope, our joy, our crown…our glory and joy!" That prize for the athletic victors in their ancient games is Paul's metaphor for his gospel boasting in this fruit of his ministry in Thessalonica.

Viewing other believers this way radically changes everything, from our motivation to gather no matter the risk, to our motivation to fellowship, minister, serve and care for one another. What joy can compare to this, to know that God used you to help another believer grow and mature. Paul is telling them, 'You are what I live for, I take pride in you, you make life worth living, you are what gets me up in the morning and keeps me going!'

Says Barclay, "The glory of any teacher lies in his scholars and students; and should the day come when they have left him far behind, the glory is still greater. A man's greatest glory lies in those whom he has set or helped on the path to Christ."

When we approach Sundays this way – not just as occupying a seat, or going through the motions, but building into one another's lives – with that attitude, *nothing can keep us apart!* Our brothers and sisters are our reward.

(4) Fight for Face-to-face Fellowship *Because of the Unbearable Risk*:

Therefore when we could endure it no longer, we thought it best to be left behind at Athens alone, and we sent Timothy, our brother and God's fellow worker in the gospel of Christ, to strengthen and encourage you as to your faith, so that no one would be disturbed by these afflictions; for you yourselves know that we have been destined for this. For indeed when we were with you, we kept telling you in advance that we were going to suffer affliction; and so it came to pass, as you know. For this reason, when I could endure it no longer, I also sent to find out about your faith, for fear that the tempter might have tempted you, and our labor would be in vain.

But now that Timothy has come to us from you, and has brought us good news of your faith and love, and that you always think kindly of us, longing to see us just as we also long to see you, for this reason, brethren, in all our distress and affliction we were comforted about you through your faith; for now we really live, if you stand firm in the Lord. For what thanks can we render to God for you in return for all the joy with which we rejoice before our God on your account, as we night and day keep praying most earnestly that we may see your face, and may complete what is lacking in your faith? (1 Thess. 3:1-10)

Your Faith Matters!

Of all the foolish, unacceptable risks in life, here is a wise, acceptable and necessary risk, says Paul. Notice, in these ten verses, five times over he speaks of "your faith…your faith…your faith…your faith…your faith". Nothing concerned Paul more than their spiritual stability in Christ. Their faces mattered to Paul because their faith mattered! Being with them physically was essential, so that he could care for them spiritually.

Paul's burden here for these Thessalonians reminds us of some of our Lord's final words to Peter before the cross: "Simon, Simon, Satan has asked to sift you as wheat. But I have prayed for you, that your faith may not fail. And when you have turned back, strengthen your brothers" (Luke 22:31-32). Which is exactly what a restored and strengthened Peter did later on: "Be of sober spirit, be on the alert. Your adversary, the devil, prowls around like a roaring lion, seeking someone to devour. But resist him, firm in your faith…." (1 Pet. 5:8-9). Our greatest concern should be for the survival of our faith.

A dear friend and mother in the faith, who lost her elderly husband to Covid, lamented to me recently about believers caring more about the body than the soul, "I don't know why we trying harder to keep Christians out of heaven than we are to save sinners from hell!"

Avoiding Apostasy

If we stop meeting, we run the unbearable risk of apostasy. Remember the context of that severe warning in Hebrews: "And let us consider how to stir up one another to love and good works, not neglecting to meet together, as is the habit of some, but encouraging one another, and all the more as you see the Day drawing near" (Heb. 20:24-25). Why can the church never be non-essential to believers? Why is our gathering together in-person so immensely, eternally significant?

The next verse gives the reason: "For if we go on sinning deliberately after receiving the knowledge of the truth, there no longer remains a sacrifice for sins, but a fearful expectation of judgment, and a fury of fire that will consume the adversaries" (Heb. 10:26-27). God views forsaking the assembly (neglect of church gatherings) as a high-handed, wilful sin that will lead to apostasy if unchecked. It is a life-or-death, heaven-or-hell issue, and nothing less.

This helps explain Paul's urgency here in 1 Thessalonians 2-3. To see a brother or sister fall from the faith because of our neglect is an unbearable risk, says Paul. No less should that be our burden and conviction in our day.

Conclusion - A Fully Human Faith

John Wesley said, "The Bible knows nothing of solitary religion." This text proves that truth. Take Paul away from those he loved, and he calls himself an "orphan". Debruyn again applies this to our day:

> *...What is really going in those who scorn the essential nature of physical gathering for corporate worship is likely*

> *a transhumanist revisioning of human life, combined with a longstanding mind-body dualism in evangelical circles. The secular culture is happy to abolish human nature, and Christians have for some time been unsure of whether Christianity is fully human.*
>
> *...When Christianity is reduced to mere information (which is what technology transmits) it becomes another ghostly, disembodied religion of mere abstractions. And the more Christianity becomes simply informational, the more it becomes simply unbelievable. People are not primarily converted by facts and concepts, but by truth that is taught, incarnated and embodied by example, imagination, and exposure to others and their lives.*
>
> *Gladly, true Christianity is far from disembodied. The Word became flesh. We are saved not only in our souls, but in body too (1 Thess 5:23), and will one day see our Redeemer in the flesh on the earth (Job 19:25). Scripture anticipates the final and ultimate gathering with God in His presence – before His face.*

Life Together

Pastor Dietrich Bonhoeffer, who was martyred for his stand against Hitler and the Nazi tyranny, was in prison when he wrote, *Life Together*, in which he states:

> *The physical presence of other Christians is a source of incomparable joy and strength to the believer. . . . It is easily forgotten that the fellowship of Christian brethren is a gift of grace, a gift of the Kingdom of God that any day may be taken from us, that the time that still separates us from utter loneliness may be brief indeed....*
>
> *Therefore, let him who until now has the privilege of living in common Christian life with other Christians thank God on his knees*

and declare: 'It is grace, nothing but grace, that we are allowed to live in fellowship with Christian brethren.

Like Bonhoeffer and Paul, we should yearn for face-to-face fellowship with other believers and ultimately with our Lord and Saviour. This is not a euphemism; it is a bodily reality that we must preserve as God's image-bearers. We need to see each other's faces! Separation is unbearable for the saints. Praying earnestly night and day and making every effort to be reunited is expected of believers who have a godly desire for togetherness. We should be resisting satanic schemes to keep us apart. The perseverance of our faith is at risk when we allow the world to divide us. The reward will be worth the fight!

As a pastor and as a Christian, I can truly testify with the hymnwriter:

I love Thy Church, O God! Her walls before Thee stand,
Dear as the apple of Thine eye, and graven on Thy hand.
For her my tears shall fall; for her my prayers ascend;
To her my cares and toils be giv'n till toils and cares shall end.
(Timothy Dwight, 1797)

FURTHER RESOURCES

<u>Four excellent examples of standing against tyranny and upholding human dignity</u>:

1. A Catholic nun reminds us Protestants of a biblical theology of the face:

An unmasked face has become a threat of illness and a reminder of death. Yet it is wholly un-Christian to consider any other human person first as a threat to oneself. Before the Wuhan Virus came into the public view, someone who habitually considered any other as a potential threat to his own physical health was rightly labelled paranoid. Before Wuhan, being paranoid in that manner was considered abnormal, contrary to the common good, and opposed to the communion which ought to exist between men.

Man is called to love his neighbour and to be in communion with him. The mask obstructs the development of genuine community, which is the basis of human society: it muffles the human voice; it hides the human smile; it obscures the deeply human facial expressions which are integral to forming human friendships. Man is by nature a social animal. The spiritual dimension of man—the fact that he has a rational soul—is expressed most pointedly, profoundly, and truly in his face. A man recognizes his wife, his children, his brothers, and his friends not primarily by their elbows or knees, nor even by their hands (as unique as each person's fingerprints are).

No; a man knows the people he loves by their faces and by their voices. Man communicates most profoundly with his face—with words, looks, facial expressions. When faces are hidden and voices are muffled, the person himself is obscured. It is precisely for this reason that burglars wear masks; they do not want their identity to be known.

Upon encountering a masked person, one's gaze is drawn to the body rather than to the face. When one looks at the body, to the exclusion of the face, one encounters an object, a thing, rather than a person. Seeing arms, legs, a body, and a third of a face, the intellect categorizes this thing as a human being. That category is objective, not subjective. Without the view of the face—that essentially personal and subjective element of the human body—how can one avoid objectifying the rest of the body and the person whose body one sees?

To illustrate the point, often, during serious operations and autopsies, the face of the patient is covered to help the doctor or coroner make a mental separation between the task at hand and the person (or former person) into whom (or into which) they are cutting. The doctor is objectifying the person, in a sense, in order to complete the operation. What is true in this legitimate use of face coverings during medical procedures is likewise true in the current context: masks objectify human subjects.

Furthermore, masks indirectly promote thinking of others in terms of oneself. "You are not wearing a mask; you are a danger to me. You are making me feel uncomfortable by failing to wear a mask." Objects are meant to be used; that is, to be used as a means to an end. Persons are primarily subjects to be known and loved. When the face is obscured, the person is obscured. However, the only proper response to persons is not use, but love. Love which establishes communion is at the heart of the Christian life; for, God is a communion of three Persons. The Evil One seeks always to separate and to isolate, and the mask is presently his useful instrument to that end. While one must take reasonable measures to ensure one's health, physical health is neither the primary nor the sole determinant of a man's actions. There are more important realities than bodily health, especially spiritual health.

A mask worn at all times and in all places conveys the message that physical health is the primary good. There have been numerous saints who, motivated by supernatural charity, contracted contagious diseases and died in service to those who had these diseases. Such persons were canonized because they had a right ordering of goods: physical health, while important, is less important than and must be subordinated to spiritual health.

...From the depths of our hearts, each Christian unites himself with the Psalmist in saying: "My face hath sought Thee: Thy Face, Lord, will I still seek. Turn not away Thy Face from me; decline not in Thy wrath from Thy servant. Be Thou my helper, forsake me not; do not Thou despise me, O God my Saviour... O God of hosts, covert us: show us Thy Face, and we shall be saved." The Psalmist seeks the face of God with his own face.

The face, more than other body part, represents the fullness of the person. It is from his face that man speaks, sees, listens. It is with his face that man communicates. It is by means of his face that he is in relationship with others. An infant knows his mother's face and develops under the gaze of his mother. The Psalmist understands that the turning of one's face to God represents the turning of the whole self. He turns himself to God and begs that God would turn towards him.[213]

2. The Amish illustrate for us human community, and non-conformity to the mainstream, being willing to stand alone against the mob and the lies. Here's the latest from a recent study:

'To shut down and say that we can't go to church, we can't get together with family, we can't see our old people in the hospital, we got to quit working.... It's going completely against everything that we believe in and you're changing our culture completely in asking us to act like they wanted us to act the last year. We're not going to do it.' ...there is no evidence that there was any more death amongst the Amish than in any place that shut down their economies, wore masks, and were vaccinated.[214]

3. Canadian author, Jules Ruechel, is clear and helpful in understanding the times in which we live. Here he shows that we're asking the wrong question if asking, "Should churches be allowed to meet?"

This seemingly innocent question should terrify us because it completely misses the broader issue that is actually at stake. This is not a controversy over how a religious community should best practice their faith during a pandemic. What is at stake is the question of who should be allowed to decide what choices each of these citizens is allowed to make. And the government's emerging answer to that question should concern every single citizen, from the most fundamentalist believer to the most hardcore atheist, because at its heart this is not a question about religion.

The moment that the government switched from making public health recommendations to issuing police-enforced public health orders, this controversy stopped being about open church doors. At that moment, it

---

213 https://rorate-caeli.blogspot.com/2020/12/the-case-against-masks-presented-by.html?m=1#_ednref4

214 https://thepulse.one/2021/11/25/the-amish-took-a-different-approach-to-covid-it-appears-to-have-worked/

became a question about what role the government should be allowed to play in our lives. At that moment, it became a question about whether the government should be allowed to force citizens to surrender their individual autonomy to the will of politicians, health authorities, and bureaucrats if our leaders (or our frightened neighbors) decide that it serves a "greater good".

The moment that the government strips anyone of any constitutionally-guaranteed right, in the name of "safety", all rights are instantly downgraded to mere privileges. A right ceases to be a right if it becomes conditional. And if even a single fundamental right can be suspended at the discretion of the government, it signals that any right and all rights can be suspended. The precedent has been set. A right is set in stone; a privilege can be withdrawn. Now everyone's rights are in jeopardy, even if the government's focus is not turned in your direction today. Once the government gave itself the power to turn rights on and off, we're all at risk of getting a turn under the jack boot.

The idea of inalienable natural (individual) rights was arguably the most important cultural innovation of the Enlightenment era because, for the first time in history, it gave society a mechanism to protect individuals from the appetites of mobs, bishops, dictators, and kings. Inalienable individual rights were purposely designed to put strict limits on government powers precisely because, without those limits, a frightened, angry, or self-serving majority will inevitably find an excuse to permit (or even demand) that its leaders ride roughshod over the rights and freedoms of individuals who are out of lockstep with majority opinion.

The greater the crisis, the more important those limits become. Inalienable individual rights are the last defense against mass hysteria, tribalism, and the violent tendencies that lurk in the hearts of all people when differences of opinion reach extremes. Inalienable individual rights are the antidote to the appetites of the mob.

The right to attend church, to go to work, to voice unpopular opinions, or not to wear a mask ultimately all boil down to a single fundamental right - the right to individual autonomy. If we have elevated safety above all other rights, then we must accept the tethered existence of slaves.

...The fact that this question is now being asked, by so many people, and by people all across the political spectrum, reveals that our culture has lost faith in the principles of individual liberty, which form the backbone of our democratic society.

So, this never was a fight about church doors, or masks, or open businesses. From the moment the government issued its first public health order, this was a cultural battle about whether we are still willing to defend the often-challenging principles that are essential to a healthy liberal democracy, or whether we want to let the government close the door on the Enlightenment and open a different and altogether darker chapter to something else. Liberty is precious. And very fragile. Do not let the candle blow out.[215]

4. This critic captures well a righteous indignation about the long-term effects of social distancing:

Many say, 'We're only doing it out of politeness. You can hardly blame these people if they've been frightened witless by the government's propaganda. If my wearing a mask helps them be less scared and eases them back into normal life, well, that's a sacrifice I'm happy to make.' I disagree. Apart from being injurious to your own health, claustrophobic, unsanitary, sinister, unconducive to communication, alienating, atomising and quite incapable of doing the one thing they're supposed to do: stop anyone getting Coronavirus masks are a symbol of collective surrender to oppression. They're a sign that the enemy has won.

...Who is the enemy?...Anyone who thinks it's right to force the population to wear pointless, obtrusive muzzles in shops, train carriages or even school classrooms. Anyone who thinks it's right to use the alleged emergency as an

---

[215] https://www.juliusruechel.com/2021/05/why-cant-they-just-attend-church-over.html. See Essay #2 about how this idea of inalienable rights came from the Bible.

excuse to turn car routes into cycle lanes and city centres into pedestrian zones, even though nobody actually voted for any of this stuff. Anyone who thinks people who've gone on holiday to the 'wrong' destination or shared air-space in a pub or restaurant with a sick person should spent two weeks in quarantine. Anyone who thinks it's acceptable or proportionate to put an entire nation or sections of that nation under house arrest, when there's no evidence lockdowns do anything other than kick the can down the road while doing enormous damage to the economy.

Anyone who obsesses about people who died 'with Covid' on their death certificates, while completely ignoring: the elderly dying of loneliness and despair; people committing suicide; people dying of untreated cancer. Anyone who thinks it's the business of the state to decide which goods qualify as 'essential' and which you should be unable to buy from the supermarket during your random lockdown, now rebranded a 'circuit breaker' (because it doesn't sound like 'lockdown'), etc. None of this stuff is remotely normal. Yet we're being encouraged to accept that all this incredibly weird, outrageously oppressive, cruel, destructive, divisive nonsense is not just necessary but something we should welcome as, well, our new normal.[216]

---

[216] https://lockdownsceptics.org/mask-non-compliance-is-a-moral-duty/; see also: https://thecritic.co.uk/face-masks-make-you-stupid/; https://lockdownsceptics.org/we-shall-everyone-be-maskd/

5
ASSEMBLY REQUIRED
A Case for Churches Standing Up, Not Locking Down
(July 2021)

More waves and variants of Covid, more lockdowns, and more bans on churches – all of these beg for more biblical teaching and wise counsel for confused saints. Parts of our country are in flames[217], and yet churches are shut down? When our nation most needs prayer, houses of prayer are bolted shut? As the darkness worsens and the light of Christ is most needed, church lampstands are snuffed out (Rev. 1:20)?! What happened to not hiding our light under a bushel (Matt. 5:14-16)?

One of our seminary faculty and a fellow pastor, David de Bruyn, back in January 2021 predicted well our current situation (from Essay #2 of this book):

> *...The difficulty we are going to face in the coming months, and maybe even years, is that as wave after wave of the virus comes our way, the government may keep banning religious gatherings.... We cannot live through another year where we are tossed to and fro by every announcement coming from Pretoria. At least one thing needs to remain certain in our lives, and that is our covenant with Christ and His people. We need the rock-solid pillar of the church, the*

[217] During 9-11 July in our Kwa-Zulu Natal and Gauteng provinces, political rioting and looting mobs caused the worst violence in South Africa since the end of apartheid nearly 30 years ago.

> *pillar and ground of the truth (1 Tim. 3:15), not the shifting sands of whatever happens with Covid-19.*

Aim of this Essay

From a pastor's heart, here are biblical answers to six burning questions so that we don't disassemble what God has assembled:

(1) Why meet 'illegally'?
(2) Why no livestream, 'on-line' church?
(3) Should we meet publicly or not?
(4) Does it matter if lockdowns are persecuting/targeting Christians or not?
(5) By meeting, are we denying the reality and risk of Covid and minimizing all the pain and loss (and harming our Christian witness)?
(6) Should I get the vaccine? Or is it the 'mark of the beast'?

(1) Why meet 'illegally'?[218]

Like our Lord, let's answer that question with another question, from Christ Himself to Peter and to us all, "But who do you say that I am?" (Mk 8:29). A clear answer to that ultimate question is found in these opening lines from the elders of Grace Community Church (in Sun Valley, California):

> *Christ is Lord of all. He is the one true head of the church (Eph.1:22; 5:23; Col. 1:18). He is also King of kings—sovereign over every earthly authority (1 Tim. 6:15; Rev. 17:14; 19:16). GCC has always stood immovably on those biblical principles. As His people, we are subject to His will and commands as revealed in Scripture. Therefore we cannot and will not acquiesce to a government-imposed moratorium on our weekly congregational*

[218] In a constitutional democracy (e.g., South Africa), no temporary public health orders (or martial law, emergency regulations, etc.) supersede the highest authority in this land, our Constitution. The law-abiding citizens are actually those obeying the Constitution and upholding our basic human rights, such as religious freedom (see Section 15 in our Bill of Rights, and Section 31 in our Constitution).

> *worship or other regular corporate gatherings. Compliance would be disobedience to our Lord's clear commands.*[219]

Our Supreme Sovereign

The Church cannot have two sovereigns. What does our Lord command as head of His Church? From Mt. Sinai to Pentecost and the early church, God made it very clear that He requires His people to gather and worship Him at least once a week. (See: Exod. 20:1-11; Heb. 10:24-25; Acts 2:42-47; 1 Cor. 11:17-20,33). When our government contradicts this command by forbidding gathering, it is stepping out of its jurisdiction.

Thankfully, we live in a constitutional democracy here in South Africa. We still have the chance to prove in court that the temporary public health orders (or martial law, emergency regulations, etc.) are actually illegal according to the constitution and Christians who are practicing their religion are upholding the highest law of the land which recognizes our basic human right to freedom of religion (see Section 15 in our Bill of Rights, and Section 31 in our Constitution). But whether gathering is legal or illegal, it is essential for Christians.

Gathering is Non-Negotiable

As Owen Strachan writes:

> *We need church. Embodied congregational worship of Christ is essential--in all seasons. Should we be wise, and thoughtful, and even careful? Yes we should. Wisdom is not the enemy of divine commands, however. We modern Christians may have many "options" regarding whether we go to church or not, but outside of serious health concerns (and even possibly including them on a case-by-case basis), we do not have the "option" of skipping congregational worship.*

[219] https://www.gty.org/library/blog/B200723

There have been times in history when churches have been unable to meet because of a plague. But to this day, there is still no scientific proof that the pandemic is driven by asymptomatic spread and super-spreader events.[220] There is no evidence that church services cannot be held without effective safety measures. Love compels us to care for the whole person, body and soul; but the first duty of the Church is to rescue souls from the worst dangers of all, which are of eternal consequence – the world, the flesh, and the devil (1 Jn. 2:15-17; Eph. 2:1-3; 6:10-12, etc.). The job of the shepherd is to gather, not to scatter the sheep (Jer. 23; Jn. 10; Acts 20:18-35; 1 Pet. 5:1-4).

Defining Church

As the GCC elder's statement goes on to say:

> *The church by definition is an assembly. ...A non-assembling assembly is a contradiction in terms. Christians are therefore commanded not to forsake the practice of meeting together (Heb. 10:25)—and no earthly state has a right to restrict, delimit, or forbid the assembling of believers. We have always supported the underground church in nations where Christian congregational worship is deemed illegal by the state.*

Christians should indeed be the best citizens of the state, true "salt" and "light" in the most dark and decaying cultures (Matt. 5:13-16). That means our default position is one of submitting to God by our civil obedience to government (Rom. 13:1-7; 1 Pet. 2:13-17). But when the state asks us to do what Scripture forbids, or forbids from doing what Scripture requires, we must "obey God rather than men" (Acts 5:29). As my pastor-friend, Joel James, writes, "I would rather explain to the government why we *do* meet, than explain to God why we do *not* meet."[221]

---

[220] https://www.pandata.org/are-asymptomatics-sick-until-proven-healthy/ https://jamanetwork.com/journals/jamanetworkopen/fullarticle/2774102 https://www.sciencemag.org/news/2020/02/paper-non-symptomatic-patient-transmitting-coronavirus-wrong ; https://www.ncbi.nlm.nih.gov/pmc/articles/PMC7219423/#

[221] https://thecripplegate.com/church-vs-covid-part-6-lessons-from-history/

Statism's Lie

It's been said that Covid lockdowns have converted modern Christians to the age-old lie of statism, with its slogan: 'The State gives, the State takes away, blessed be the name of the State' (contra Job 1:21). For more on this subject, and the correct use of Romans 13, see Essay #2 in this book. Praise God for the brave examples of our brothers in Canada. May their tribe increase! Watch their story here; your church or mine could be next: https://www.jccf.ca/the-government-war-on-worship/.[222]

(2) Why no livestream, 'on-line church'?

Answer: Because there is no such thing, despite all of today's digital delusions, 'technopoly', and Big Tech takeover.[223] It is a contradictory oxymoron (as stated above) to speak of a separated gathering, an isolated assembly. How about a virtual honeymoon for the newlyweds? That's why our church cannot offer 'virtual communion'; because in 1 Cor. 11, *four times* Paul states that the Lord's Supper is a church ordinance for "when you come together", not for private participation. And in 1 Thess. 2-3, Paul is emphatic about the need for "face to face" fellowship (see Essay #4 in this book).[224]

Biblical Christianity is incarnational; all else is false religion. We worship an incarnate Lord, the eternal Word who "became flesh and dwelt among us" (Jn 1:14). And so His means of grace to us are also incarnational and 'enfleshed', not pixelated. God has uniquely made His image-bearers to be body-and-soul creatures. As de Bruyn warns:

---

[222] Another Canadian pastor warns: "Based upon the logic I've heard from other pastors over the past 15 months, if experts and elected officials declare Climate Change a global emergency, pastors will close their churches again." https://twitter.com/DrAaronRock

[223] As Neil Postman warned way back in 1993, in his book, *Technopoly: The Surrender of Culture to Technology*: "The uncontrolled growth of technology destroys the vital sources of our humanity. It creates a culture without a moral foundation. It undermines certain mental processes and social relations that make human life worth living."

[224] See here: https://youtu.be/fzQ5Pf45Lsc ("Face to Face: Against Disembodied Christianity")

> *Screens have colonized us. And it appears that Christianity...has likewise been screenified. It is primarily a debate over what a fully human Christianity is. It is the Christian view of the body that is behind these debates. ...does 'virtual' presence still constitute a true, human presence? ...the images might be 'live', but they are not living. ...worship is more than communication; it is the communion of living persons with one another.*[225]

Many of us as pastors/elders had to learn this lesson the hard way last year, seeing how on-line ministry (despite the best motives) becomes a crutch and convenient excuse. While some may benefit temporarily, others form bad spiritual habits that are hard to break, depriving them of the love, care and accountability they need, and that their church family needs from them.

We have also seen the rich benefit from the flock no longer having the livestream option, giving them greater incentive and a warm invitation to return to in-person fellowship. What a joyful reunion it has been each time to welcome our dear brothers and sisters back! No wonder the New Testament puts such a high premium on warm and affectionate Christian greetings (Rom. 16; 1 Cor. 16:19-20, etc.).

(3) Should we meet publicly or not?

I wish *this* were the bigger debate among Christians – not about *if* we should obey Christ, but *where* and *how*. Here is a genuine area of Christian freedom and godly wisdom in how we apply biblical principle, as summed up in Jesus' command: "Behold, I send you out as sheep in the midst of wolves; so be shrewd as serpents and innocent as doves" (Matt. 10:16).

We must carefully weigh up many factors, such as: the legal recourse and avenues available (e.g., a constitutional democracy vs. a communist state); the visibility of a church's location; the extent of police threat; the spiritual needs and maturity of a church flock at that time; the godly consensus of a

---

[225] See Essay #4 for much more on this.

church's elders; number of people gathering; other available venues, and their location, capacity and ventilation; plus other realities.

In God's Word, there are times we are told to "flee to the mountains", to avoid danger, to find safe refuge from physical harm (Mk. 13:14; Prov. 22:3; 27:12). But there are other times we are called to "stand", to face the enemy head on, to lay down our lives (Mk. 8:34-38; Jn. 15:18-20; Acts 5:41; 1 Pet. 4:12-19; 2 Tim. 3:12; Heb. 10:32-34; 13:13; Rev. 12:11).

Rightly do we admire the open defiance of Daniel and his three friends against the self-worship and idolatry of Nebuchadnezzar, with Daniel deliberately praying by his open window (Dan. 3, 6). Yet the early church often hid in the Roman catacombs so that their meetings would not be interrupted, to preach the gospel, expound Scripture, practice the ordinances, bring comfort, love one another, and prepare Christ's soldiers for persecution. Church history is also full of accounts of underground weddings and funerals amidst state persecution. This was one reason that churches owned their own graveyards for centuries.

In a country like South Africa, if more churches would unite together to stand up for our religious liberties and against government overreach, it would be impossible for the police to arrest all the worshippers or even disburse all the services. However, those committed to meeting are a tiny minority, so we have no such strength in numbers.

The Scottish Covenanters would meet secretly out in the moors and highlands. When these underground meetings were found out, Christians courageously faced their persecutors, like our Lord in Gethsemane when He prayed to be spared, yet rose to meet His betrayer and the police (Mk. 12:43ff). Our Lord especially promises to give us wisdom for such decisions, and the words to speak as we bear witness for Him before our foes (Jm. 1:5-8; Matt. 10:16-20).

(4) Does it matter if lockdowns are persecuting/targeting Christians or not?

Defining Persecution

Let's answer again with another question, 'How does that make any difference in whether we obey the highest Government and most supreme Court of Christ our Lord and King when He commands us to gather in worship?' Whether churches are banned by indiscriminate tyranny or discriminate persecution, we "must obey God rather than man" in either case. Since when did Christians wait until it was obvious persecution *before* obeying Christ? The Church is usually persecuted *because* she is already obeying Christ.

In fact, that's the definition of persecution: "if anyone suffers as a Christian" (1 Pet. 414-16), i.e., getting in trouble for obeying Jesus. Going to church is what Christians do in obedience to Jesus. "Blessed are those who have been persecuted for the sake of righteousness" (Matt. 5:10). "Righteousness" in the Bible is doing what God requires. And if doing what is right by going to church is criminalized, how is that not state persecution?

Exposing Inconsistencies

Here in South Africa, government is hardly playing fair, with a total ban on churches while crowded airplanes, taxis, buses, mines, malls, shops and businesses, restaurants and gyms carry on (as we believe they should); not to mention mass political rallies and protests.[226] Caesar's theology is again obvious – making money is essential, not caring for souls or worshipping God. That is the essence of atheistic secularism, that this age is all that matters; there is no unseen, spiritual or eternal realm; there is no God (Ps. 14:1; Prov. 1:7).

[226] https://joynews.co.za/churches-remain-shut-while-anc-eff-defy-lockdown-rules/

Opposing Tyranny

Consider also: we hate all forms of evil and tyranny, not just against churches (Prov. 8:13; Ps. 97:10; Rom. 12:9; Amos 5:15). Since when did this become a Sunday-only debate? We should also support business owners on Monday-Saturday who believe that God's Word requires civil disobedience of them too, defying unconstitutional lockdowns for the sake of putting bread on the table for their family and employees (1 Tim. 5:8). Lockdowns are a gross human rights violation; they are super-spreaders of oppression, death, despair, economic collapse, delayed immunity and prolonged health risk.[227] More and more evidence is proving that lockdowns don't work, they destroy.[228]

Yet we have become complacent about all the liberties we've enjoyed in the West. We've raised Christians who will not resist tyranny because they cannot even recognise or define it. Scripture speaks about the tyranny, or "cruel dominion", of sin (Rom. 6:18,22).[229] The Bible and history tell the bloody tale of both individuals, groups, and the masses abusing power over others. In the words of James Madison (one of America's founding fathers): "The accumulation of all powers, legislative, executive, and judiciary, in the same hands...may justly be pronounced the very definition of tyranny."[230]

---

[227] https://www.amazon.com/UNREPORTED-TRUTHS-ABOUT-COVID-19-LOCKDOWNS/dp/1953039103/ ; https://www.amazon.com/Liberty-Lockdown-Jeffrey-Tucker/dp/1630692123/; https://www.amazon.com/Price-Panic-Tyranny-Pandemic-Catastrophe/dp/B08G1Y764G/; https://www.amazon.com/State-Fear-government-weaponised-Covid-19-ebook/dp/B08ZSYN14J/; https://www.theguardian.com/world/2021/jul/08/new-zealand-children-falling-ill-in-high-numbers-due-to-covid-immunity-debt

[228] A recent study looking at 43 countries plus all 50 states in the USA concluded: "We failed to find that countries/states that implemented SIP (shelter-in-place) policies earlier, and in which SIP policies had longer to operate, had lower excess deaths than countries/states that were slower to implement SIP policies. We also failed to observe differences in excess death trends before and after the implementation of SIP policies based on pre-SIP COVID-19 death rates." (https://www.nber.org/papers/w28930) See also: https://www.pandata.org/lockdowns-dont-work-why/; https://www.biznews.com/undictated/2021/03/30/covid-19-lockdown-panda; https://www.bmj.com/content/371/bmj.m4263

[229] https://biblehub.com/topical/t/tyranny.htm

[230] https://www.pbs.org/tpt/constitution-usa-peter-sagal/we-the-people/separation-of-powers/. James Madison became convinced of religious liberty as a boy, after hearing a fearless Baptist

And our Protestant forefather, John Knox, famously declared, "Resistance to tyrants is obedience to God."[231]

Our Ultimate Enemy

We also know that behind all worship bans is our archenemy himself, Satan, the supreme tyrant. Regardless of whatever stated or unstated reasons the state gives, we know that any obstacle to the gathering of God's people originates in the Devil himself (1 Thess. 2:18; 3:5). As Spurgeon stated, "Satan always hates Christian fellowship; it is his policy to keep Christians apart. Anything which can divide saints from one another he delights in."[232] Or in the words of R.C. Sproul:

> *The church is the most important organization in the world. It is the target of every demonic, hostile attack in the universe. Jesus personally guaranteed that the gates of hell will never prevail against the church. He made no guarantee that the gates of hell would not be unleashed against it, however.*[233]

Tell me Satan does not have the church in his crosshairs when our government Health Department sent out this notice to health workers: "…unrepentant behavioural patterns such as social gatherings remain a recipe for disaster and should be discouraged at all costs". To which God says, "Woe to those who call evil good and good evil", rebuking worshippers for not repenting of their churchgoing (Isa. 5:20)! May Christ our Captain

---

minister preaching the gospel from the window of his prison cell. As one historian states, "Freedom of conscience, unlimited freedom of mind, was from the first the trophy of the Baptists." (pp. 14-16, *What I Like About Baptists*, by George Vandeman, 2003)

[231] https://www.goodreads.com/quotes/135100-resistance-to-tyranny-is-obedience-to-god. "Tyrants seek control, but apathetic citizenries allow it. Tyranny is only the victor when the citizenry abdicates the freedom they fail to cherish. Or perhaps they do cherish their freedom but are simply too naïve to see the preface of tyranny right in front of them." (https://www.standingforfreedom.com/2021/07/05/proclaiming-liberty-with-the-reverberating-courage-of-our-founders/)

[232] https://www.spurgeon.org/resource-library/sermons/satanic-hindrances/#flipbook/

[233] https://www.ligonier.org/blog/great-quotes-renewing-your-mind/

strengthen us to stand against every demonic scheme to use this anti-church virus to scatter Jesus' blood-bought sheep.

(5) By gathering are we denying the deadly reality and risk of Covid and minimizing all the pain, loss and heartache (and harming our Christian witness)?

Right now in our province of South Africa, everybody knows someone who has died of Covid in the last month. There is no longer any debate about the deadliness of this virus, the terrible way its victims die, or the immense strain on hospitals and healthcare workers. Every church has had a funeral, every workplace a tragedy, every family affected, some severely.

I recently attended a gut-wrenching funeral for a dear brother in Christ, leaving behind a wife and two young children. As we buried him at West Park cemetery, I noticed many other fresh graves – a sobering reminder of our mortality and of the ravages of Covid. The question is *not* the grim reality of Covid; it is *only* about the best solutions and right response.[234]

What About Our Witness?

Related to this is also the frequent question amongst believers about our witness to a watching world: 'Are we being a bad example of the gospel by (supposedly) putting lives at risk in our church gatherings?' But in light of our answers to questions #1-2 above, it should be clear that we cannot reach a lost world by disobeying Christ. The "first and greatest commandment" is not loving our neighbour; that is second to loving our God wholeheartedly (Matt. 22:34-40).

How does the world know that we are Christ's disciples? By our "love for one another", even more than our love for them (Jn. 13:35). We should not expect that the world will understand that our highest good is not physical safety, that we are not paralysed by the fear of death, and that we are fervent

---

[234] https://www.pandata.org/south-african-er-and-third-wave/

in our love for one another (1 Pet. 1:22; 1 Jn. 3:1; 1 Cor. 2:14; Heb. 2:15). The world will always accuse and slander believers; but we can have a clear conscience if we are only doing what is right in God's eyes – whether it be Sunday worship or any Christian fellowship, hospitality, or good works (1 Pet. 2:18-20; 4:14-16,19; Acts 2:42-47; 1 Pet. 4:9; Tit. 2:14; 3:14).

Harmful Remedies

Since when did compassion for the sick equal isolation from other believers, when prayer, worship, comfort and the human touch are most needed? Only a post-Christian, godless society could invent such cruel therapy. We have two whole chapters in the Bible calling for a quarantine of the sick, but never of the healthy (Lev. 13-14). The more burdens, the more need to "bear one another's burdens, and thus fulfil the law of Christ" (Gal. 6:2).

Constructive Debate

It is slanderous to falsely accuse anyone of being 'a Covid denier' or 'Covidiot' or 'conspiracy theorist' simply when they don't agree with the mainstream solutions, appointed experts, and government responses. God's Word forbids us from "bearing false witness" against others (Exod. 20:16; 23:1,7). Open debate and constructive disagreement over lockdowns and protocols is one thing; denouncing others as heartless 'Grandma-killers' is another thing altogether. This sin of slander should not be named among God's people (Lev. 19:16; Ps. 101:5; Prov. 10:18; Col. 3:8; Eph. 4:31; Jam. 4:11).

Christians are welcome to defend state lockdowns, protocols, and church shutdowns, if they believe there are good and godly reasons to do so. Their church will answer to God for how they've handled this crisis, and so will we. Out of Christian love and conviction, we may also zealously try and persuade one another of our position.

Helpful Materials

Speaking of which, here are a few sources our church elders have found proven and credible over the past 16 months in reaching an anti-lockdown position of focused protection for the vulnerable, instead of shutting down society. (Note, these are helpful medically, scientifically and politically; see above for theological sources already recommended.):

https://www.pandata.org/time-to-reopen-society/
https://www.pandata.org/covid-and-the-clash-of-ideologies/
https://gbdeclaration.org/
https://swprs.org/

Truth Matters

As God's people, we serve a "God of truth", and are followers of Truth incarnate, and are led by His "Spirit of truth" (Ps. 31:5; Jn. 14:6; 16:13). Only His Word is perfect, infallible truth. But we then measure all things by this biblical standard of truth, we stand for truth in every realm, and we oppose all lies, wherever we find them – theologically, scientifically, politically or anywhere.

Temporary Isolation

Churches should surely allow for a wide range of consciences and convictions on matters of personal healthcare (Rom. 14-15; 1 Cor. 8,10). Who cannot sympathise with older folk who fear gathering when at the peak of another Covid wave? Yet such isolation from worship and fellowship should not be indefinite. And often, when vulnerable people are weaned off of the mainstream panic narrative and taught further facts about the virus, they may find ways to return to church sooner rather than later.

(6) Should I get the vaccine; or is it the mark of the beast?

This question may not be as decisive in whether a church gathers or not; but it is a volatile issue dividing churches, and all of society. In our church for many months now we've taught about the three biblical spheres of God-given authority: the family, church, and state, each with their own assigned jurisdiction (see Essay #2 in this book). We've held that mask-wearing and social distancing is a personal health decision, outside of both state and church authority. The vaccine choice then falls under this same family sphere.

At the same time, since it is widely known that the vaccines are a new technology, not yet undergoing the same rigorous trials as previous vaccines, we recommend:

(a) Consult your doctor as to the potential pros and cons for your particular health profile. Consider also seeking a 2nd opinion, given the rushed nature of this new technology.[235]

(b) Do your homework and research to ensure best stewardship of your bodily "temple" the Lord has entrusted to you (1 Cor. 6:19). Ensure you have examined the adverse outcomes of the vaccine being reported around the world and have understood the benefits of natural immunity.[236]

---

[235] *For* the vaccine: https://www.thegospelcoalition.org/article/covid-vaccine-christian-unity/; *Against* the vaccine: https://www.deconstructingconventional.com/post/18-reason-i-won-t-be-getting-a-covid-vaccine

[236] "The human immune system is one of the most sophisticated achievements.... The survival of our species has depended on it for millennia. And today, we are still very much relying on it. For the record, 99% of people infected with SARS-CoV-2 recover without treatment. Only 1% of SARS-CoV-2 patients, who did not receive early home-based treatment, end up hospitalised. In other words, the immune system overwhelmingly protects. Even vaccines depend entirely on the immune system: vaccines essentially teach our immune systems what viral markers to be prepared for, they are not cures per se. Without a functional immune system, there can be no effective vaccine."
(https://www.pandata.org/should-covid-recovered-take-vaccine/)
See also: https://www.biznews.com/health/2021/06/28/covid-19-vaccine-immunity

(c) As with all of the Christian life, examine your motive: Is it only medical? Is it caving into social pressure? Is it job security? Coercion by government, employers or social memberships of any kind is wrong and tyrannical.[237] As with masks, the vaccine has become society's next pillar of a new moralism and virtue-signalling, all in the name of the public good: 'I didn't get the jab for myself, but to protect others.' In every age, the Church must be vigilant against all manmade forms of self-righteousness and extra-biblical spirituality (Matt. 15:1-20; Col. 2:16-23; Gal. 3:3; 4:8-11; 5:1-26; 6:12-15).

No, the vaccine is not the "mark of the beast" (666) in Revelation 13, that sign of loyalty to Antichrist's kingdom.[238] "666" will not be some accidental allegiance that true believers are tricked into accepting, without knowing it or being able to reverse it. Satan and his antichrist empire will be very deceitful, and many false converts and pretend believers will fall; but God's faithful will "endure to the end" and not be overcome (Mk 13:13; Rev. 12:11; 13:10,18). Getting the 'Covid jab' is not the beast's mark; but it could

---

https://www.wsj.com/articles/how-to-end-lockdowns-next-month-11608230214?reflink=desktopwebshare_twitter
https://www.medrxiv.org/content/10.1101/2021.04.20.21255670v1
https://gbdeclaration.org/frequently-asked-questions/
https://www.pandata.org/you-asked-we-answered/ (see helpful section on vaccines)
https://swprs.org/covid-vaccines-deaths/

[237] Benjamin Franklin said, "Those who would give up essential liberty to purchase a little temporary safety, deserve neither liberty nor safety." (https://www.goodreads.com/quotes/140634-those-who-would-give-up-essential-liberty-to-purchase-a). We face the potential for gross abuses of authority and violation of human rights and civil liberties through vaccine passports, medical apartheid, etc. See also: https://www.newsafrica.net/world/vaccine-passports-a-ticket-to-apartheid-and-racism; https://www.wsj.com/articles/declining-a-covid-19-vaccine-risks-penalties-in-some-countries-11613998997

[238] https://www.gty.org/library/bibleqnas-library/QA0174/what-is-the-mark-of-the-beast
https://www.crossway.org/articles/what-is-the-mark-of-the-beast-revelation-13/

become the beast's tool.[239] So the Church must stay alert against tyrannical coercion and persecution, and never compromise.

Conclusion - Trusting Our Sovereign Lord

No one loves His Church more than her Head who gave His life to save us, whose Father sent Him to redeem us, and whose Holy Spirit indwells us. May our faithful Lord use these six answers to exalt His name, preserve His Church, and advance His gospel. May He also give us much grace and patience wherever we disagree with one another as fellow members of His body. If ever there was a time our dying world needs to hear God's life-giving Word proclaimed by His Church, it is now. We must not be silenced!

Aren't you grateful that our God can always be trusted, no matter what? He is the 'Christ of the Crises', the Lord of the wind and the waves (Mk. 4:35-41; 6:47-50). Beneath all of the above questions (and many others) about going to church lurks a deeper, underlying question: 'Can I trust God with my doubts and fears?'

Better Than All Our Fears

As we stand for truth and continue in the clear path of biblical duty, we can be assured that He will prove faithful to provide for us and our loved ones, as He always has. Our God does not need my scheming or my anxieties to plan for every contingency before I take any risks in obeying Him. Our Lord Jesus truly declared:

> *If anyone wishes to come after Me, he must deny himself and take up his cross and follow Me. For whoever wishes to save his life will*

---

[239] From a Bulgarian living under a communist regime: "You cannot understand and you cannot know that the most terrible instrument of persecution ever devised is an innocent ration card. You cannot buy and you cannot sell except according to that little, innocent card. If they please, you can be starved to death, and if they please, you can be dispossessed of everything you have; for you cannot trade, and you cannot buy and you cannot sell, without permission." (W. A. Criswell, *Expository Sermons on Revelation*, 4:120–21).

> *lose it, but whoever loses his life for My sake and the gospel's will save it.* (Mk. 8:34-35)

As Mary Moffat of Kuruman once testified, after all the dangers they faced serving the Lord for 52 years in the Northern Cape: 'My Lord was better to me than all my fears.' His absolute promise still stands: "My God will supply all your needs according to His riches in glory in Christ Jesus" (Php. 4:19).

O Church arise and put your armour on
Hear the call of Christ our Captain;
For now the weak can say that they are strong
In the strength that God has given. (Getty)

POSTSCRIPT

Once Hitler announced in 1933 that any criticism of his Nazi Third Reich was a crime, most of the churches in Germany went silent (or openly supported him). Only a few faithful voices, like Pastor Martin Niemoller, who would spend time in a concentration camp for his boldness, dared to oppose the system. Here's what he told his flock:

> *We have all of us – the whole Church...been thrown into the Tempter's sieve, and he is shaking and the wind is blowing, and it must now become manifest whether we are wheat or chaff! ...It is now springtime for the hopeful and expectant Christian Church – it is testing time, and God is giving Satan a free hand, so he may shake us up and so that it may be seen what manner of men we are!*[240]

To that end, here are a few closing thoughts and burdens about blind spots in the modern church, *three final challenges we face in formulating a Christian response to Covid tyranny*:

(1) The Tyranny of the Weaker Brother

For the past two years, numerous Christian voices have been calling us to enforce new rules (mask-wearing and social-distancing protocols) in our

---

[240] pp. 261-262, qtd in E. Lutzer, *We Will Not Be Silenced* (Harvest House, 2020).

churches as a means of "care for the weaker brother."[241] Is this truly the most loving route to take? Is it appropriate to change the way we do church in order to follow the ever-changing moralism of the prevailing narrative? Or are we unconsciously giving in to another kind of tyranny? R.C. Sproul calls it the "Tyranny of the Weaker Brother."[242]

Sproul wisely warned us that when well-meaning believers make fellowship dependent on adherence to an extrabiblical moral code, they join with Peter who refused to eat with Gentile believers who were uncircumcised. For this he was publicly rebuked by the apostle Paul (Gal. 2). Paul goes on to say, "It was for freedom that Christ set us free; therefore keep standing firm and do not be subject again to a yoke of slavery. Behold I, Paul, say to you that if you receive circumcision, Christ will be of no benefit to you" (Galatians 5:1,2). Scripture takes bondage to legalism very seriously.

Enslaving One Another?

For example, I can personally love a weaker brother by choosing to give up my right to drink alcohol to avoid him following my example and falling back into sin. But it would not be loving for us as a church to put up signs saying, "Only teetotalers allowed!" This would be tyranny of the weaker brother, or what Paul calls, "placing a yoke of slavery" on free men. It would be an abuse of church authority (whether the regulation came from civil authority, or any other manmade laws). We do not protect the weaker brother by allowing him to dictate terms for the entire church and set rules that go "beyond what his written" (1 Cor. 4:6).

Indeed, 1 Corinthians 8-10 and Romans 14 give detailed warnings about Christian love prevailing amidst differences of opinion in the church around deeply cherished Old Testament Laws and extrabiblical matters of personal preference. If you are my brother/sister in Christ, I must be willing to give

---

[241] https://www.thegospelcoalition.org/blogs/erik-raymond/are-masks-a-conscience-issue/; https://www.thegospelcoalition.org/article/4-reasons-wear-mask/
[242] https://www.ligonier.org/learn/conferences/peace-purity-unity-church-2010-pastors/tyranny-weaker-brother/

up my freedoms when the practice of my liberty might tempt you to violate your conscience and stumble into sin. But no believer, and especially no church leader, has the right to add to the gospel by imposing Old Testament Law or any man-made regulation (whether medical, legal, etc.) on Christians who want to gather to worship our risen Christ (cf. Matt. 15:1-9).

Not Bearing False Witness

The helpful *Warrenton Declaration on Medical Mandates, Biblical Ethics & Authority* states:

> *XXX. WE DENY that an individual Christian's obligation to the weaker brother (1 Cor. 8:1-12) compels any Christian to violate his or her conscience (Rom. 14:3; 1 Cor. 10:31) regarding the wearing of masks or injecting a substance into their body. Such action may be regarded by Christians both as contrary to sound and loving health practices for themselves and their family. Specifically with masks which are worn visibly on the body, Christians may also have concern in their conscience about the message they believe wearing the mask sends to the world. They may regard the wearing of masks as bearing false witness (Ex. 20:16; 23:2) or as an unloving, tacit endorsement of what they see as propaganda surrounding their use and enforcement upon their neighbor.*
>
> *XXXI. WE AFFIRM that those who seek to bind the conscience of the believer by insisting that conformity with mask or vaccination mandates is the only way for a Christian to fulfill the command to "love one's neighbor as oneself" are treating the traditions of man as the commandments of God (Mk 7:6-9). These individuals are themselves guilty of twisting the Scriptures and are effectively subjecting the law of God to the ever-changing and conflicting whims of "public health" agencies, the latest medical study, or majority opinion.*[243]

---

[243] https://warrentondeclaration.com/

(2) Hatred of Evil

One of the underlying causes of so much Christian indifference toward tyranny can be traced to our worldliness and weakened sense of moral outrage and righteous revulsion. "Woe to those who call evil good and good evil, who put darkness for light and light for darkness, who put bitter for sweet and sweet for bitter!" (Isa. 5:20). Yet today we are losing the biblical discernment that should shape our affections and emotions, causing us to love what God loves and hate what He hates.[244]

Dr. Erwin Lutzer, veteran pastor of the historic Moody Church in Chicago, and author and evangelical leader, has written a timely book (not only for America), *We Will Not be Silenced: Responding Courageously To Our Culture's Assault on Christianity*. He states:

> *It's vital for us to understand that behind the headlines is a raging spiritual battle that can be confronted only by prayer and repentance followed by action in keeping with repentance. Only then can we hope to be a powerful voice in this nation. I am skeptical about our willingness to stand against the headwinds we face. We are so much a part of our culture that it might be difficult for us to know where to begin in our resolve to remain firm. We are like a fish swimming in the ocean wondering where the water is. Perhaps we have lost our capacity to despise sin, whether it be our own or the sin prevalent in our culture.*[245]

Apathy Not Allowed

Yet God's Word makes very clear what our response to evil should be. Whether it is wickedness in the ethical, moral, or doctrinal realm, apathy and complacency is not an option for the child of God. For example:

---

[244] For example, Psalm 5 says of God: "You hate all who do iniquity, You destroy those who speak falsehood; the LORD abhors the man of bloodshed and deceit" (vv. 5-6)."

[245] pp. 37-38

Psalm 97:10, "Hate evil, you who love the Lord."

Proverbs 8:13, "The fear of the Lord is to hate evil."

Proverbs 13:5, "A righteous man hates falsehood."

Amos 5:15, "Hate evil, love good."

Romans 12:9, "Abhor what is evil."

1 Thess. 5:22, "Abstain from every form of evil."

Like Phinehas purging Israel of sexual immorality, with sword in hand, consumed with jealousy for God's glory (Num. 25). Like Jesus, twice with a whip in His hand, overturning tables, cleansing the evil from God's house (Jn. 2:13-22; Matt. 21:12-17). God has given us a clear pattern in both Old and New Testaments of what a righteous reaction to evil should be.

Why then would medical tyranny and a cruel empire of scientific elites be any different? But as my friend, Voddie Baucham, often warns, "Today's 11th commandment is, 'Thou Shalt Be Nice'; and we can ignore the other 10 commands." No one wants to do battle in an age of emasculated men and an effeminised culture, after decades of feminism and egalitarianism.

Complacent Convictions

Thomas Aquinas wrote, "He who is not angry when there is just cause for anger is immoral. Why? Because anger looks to the good of justice. And if you can live amid injustice without anger, you are immoral as well as unjust."

I confess that God has used the Covid attack on our church to convict me of other evils that for too long I've not cared enough about (e.g., abortion, genocide, oppression, syncretism, false doctrine), not leading my family and church in praying against, preaching against, and standing against wickedness in every place. In no way does this change the gospel mission or message of the church; but it does sharpen our application of God's Word to this generation.

Turning the Other Cheek?

Throughout church history, Jesus' call for us to "turn the other cheek" has been wrongly interpreted as a mandate for total pacifism and non-resistance toward all evil (Matt. 5:39). Erasmus, Tolstoy and Gandhi have all perpetuated this myth that Christian love equals passivity towards tyrants.

Yet that view goes far beyond the command of our Lord, which is clearly in the context of interpersonal relations and loving your own personal enemy. Nothing Jesus taught cancels biblical teaching about government "bearing the sword", about the death penalty for murderers, about Christians serving in the military, about excommunication in the church, about corporal discipline in the home, and about personal self-defence (Rom. 13:1-7; Gen. 9:6; Matt. 18:15-18; Prov. 22:15; Exod. 22:2-3; Neh. 4:14-23; 1 Tim. 5:8).

'Blessing those who curse us' and 'returning good for evil' are essential Christian responses to our persecutors and personal enemies (Matt. 5:43-47; Rom. 14:18-21). But that does not negate the responsibility of Christian citizens to participate in the constitutional democracy they have inherited, in order to oppose public evils and love our neighbour – wrongs such as abortion, crime, corruption, racism and any violation of the God-given, inalienable rights of humanity, as His image-bearers. We may each oppose evil in differing ways, but indifference toward what God calls lawlessness is unacceptable for the believer. How can we pray, "Deliver us from evil", until we recognise and despise it as we ought?[246]

[246] For example: "Established western democracies are hosting the overt expression of hate – in words and deeds – directed at a minority outgroup, the likes of which have not been observed for almost a century. The victims of this onslaught are those people who have made the decision not to accept the offer of a Covid-19 gene-based 'vaccine'. ...So who is responsible for this persecution of a minority group? HART believes that responsibility for unleashing this tyrannical monster lies mainly at the door of the behavioural scientists who for the last two years, from their privileged position embedded at the heart of government, have

(3) The Danger of Pietism

I believe the Church's weak response to Covid tyranny can also be traced back to a major movement in the past 200 years of church history, called Pietism. God has used these past two years of lockdowns and worship bans to reveal the 'Pietistic Captivity of Christianity'.

Pietism came out of Germany in the 1700s, as a good reaction to dead orthodoxy. Yet as is so often the case in our pendulum tendencies as fallen creatures, the reaction went too far, beyond Scripture. Who can argue with a call for greater holiness, godliness and pure piety in our churches? Yet Pietism became a mindset of abandoning Christian involvement in the public sphere, of minimising the role of believers in the marketplace as salt and light, of handing over much of civic life to the world, such as politics, education, law, science, media and journalism (Matt. 5:13-16). Francis Schaeffer rightly stated in *A Christian Manifesto*:

> *Most fundamentally, our culture, society, government, and law are in the condition they are in, not because of a conspiracy, but because the church has forsaken its duty to be the salt of the culture.*

Protestant Monks

Pietism became a spiritual retreat, another kind of monasticism, instead of a godly advance for Christ. It led to cloistering away from the nations instead of "discipling" them in obedience to our Lord's Great Commission (Matt. 28:18-20). Privatising the faith and turning the church into a secret ghetto, Pietism forgot the church's biblical calling as a "pillar and support of the truth" publicly, an open lampstand lighting up a dark world (1 Tim. 3:15-16; Matt. 5:14-16).

---

skilfully orchestrated the unprecedented propaganda campaign."
https://www.hartgroup.org/the-persecution-of-the-unvaccinated/

Pietism effectively says, 'God's Law has nothing to say to society; it's for Sundays and for private spirituality.' Yet often we hear God's Word speaking to unbelievers; for example, about the duties of civic rulers: "O kings, show discernment. Take warning, O judges of the earth…." (Psalm 2:10-12; cf. Prov. 8:15; 11:11; 16:12; 20:28; 27:11; 29:4,14; Deut. 17; 1 Sam. 8, etc.).

A Compartmentalised Church

State authorities *love a pietistic, compartmentalised church* that will leave them alone, unbothered and unrebuked, with no prophetic voice heralding the Word of God. Caesar loves to be undisturbed by any rival authority, not having to tremble before a greater King, in the very courtroom of Almighty God. Satan himself loves a church that is retreating instead of advancing for Christ in this world, not "turning upside down" their city like the apostles of old (Acts 17:6-7).[247]

As C.H. Spurgeon preached to his 19th century London congregation:

> *I often hear it said, 'Do not bring religion into politics.' This is precisely where it ought to be brought! I would have the Cabinet and Members of Parliament do the work of the nation as before the Lord, and I would have the nation, either in making war or peace, consider the matter by the light of righteousness. We have had enough of clever men without conscience. Now let us see what honest, God-fearing men will do.*[248]

D. James Kennedy makes this worthy appeal:

> *How great it would be for more Christians to be involved in the various spheres of national life. In every sphere of life, whether it be the spheres of law or of government or of education or science, the*

---

[247] https://defytyrants.com/a-brief-history-on-pietism-and-statist-rulers/; https://defytyrants.com/the-destructive-influence-of-pietism-in-american-society/

[248] Sermon, "The Candle", Metropolitan Tabernacle Pulpit, Vol. 27, #1594

> *arts, television, motion pictures, journalism, whatever it is, we Christians need to get in there and we need to make our influence felt. We need to bear our witness for Jesus Christ and bring the teaching of Christ to bear on all of these spheres of life that He might receive the glory. After all, this is His world.*[249]

Seize the Day!

O that our risen Lord would alert us to the tyranny of the weaker brother, awaken us out of our pietistic slumber, and increase our holy hatred of evil and our zeal for His glory. As Erwin Lutzer again states:

> *A Christianity without courage is cultural atheism. ...We fear suffering – not the flames that past martyrs endured, but the cultural flames of shame and ridicule.*
>
> *...What a special privilege it is to be called to represent Christ at this pivotal moment of history! We are called for such a time as this. And we must pray that our light might shine more brightly than ever in our darkening world.*[250]

Let us keep this hymn of hope on our lips, come what may:

This is my Father's world.
O let me ne'er forget
That though the wrong
Seems oft so strong,
God is the ruler yet.

This is my Father's world:
The battle is not done:

---

[249] https://www.djameskennedy.org/devotional-detail/20170818-every-sphere-for-christ

[250] pp. 18, 262, *We Will Not Be Silenced*

Jesus who died shall be satisfied,
And earth and Heav'n be one.
(Maltbie Babcock, 1901)

FURTHER DEBUNKING OF FAUCI & HIS COVID CATASTROPHE

(By R. Kennedy, *The Real Anthony Fauci: Bill Gates, Big Pharma, and the Global War on Democracy and Public Health,* November 2021)

Fauci dictated a series of policies that resulted in some of the most deaths and one of the highest percentages of covid-19 body counts of any nation on the planet. Only relentless propaganda and wall-to-wall censorship could conceal his disastrous mismanagement during covid 19's first year.
Fauci's lockdown policies during covid-19 bankrupted a massive amount of small businesses, including 40% of black-owned businesses, some of which took generations of investment to build. The interest payments on the national debt due to some of these closure policies will cost up to one trillion dollars annually. Kennedy predicts that debt will likely permanently bankrupt the new deal programs, the social safety net that, since 1945, fortified nurtured and sustained America's middle class.

Business closures pulverized America's middle class and engineered the nation's largest upward transfer of wealth in history. In 2020 workers lost 3.7 trillion dollars while billionaires gained 3.9 trillion. An additional 8 million workers dropped below the poverty line.

...With fears of covid generously stoked, the dramatic and steady erosion of constitutional rights and fomenting of a global coup d'état against democracy, the demolition of our economy, the obliteration of a million small businesses, the collapsing of the middle class, the evisceration of our Bill of Rights, the tidal wave of surveillance capitalism, and the rising biosecurity state, and the stunning shifts in wealth and power going to a burgeoning oligarchy of high-tech silicon valley robber barons seemed to a dazed and uncritical America like it might be a reasonable price to pay for safety.

...Kennedy documents that the Fauci-encouraged, large-scale approach to treating patients with covid-19 was devastating. Specifically, treating patients with Remdesivir, intubation, and ventilator, was unprecedented, and racked up an unnecessarily high body count.

One of the more troubling reports from the book concerns this high death count. Dr. Peter McCullough (Baylor University Medical) is the most peer-reviewed published medical professional in history. McCullough wrote that we could have drastically reduced hospitalizations and deaths by early treatment medications like ivermectin and hydroxychloroquine. His work demonstrates that some 80% of deaths could have been avoided with these and other relatively inexpensive treatments.

...Five medical professionals, including some of the nation's most highly published and experienced physicians and frontline covid specialists (Dr. McCullough, Dr. Kory, Dr. Ryan Cole, Dr. Brownstein, and Dr. Harvey Rish) independently reported that Dr. Fauci's suppression of aforementioned early treatments and off-patent remedies was responsible for up to 80% of the deaths attributed to covid-19 in the US. The relentless malpractice of deliberately withholding these effective, early covid-19 treatments, and forcing the use of Remdesivir (which costs a few thousand dollars per dose) may have unnecessarily killed up to 500,000 Americans.

...Dr. Fauci led an effort to deliberately derail America's access to life-saving drugs and medicines that might have saved hundreds of thousands of lives, and dramatically shortened the pandemic. There is no other aspect of the covid crisis that more clearly reveals the malicious intentions of a powerful vaccine cartel led by Dr. Fauci and Bill Gates to prolong the pandemic and amplify its mortal effects in order to promote their mischievous inoculations."

...Covid-19 is not the problem; it is a problem, one largely solvable with early treatments that are safe, effective, and inexpensive. The problem is endemic corruption in the medical-industrial complex, currently supported at every turn by mass-media companies. This cartel's coup d'état has already

siphoned billions from taxpayers, already vacuumed up trillions from the global middle class, and created the excuse for massive propaganda, censorship, and control worldwide. Along with its captured regulators, this cartel has ushered in the global war on freedom and democracy.[251]

[251] https://thecripplegate.com/book-review-the-real-anthony-fauci/

APPENDICES

APPENDIX A

CHRIST, NOT CAESAR, IS HEAD OF THE CHURCH

A Biblical Case for the Church's Duty to Remain Open

(A statement from John MacArthur and the elders of Grace Community Church - July 2020)

Christ is Lord of all. He is the one true head of the church (Ephesians 1:22; 5:23; Colossians 1:18). He is also King of kings—sovereign over every earthly authority (1 Timothy 6:15; Revelation 17:14; 19:16). Grace Community Church has always stood immovably on those biblical principles. As His people, we are subject to His will and commands as revealed in Scripture. Therefore we cannot and will not acquiesce to a government-imposed moratorium on our weekly congregational worship or other regular corporate gatherings. Compliance would be disobedience to our Lord's clear commands.

Some will think such a firm statement is inexorably in conflict with the command to be subject to governing authorities laid out in Romans 13 and 1 Peter 2. Scripture does mandate careful, conscientious obedience to all governing authority, including kings, governors, employers, and their agents (in Peter's words, "not only to those who are good and gentle, but also to those who are unreasonable" [1 Peter 2:18]). Insofar as government authorities do not attempt to assert ecclesiastical authority or issue orders that forbid our obedience to God's law, their authority is to be obeyed whether we agree with their rulings or not. In other words, Romans 13 and 1 Peter 2 still bind the consciences of individual Christians. We are to obey our civil authorities as powers that God Himself has ordained.

However, while civil government is invested with divine authority to rule the state, neither of those texts (nor any other) grants civic rulers jurisdiction over the church. God has established three institutions within human society: the family, the state, and the church. Each institution has a sphere of authority with jurisdictional limits that must be respected. A father's authority is limited to his own family. Church leaders' authority (which is delegated to them by Christ) is limited to church matters. And government is specifically tasked with the oversight and protection of civic peace and well-being within the boundaries of a nation or community. God has not granted civic rulers authority over the doctrine, practice, or polity of the church. The biblical framework limits the authority of each institution to its specific jurisdiction. The church does not have the right to meddle in the affairs of individual families and ignore parental authority. Parents do not have authority to manage civil matters while circumventing government officials. And similarly, government officials have no right to interfere in ecclesiastical matters in a way that undermines or disregards the God-given authority of pastors and elders.

When any one of the three institutions exceeds the bounds of its jurisdiction it is the duty of the other institutions to curtail that overreach. Therefore, when any government official issues orders regulating worship (such as bans on singing, caps on attendance, or prohibitions against gatherings and services), he steps outside the legitimate bounds of his God-ordained authority as a civic official and arrogates to himself authority that God expressly grants only to the Lord Jesus Christ as sovereign over His Kingdom, which is the church. His rule is mediated to local churches through those pastors and elders who teach His Word (Matthew 16:18–19; 2 Timothy 3:16–4:2).

Therefore, in response to the recent state order requiring churches in California to limit or suspend all meetings indefinitely, we, the pastors and elders of Grace Community Church, respectfully inform our civic leaders that they have exceeded their legitimate jurisdiction, and faithfulness to Christ prohibits us from observing the restrictions they want to impose on our corporate worship services.

Said another way, it has never been the prerogative of civil government to order, modify, forbid, or mandate worship. When, how, and how often the church worships is not subject to Caesar. Caesar himself is subject to God. Jesus affirmed that principle when He told Pilate, "You would have no authority over Me, unless it had been given you from above" (John 19:11).

And because Christ is head of the church, ecclesiastical matters pertain to His Kingdom, not Caesar's. Jesus drew a stark distinction between those two kingdoms when He said, "Render to Caesar the things that are Caesar's, and to God the things that are God's" (Mark 12:17). Our Lord Himself always rendered to Caesar what was Caesar's, but He never offered to Caesar what belongs solely to God.

As pastors and elders, we cannot hand over to earthly authorities any privilege or power that belongs solely to Christ as head of His church. Pastors and elders are the ones to whom Christ has given the duty and the right to exercise His spiritual authority in the church (1 Peter 5:1–4; Hebrews 13:7, 17)—and Scripture alone defines how and whom they are to serve (1 Corinthians 4:1–4). They have no duty to follow orders from a civil government attempting to regulate the worship or governance of the church. In fact, pastors who cede their Christ-delegated authority in the church to a civil ruler have abdicated their responsibility before their Lord and violated the God-ordained spheres of authority as much as the secular official who illegitimately imposes his authority upon the church. Our church's doctrinal statement has included this paragraph for more than 40 years:

We teach the autonomy of the local church, free from any external authority or control, with the right of self-government and freedom from the interference of any hierarchy of individuals or organizations (Titus 1:5). We teach that it is scriptural for true churches to cooperate with each other for the presentation and propagation of the faith. Each local church, however, through its elders and their interpretation and application of Scripture, should be the sole judge of the measure and method of its cooperation. The elders should determine all other matters of membership, policy, discipline, benevolence, and government as well (Acts 15:19–31; 20:28; 1 Corinthians 5:4–7, 13; 1 Peter 5:1–4).

In short, as the church, we do not need the state's permission to serve and worship our Lord as He has commanded. The church is Christ's precious bride (2 Corinthians 11:2; Ephesians 5:23–27). She belongs to Him alone. She exists by His will and serves under His authority. He will tolerate no assault on her purity and no infringement of His headship over her. All of that was established when Jesus said, "I will build My church; and the gates of Hades will not overpower it" (Matthew 16:18).

Christ's own authority is "far above all rule and authority and power and dominion, and every name that is named, not only in this age but also in the one to come. And [God the Father has] put all things in subjection under [Christ's] feet, and gave Him as head over all things to the church, which is His body, the fullness of Him who fills all in all" (Ephesians 1:21–23).

Accordingly, the honor that we rightly owe our earthly governors and magistrates (Romans 13:7) does not include compliance when such officials attempt to subvert sound doctrine, corrupt biblical morality, exercise ecclesiastical authority, or supplant Christ as head of the church in any other way.

The biblical order is clear: Christ is Lord over Caesar, not vice versa. Christ, not Caesar, is head of the church. Conversely, the church does not in any sense rule the state. Again, these are distinct kingdoms, and Christ is sovereign over both. Neither church nor state has any higher authority than that of Christ Himself, who declared, "All authority has been given to Me in heaven and on earth" (Matthew 28:18).

Notice that we are not making a constitutional argument, even though the First Amendment of the United States Constitution expressly affirms this principle in its opening words: "Congress shall make no law respecting an establishment of religion, or prohibiting the free exercise thereof." The right we are appealing to was not created by the Constitution. It is one of those unalienable rights granted solely by God, who ordained human government and establishes both the extent and the limitations of the state's authority (Romans 13:1–7). Our argument therefore is purposely not grounded in the First Amendment; it is based on the same biblical principles that the Amendment itself is founded upon. The exercise of true religion is a divine duty given to men and women created in God's image (Genesis 1:26–

27; Acts 4:18–20; 5:29; cf. Matthew 22:16–22). In other words, freedom of worship is a command of God, not a privilege granted by the state.

An additional point needs to be made in this context. Christ is always faithful and true (Revelation 19:11). Human governments are not so trustworthy. Scripture says, "the whole world lies in the power of the evil one" (1 John 5:19). That refers, of course, to Satan. John 12:31 and 16:11 call him "the ruler of this world," meaning he wields power and influence through this world's political systems (cf. Luke 4:6; Ephesians 2:2; 6:12). Jesus said of him, "he is a liar and the father of lies" (John 8:44). History is full of painful reminders that government power is easily and frequently abused for evil purposes. Politicians may manipulate statistics and the media can cover up or camouflage inconvenient truths. So a discerning church cannot passively or automatically comply if the government orders a shutdown of congregational meetings—even if the reason given is a concern for public health and safety.

The church by definition is an assembly. That is the literal meaning of the Greek word for "church"—ekklesia—the assembly of the called-out ones. A non-assembling assembly is a contradiction in terms. Christians are therefore commanded not to forsake the practice of meeting together (Hebrews 10:25)—and no earthly state has a right to restrict, delimit, or forbid the assembling of believers. We have always supported the underground church in nations where Christian congregational worship is deemed illegal by the state.

When officials restrict church attendance to a certain number, they attempt to impose a restriction that in principle makes it impossible for the saints to gather as the church. When officials prohibit singing in worship services, they attempt to impose a restriction that in principle makes it impossible for the people of God to obey the commands of Ephesians 5:19 and Colossians 3:16. When officials mandate distancing, they attempt to impose a restriction that in principle makes it impossible to experience the close communion between believers that is commanded in Romans 16:16, 1 Corinthians 16:20, 2 Corinthians 13:12, and 1 Thessalonians 5:26. In all those spheres, we must submit to our Lord.

Although we in America may be unaccustomed to government intrusion into the church of our Lord Jesus Christ, this is by no means the first time in church history that Christians have had to deal with government overreach or hostile rulers. As a matter of fact, persecution of the church by government authorities has been the norm, not the exception, throughout church history. "Indeed," Scripture says, "all who desire to live godly in Christ Jesus will be persecuted" (2 Timothy 3:12).

Historically, the two main persecutors have always been secular government and false religion. Most of Christianity's martyrs have died because they refused to obey such authorities. This is, after all, what Christ promised: "If they persecuted Me, they will also persecute you" (John 15:20). In the last of the beatitudes, He said, "Blessed are you when people insult you and persecute you, and falsely say all kinds of evil against you because of Me. Rejoice and be glad, for your reward in heaven is great; for in the same way they persecuted the prophets who were before you" (Matthew 5:11–12).

As government policy moves further away from biblical principles, and as legal and political pressures against the church intensify, we must recognize that the Lord may be using these pressures as means of purging to reveal the true church. Succumbing to governmental overreach may cause churches to remain closed indefinitely. How can the true church of Jesus Christ distinguish herself in such a hostile climate? There is only one way: bold allegiance to the Lord Jesus Christ.

Even where governments seem sympathetic to the church, Christian leaders have often needed to push back against aggressive state officials. In Calvin's Geneva, for example, church officials at times needed to fend off attempts by the city council to govern aspects of worship, church polity, and church discipline. The Church of England has never fully reformed, precisely because the British Crown and Parliament have always meddled in church affairs. In 1662, the Puritans were ejected from their pulpits because they refused to bow to government mandates regarding use of the Book of Common Prayer, the wearing of vestments, and other ceremonial aspects of state-regulated worship. The British Monarch still claims to be the supreme governor and titular head of the Anglican Church.

But again: Christ is the one true head of His church, and we intend to honor that vital truth in all our gatherings. For that preeminent reason, we cannot accept and will not bow to the intrusive restrictions government officials now want to impose on our congregation. We offer this response without rancor, and not out of hearts that are combative or rebellious (1 Timothy 2:1–8; 1 Peter 2:13–17), but with a sobering awareness that we must answer to the Lord Jesus for the stewardship He has given to us as shepherds of His precious flock.

To government officials, we respectfully say with the apostles, "Whether it is right in the sight of God to give heed to you rather than to God, you be the judge" (Acts 4:19). And our unhesitating reply to that question is the same as the apostles': "We must obey God rather than men" (Acts 5:29).

Our prayer is that every faithful congregation will stand with us in obedience to our Lord as Christians have done through the centuries.

Addendum

The elders of Grace Church considered and independently consented to the original government order, not because we believed the state has a right to tell churches when, whether, or how to worship. To be clear, we believe that the original orders were just as much an illegitimate intrusion of state authority into ecclesiastical matters as we believe it is now. However, because we could not possibly have known the true severity of the virus, and because we care about people as our Lord did, we believe guarding public health against serious contagions is a rightful function of Christians as well as civil government. Therefore, we voluntarily followed the initial recommendations of our government. It is, of course, legitimate for Christians to abstain from the assembly of saints temporarily in the face of illness or an imminent threat to public health.

When the devastating lockdown began, it was supposed to be a short-term stopgap measure, with the goal to "flatten the curve"—meaning they wanted to slow the rate of infection to ensure that hospitals weren't overwhelmed. And there were horrific projections of death. In light of those factors, our pastors supported the measures by observing the guidelines that were issued for churches.

But we did not yield our spiritual authority to the secular government. We said from the very start that our voluntary compliance was subject to change if the restrictions dragged on beyond the stated goal, or politicians unduly intruded into church affairs, or if health officials added restrictions that would attempt to undermine the church's mission. We made every decision with our own burden of responsibility in mind. We simply took the early opportunity to support the concerns of health officials and accommodate the same concerns among our church members, out of a desire to act in an abundance of care and reasonableness (Philippians 4:5).

But we are now more than twenty weeks into the unrelieved restrictions. It is apparent that those original projections of death were wrong and the virus is nowhere near as dangerous as originally feared. Still, roughly forty percent of the year has passed with our church essentially unable to gather in a normal way. Pastors' ability to shepherd their flocks has been severely curtailed. The unity and influence of the church has been threatened. Opportunities for believers to serve and minister to one another have been missed. And the suffering of Christians who are troubled, fearful, distressed, infirm, or otherwise in urgent need of fellowship and encouragement has been magnified beyond anything that could reasonably be considered just or necessary. Major public events that were planned for 2021 are already being canceled, signaling that officials are preparing to keep restrictions in place into next year and beyond. That forces churches to choose between the clear command of our Lord and the government officials. Therefore, following the authority of our Lord Jesus Christ, we gladly choose to obey Him.

APPENDIX B

FACING COVID-19 WITHOUT FEAR

(A statement from John MacArthur and the pastoral staff of Grace Community Church - September 2021)

Introduction

We get many requests from church leaders around the world asking for advice as they deal with COVID-19 lockdown orders and other government-mandated restrictions on worship. This is a short record of how our church responded to the government's efforts to keep our congregation from gathering, an index of some things we have learned, and a few important biblical principles to bear in mind as you consider how you and your church must respond biblically.

We are convinced that governmental encroachment on basic human freedoms constitutes a more intimidating threat to individuals, a greater impediment to the work of the church, and a larger calamity for all of society than any pestilence or other natural disaster. These are difficult times, calling for a thoughtful, biblical, and wise response from church leaders and their congregations.

A Short History

COVID-19 began to make international headlines in early 2020, and by mid-March, state and local governments across America were issuing emergency orders restricting large gatherings of people. At the time, health officials were warning that COVID might cause a wave of death and disaster ranking high on the spectrum between the 1918 Spanish flu epidemic and the Black Death in 14th-century Europe. Major media outlets reported that people were literally dying on the streets in China. One report featured a morgue in New York City where bodies were stacked like cordwood. Naturally, such stories provoked a high level of public fear.

In mid-March, Californians were put under a statewide mandatory lockdown. Initially, government health officials said they expected a two-week quarantine ("fifteen days to slow the spread"). The original goal was not to eliminate the virus completely (epidemiologists knew that was impossible), but to make sure hospitals were not overwhelmed until more treatment facilities could be set up. Since the true gravity of the threat was still unknown and the quarantine was supposed to be reasonably short, Grace Church's elders decided to suspend public services while we continued live-streaming sermons from the pulpit in the Worship Center auditorium.

More than six weeks passed with no letup on the government-ordered quarantine. While media reports and health department predictions continued to be dire, the actual impact of the virus on our congregation was only mildly worse than the annual flu. Relatively few congregants tested positive, and those who did typically recovered quickly. It was soon obvious (and CDC statistics proved it) that healthy people in their fifties or younger were not in imminent mortal danger from the spread of COVID-19.

By mid-May, large numbers of worshipers began returning on Sunday mornings spontaneously. The auditorium was well filled by early June. Hardly anyone came wearing a mask, and because of limited space on the church campus, social distancing was not an option. So county health officials stepped up their efforts to close the doors of Grace Church to worshipers. On July 24, faced with new emergency mandates aimed specifically at tightening restrictions on churches, Grace Church's elders issued a statement, "Christ, Not Caesar, Is Head of the Church." The statement gives a brief biblical rationale for why the church must gather, and concludes, "We cannot accept and will not bow to the intrusive restrictions government officials now want to impose on our congregation."

The aftermath featured a protracted court case in which the church argued that the state has no legal authority to impose such a long-term closure on places of worship. Almost exactly a year after the elders' statement was published, the court case was settled in the church's favor, thus vindicating the stance Grace Church took.

The course of action we followed reflects our unshakable biblical conviction that we must not render to Caesar that which belongs to God. The Lord has not granted to civil government any authority to regulate the terms and circumstances of the church's worship. That prerogative belongs to Christ alone.

What follows is a brief digest of some facts about COVID that convinced us the virus, while not negligible, is not so much of a threat that it warrants churches to refrain from gathering as the people of God.

COVID Facts

The death rate from COVID is nowhere near the original dire predictions. In early 2020, most policy makers were citing predictions from a researcher named Neil Ferguson, a professor at Imperial College London. Ferguson confidently predicted that more than 2.2 million people in the United States would die from COVID within three months' time. Even though that prediction quickly proved to be grossly overblown, government officials continued to cite the Ferguson model as justification for prolonging the lockdowns. Rather than acknowledging that COVID-19 is not the doomsday pandemic so many had foretold, they claimed the diminished numbers were proof that the lockdowns were working.

To put the facts in perspective: Ferguson's model predicted that more than 81 percent of Americans would be infected with the virus, and at least 1 percent of those infected would die. It was a colossal overestimate of the virus's severity. More than eighteen months later, cumulative statistics for the state of California showed that fewer than 12 percent had tested positive for the virus, and the death rate among infected people was only about one-tenth of what Ferguson's model predicted.

Furthermore, the figures currently on record are likely inflated and certainly over-sensationalized by the media in comparison with recent flu epidemics, as well as the SARS and MERS outbreaks. Researchers acknowledged early on that a relentless pattern of exaggerated reports and inflated statistics was unnecessarily elevating public fear and fostering bad government policy. A paper published in April 2020 by the US National Library of Medicine at the National Institutes of Health (NIH) listed a dozen ways false, sensational, and exaggerated media reports were making it difficult to assess the COVID situation objectively. In part, the paper said, "This year's coronavirus outbreak is clearly unprecedented in amount of attention received. Media have capitalized on curiosity, uncertainty and horror. . . . Other coronaviruses probably have infected millions of people and have killed thousands. However, it is only this year that every single case and every single death gets red alert broadcasting in the news."

Childhood mortality from COVID is significantly lower than normal flu levels. More than eighteen months after nearly all schools in the country were closed (and with many still not yet open), the Centers for Disease Control (CDC) counted just over 400 young people (0–17 years old) who died from COVID. By comparison, during just six months at the peak of the 2017–18 flu season, an estimated 643 from that same age group succumbed to the flu—meaning the typical flu bug is about five times more deadly for children than COVID-19.

Shootings of children in Chicago alone have greatly outnumbered pediatric COVID deaths across the state of Illinois. In the first eight months of 2021, 35 children died from gun violence in Chicago. In the entire state during that same time span, 15 children died from COVID.

Meanwhile, government-imposed lockdown policies have been catastrophic for the mental health of children. Harsh restrictions imposed on common childhood activities impede every child's normal physical, spiritual, and intellectual development. The mandatory closure of churches, schools, playgrounds, and even beaches has therefore done far more actual damage to the well-being of children than COVID by several orders of magnitude. According to the CDC, suicide attempts by girls aged 12–17 rose 50.6 percent between February 21 and March 20, 2021. Virtually all public school children missed more than a year of in-person instruction, and a host of other physical and mental health problems rose by large margins as well. A plethora of statistical information exists to show that among children and teenagers the lockdowns have caused a dramatic rise in drug addiction, alcoholism, depression, self-harm, and other unhealthy compulsions—including eating disorders, sleep disorders, clinginess, irritability, and inordinate fear. Nationwide statistics also reveal a precipitous rise in domestic violence and child abuse (including neglect) during the COVID quarantine.

In short, while COVID-19 was not the fierce pandemic that was originally forecast, the lockdowns have been highly injurious to public health on numerous levels.

To be clear: COVID is indeed a dangerous virus for people in certain demographics. It can cause serious (potentially fatal) pulmonary, renal, and cardiovascular impairment, especially among those who are elderly, infirm, obese, or afflicted with other co-morbidities. But the threat posed to the general public by COVID is not an emergency sufficient to warrant the quarantining of healthy people, the isolation and virtual imprisonment of children, the permanent closure of countless businesses, the destruction of whole economies, or the indefinite suspension of public worship and face-to-face fellowship.

The public has repeatedly been force-fed misinformation from the media and government officials—not only about COVID, but about other matters as well. In March 2020, Dr. Anthony Fauci, Chief Medical Advisor to the White House, famously said on "60 Minutes" that masking the general populace would not help slow the spread of the virus and could even be detrimental to the wearer. "There's no reason to be walking around with a mask," he said. "Often there are unintended consequences—people keep fiddling with the mask and they keep touching their face." When Fauci reversed himself a few months later, he explained that he had discouraged the wearing of masks because he didn't want to say anything that might diminish the supply of masks for medical workers. In an interview with InStyle magazine, he said, "We were told in our task force meetings that we have a serious problem with the lack of PPEs and masks for the health providers." He indicated that his task force had met and agreed to be less than candid with the public. In

Fauci's words, concerns about a shortage of masks "led all of us, not just me but also [U.S. Surgeon General] Jerome Adams, to say, 'Right now we really need to save the masks for the people who need them most.'" That is an admission that truth was not health officials' first concern; public policy was. By January 2021, Fauci was advising people to wear layers of multiple masks.

The fundamental question of where the COVID-19 virus originated was either deliberately obscured or handled with gross ineptitude in 2020 by Dr. Fauci and other leading scientists, government officials, health departments, and the major news media. At the time, common sense and publicly known facts seemed to point to what officials did not want people to see—namely, that the virus originated in the Wuhan Institute of Virology. Many experts now acknowledge that is probably where the virus came from. But for nearly a full year, those who even wondered aloud whether the virus originated in the Wuhan lab were automatically silenced or suppressed in virtually (if not literally) all major scientific, academic, and social media forums.

Dr. Fauci also gave a misleading and possibly false reply in sworn testimony before Congress when asked about how US taxpayer money was being used to fund research at the Wuhan lab.

Vaccines began to be available near the end of 2020. For weeks, health officials assured the public that the new vaccines were effective and life would soon return to normal without masks. But in July 2021, the CDC released a report saying, "Emerging evidence suggests that fully vaccinated persons who do become infected with the Delta variant are at risk for transmitting it to others; therefore, CDC also recommends that fully vaccinated persons wear a mask in public indoor settings in areas of substantial or high transmission." Rather than providing data to support the revised opinion, the CDC document gave this citation: "CDC COVID-19 Response Team, unpublished data, 2021."

We now have ample evidence (including data from the CDC's own reports) that the vaccines don't work as advertised. By September

2021, 70 percent of Californians had been vaccinated, but statewide numbers of people who tested positive were still rising. In August 2021, 364 people at Duke University tested positive for the virus. Only 8 were unvaccinated. All the rest—356 people—were fully vaccinated but became infected with the virus anyway. The university's response was to tighten their mask mandate. Oddly, the people in our community who seem most fearful of the virus are those who have already been vaccinated—many of them now clamoring for more mask mandates and renewed restrictions—which indicates that they do not trust the vaccination to protect them as they were promised before they took it.

No wonder. Sources purported to be reliable voices of authority have repeatedly shown themselves untrustworthy. Heads of state impose rules on the populace that they themselves refuse to submit to. The rules suddenly change on someone's whim. It turns out even "the science" is not very dependable. There is even reason to doubt the accuracy of COVID testing. Major media sources are notoriously biased and inaccurate. Narratives aggressively touted by the media about this (and practically every politically charged subject) often prove false.

Large pharmaceutical companies, the US Food and Drug Administration (FDA), the World Health organization (WHO), and various influencers in government and media have actively tried to suppress discussion about the usefulness of drugs like Ivermectin, chloroquine, and hydroxychloroquine as early treatments for COVID-19—even though many physicians report using those compounds successfully. It is widely understood that the debate over these medications (more precisely: the lack of any open exchange of information about them) is largely driven by economic and political concerns, not scientific studies. In fact, the WHO halted their studies of hydroxychloroquine, and the FDA revoked their Emergency Use Authorization for the drug just days after President Trump announced it had been successfully used to treat him for COVID.

Support for and opposition to the vaccinations have changed with the transition from one political party to the next in the Oval Office. In 2020,

Democrats were openly contemptuous of Donald Trump's efforts to develop a vaccine quickly, saying they would refuse any vaccination Mr. Trump recommended. But shortly after a Democrat moved into the White House, they suddenly began lobbying for a nationwide mandate and vaccination passports.

Notice, also, that virtually nothing is ever said by health officials or reported by the media regarding the natural immunity people develop once they have actually been infected by the virus and recovered. Natural immunity is God's design for our protection. It is robust, durable, and long lasting. It's how we normally survive and ward off illnesses in a world of microscopic dangers. But to suggest that natural immunity is sufficient protection against reinfection would undermine the push for a universal vaccine mandate.

Ideologically-driven propaganda and government pressure are routinely paired with efforts by Big Tech companies to squelch all dissenting opinions. Meanwhile, throughout most of the Western world, government agencies have worked hand in hand with the media to cultivate open hostility toward biblical values while actively promoting the normalization of abortion, homosexuality, transgenderism, and various other assaults on the family structure. It is no wonder that public trust in government and media has severely eroded over the past decade.

Reasonable people know that they are being lied to. They recognize the tools of indoctrination. When what is deemed "truth" constantly changes, it is an insult to people's intelligence to expect them to swallow every new truth claim put forth by agencies and institutions that have frequently distorted or outright denied the truth.

How Should the Church Respond?

Intense disagreements have swirled among evangelicals since March 2020 regarding how the church should respond to government-mandated COVID restrictions. The clash of opinions only compounds the bewilderment of Christians already confused by conflicting media reports. It has generated a firestorm of contention on social media. And it has caused unexpected division in churches. Oddly, some of the same evangelical leaders who insisted the church must shut down on orders from the state also published essays affirming the duty and priority of congregational worship. No wonder churchgoers are confused.

Here are four non-negotiable precepts about church life that are always apropos but seem particularly suited for the current circumstances. Every sound, biblically minded congregation should affirm these principles without uncertainty or indecision:

1. The church must stand firm on the truth. Scripture says the church is "the pillar and support of the truth" (1 Timothy 3:15). In that role we are often pitted against popular opinion and media narratives. It's a task that normally calls for boldness rather than subtlety.

It would be sinfully negligent for any church to remain passive or pliant when waves of misinformation dominate popular opinion and deliberately foment anxiety. What makes the current case especially urgent is the way officials have intentionally fueled public angst with relentless propaganda, then exploited the public's fears in order to justify banning public worship—even while bars, strip clubs, and casinos remain open—and radical political protestors are permitted to swarm the streets.

If we truly believe Scripture, we cannot automatically go along with the prevailing values and beliefs of the rest of the world—especially in a culture (like ours) where biblical righteousness is constantly under fierce attack, militant unbelief dominates public discourse, and diabolical ideologies routinely influence public policy. God's people must contend earnestly for the faith. We are to be aggressively engaged in the battle to liberate people from every falsehood and every lofty argument that is raised against the knowledge of God (2 Corinthians 10:4–5). And we must bear in mind that "the wisdom of this world is foolishness before God" (1 Corinthians 3:19).

Indeed, the average person today doesn't even believe truth can be known with any degree of settled certainty. Nothing is deemed authoritatively true; truth itself is seen as merely a matter of personal perspective. That brand of skepticism permeates our news media, politics, the secular academic world, the entertainment industry, and most people's religious beliefs.

Bible-believing Christians, on the other hand, know that the Word of God is not only absolutely true; it is the ultimate standard by which all other truth claims must be tested. Christianity begins with this conviction. Jesus affirmed it in his high-priestly prayer: "Your word is truth" (John 17:17). The Psalms declare it repeatedly: "The testimony of the Lord is sure, making wise the simple" (Psalm 19:7). "The words of the Lord are pure words; as silver tried in a furnace on the earth, refined seven times" (Psalm 12:6). God's Word is more sure and more trustworthy than any other witness. Anyone who does not affirm such a high view of Scripture is not really a follower of Christ.

Again, authentic Christians cannot allow either majority opinion or government edicts to determine what we believe, especially at this moment in history. Anyone with a modicum of biblical discernment ought to be able to see that Western society has purposely waded into a deep cesspool of immorality and unbelief, just as Romans 1:22–25 describes: "Professing to be wise, they became fools, and exchanged the glory of the incorruptible God for an image . . . [And] they exchanged the truth of God for a lie."

That passage goes on to outline precisely what we see happening in contemporary Western society. And the point of the biblical text is that this moral meltdown is a judgment from God against a willfully depraved culture: God gave them over to degrading passions; for their women exchanged the natural function for that which is unnatural, and in the same way also the men abandoned the natural function of the woman and burned in their desire toward one another, men with men committing indecent acts and receiving in their own persons the due penalty of their error. And just as they did not see fit to acknowledge God any longer, God gave them over to a depraved mind, to do those things which are not proper, being filled with all unrighteousness, wickedness, greed, evil; full of envy, murder, strife, deceit, malice; they are gossips, slanderers, haters of God, insolent, arrogant, boastful, inventors of evil, disobedient to parents, without understanding, untrustworthy, unloving, unmerciful; and although they know the ordinance of God, that those who practice such things are worthy of death, they not only do the same, but also give hearty approval to those who practice them. (Romans 1:26–34)

Churches should be the last place on earth where purveyors of immoral values, half-truths, lies, and tyrannical abuses of authority find any kind of approval.

2. Joy, not fear, should dominate the fellowship of believers. The New Testament is full of instructions and encouragements for Christians to cultivate joy, even in the midst of persecution and distress. “Rejoice always” (1 Thessalonians 5:16). “Rejoice in the Lord always; again I will say, rejoice!” (Philippians 4:4). One mark of a faithful church is that they are “rejoicing in hope” (Romans 12:12), not cowering in fear.

Fear of death is abject enslavement, and that is the very thing Christ came to liberate us from. The purpose of Christ’s incarnation was so “He might render powerless him who had the power of death, that is, the devil, and might free those who through fear of death were subject to slavery all their lives” (Hebrews 2:14). As Christians, we “have not received a spirit of slavery leading to fear again” (Romans 8:15).

When the congregation of Grace Community Church was gathering for worship in defiance of the state’s lockdown orders, virtually all observers (including reporters and health officials who weren’t necessarily sympathetic with the church’s position) remarked on the joy that permeated our services. Despite the threats and legal stratagems that were brought against the church every week, the spirit of our services was exuberant—not angry, anxious, or apprehensive. That is as it should be. “God has not given us a spirit of timidity, but of power and love and discipline” (2 Timothy 1:7).

In today’s troubled world, perpetual fear has been made to seem normal, even noble. Life itself has become all about avoiding risk. But to cultivate that kind of fear, especially at the government's behest, poses a grave danger to the long-term spiritual health and ministry of the church. If young people are taught that the preservation of their own lives is more important than corporate worship and evangelism, who will go to the mission field?

Christianity does not flourish, and our collective testimony loses all credibility, when the church cowers in fear. Christians should enjoy liberty from the fear of death, hope in the midst of tribulation, and joy and gladness in all circumstances.

The dark cloud of melancholy and anxiety that COVID has brought over the world signifies an extraordinary opportunity for the church—but only if congregations can resist adopting the frame of mind that currently dominates our culture.

3. We must be "diligent to preserve the unity of the Spirit in the bond of peace" (Ephesians 4:3). The COVID crisis has been (and continues to be) a malignant source of division and conflict in otherwise sound churches. It is frankly preposterous and deeply troubling that any church leader would regard COVID as a greater threat to the church than disunity. Researchers say the recovery rate among those infected with the virus is as high as 99.75 percent. Many who test positive for COVID have no symptoms at all. The vast majority who do show symptoms are only mildly ill.

Yet some church leaders have said they will henceforth forbid worshipers to attend if they cannot show proof of vaccination. Others sequester unmasked or unvaccinated worshipers apart from the main congregation. Thus they literally rebuild a middle wall of partition between diverse groups of believers, defying the principle of Ephesians 2:11–22.

Ample data demonstrate conclusively that cloth masks cannot stop the spread of the virus. There is good reason to think the hazards of constant masking outweigh whatever benefit the masks might afford. Masking has nevertheless become the most visible and universal symbol of the COVID era. It is also the primary instrument for virtue signaling among those most fearful of the COVID virus. In some circles, masks serve as a kind of secular substitute for religious vestments. They have become the chief symbol of popular culture's sanctimonious devotion to a secularist credo.

In the context of a church gathering, masks are an obvious impediment to congregational singing, face-to-face-fellowship, and normal human interaction. Regardless, the question of whether to wear a mask in church should be treated as entirely a matter of personal conscience. Churches must not canonize rules of behavior that have no basis in Scripture. On all such matters not addressed either explicitly or by precept in Scripture, "each person must be fully convinced in his own mind" (Romans 14:5). On matters where the law of God is silent, "Who are you who judge your neighbor?" (James 4:12).

Those same principles hold true on the question of vaccines. If the vaccines worked, those who have been vaccinated would have nothing to fear from exposure to those who haven't. Ironically, as noted above, some of the most fearful people speaking out today are people who have already been vaccinated. But both the safety and the effectiveness of the vaccines is another question that is clearly debatable.

The CDC's Vaccine Adverse Event Reporting System (VAERS) was established to collect statistics on side effects and health crises that people experience after being vaccinated. In 1976, when three people died after receiving vaccinations for swine flu, nine states immediately halted the immunization program. Nine months after COVID vaccines became available, VAERS had received 7,899 reports of people who had died following vaccination. Nevertheless, the same CDC webpage that reported those figures led with the statement, "COVID-19 vaccines are safe and effective."

One leading virologist says, "Scientific analysis of the data from pivotal clinical trials for US COVID-19 vaccines indicates the vaccines fail to show any health benefit and in fact, all the vaccines cause a decline in health in the immunized groups." After reporting the world's highest percentage of people who have taken a third booster, Israel was experiencing record rates of infection. Mongolia recorded fewer than 1,000 cases of COVID in the first nine months of 2020 (among the lowest in the world), but the infection rate spiked precipitously a year later, after the Mongolian government had "administered more COVID-19 shots relative to its population than any country in Asia." So again, the vaccines clearly cannot even promise immunity against COVID.

Nevertheless, several policy makers in health departments across the country are recommending universal vaccination mandates with no exclusions (even for those who have had the virus and acquired natural immunity). Governors and local health officials intend to require churches to monitor and enforce our people's compliance.

What is the church's duty under those circumstances? The question of whether to get a vaccine should be a personal, private medical decision, between each individual and his or her physician. It is not a matter where either the church or the government ought to intrude, especially by force of law. Personal medical decisions are not something we are obliged to render unto Caesar, and the church cannot become an enforcement agency for Caesar.

For a church to demand proof of vaccination is to set a legalistic standard that is not authorized by Scripture. Again, the church is a place where the people of God come together as one, without passing judgment on one another over questions of conscience. And the issues of masks and vaccines are nothing if not matters of personal conscience. So the choice of whether to be vaccinated or not and whether to wear a mask or not should be left entirely up to each individual (Romans 14:1–23; 15:7).

4. A company of believers is not a "church" if they don't gather. The word for "church" in the original New Testament manuscripts is ekklēsia. Even before the founding of the New Testament church, that word signified an assembly, a gathering of people. It comprises two Greek roots that literally mean "called out," and more specifically, it refers to a body of people called

out from their homes (or summoned out of a larger group) in order to muster together. Like the English word congregation, the concept of a group coming together is built right into the term.

The church specifically comes together for worship, but the vital benefits of the assembly include fellowship, instruction, mutual encouragement, and accountability. Believers are commanded not to forsake the assembly (Hebrews 10:25), and that command comes immediately before the New Testament's most somber warning about apostasy.

Fellowship and corporate worship are therefore absolutely essential aspects of spiritual health for individual Christians, and they are also (obviously) vital for the very life of the church.

Believers may be forced by illness, imprisonment, warfare, natural disaster, necessary travel, or some other significant emergency to abstain from the corporate gathering temporarily. But there is no justification for quarantining healthy people, and certainly no warrant for having the entire church suspend congregational worship on a prolonged basis. Plagues, pandemics, and persecution have frequently (if not constantly) threatened the people of God since that first Pentecost. Never have faithful churches responded to such obstacles by simply shutting their doors for months at a time and declaring distance-learning technologies a sufficient substitute for corporate worship.

Christians in America and other Western democracies have been blessed and privileged to thrive for more than two centuries under governments that formally affirm and have seldom challenged the right of worshipers to assemble freely. But COVID is a wakeup call and a reminder to believers of how tenuous that liberty is. Pastors in supposedly free countries were literally jailed for weeks because they led worship services during the 2020 lockdowns. Despite court decisions favorable to churches, a strong current of public opinion favors giving governments more power to force churches to comply with restrictions inhibiting attendance, fellowship, and congregational singing. Many also think churches should be compelled to require vaccine passports and strict segregation between vaccinated and unvaccinated worshipers.

Again, the world's opposition to the church and her teaching should not catch believers off guard. "Do not be surprised, brethren, if the world hates you" (1 John 3:13). Jesus said, "Because you are not of the world... the world hates you" (John 15:19). We are citizens of heaven—mere sojourners and aliens here in this world (Philippians 3:20). And even the world sees the church that way when we are faithful to our calling.

That is one of the main reasons why the people of God need to come together regularly for mutual encouragement and instruction—and all the more as we see the day of Christ drawing near (Hebrews 10:25). Times of crisis and hardship don't make the church assembly expendable; that's when it is most essential for believers to congregate. "We must obey God rather than men" (Acts 5:29).

Faithful churches must assemble even if they have to go underground to do it. That's how churches in the first three centuries survived and flourished despite intense opposition from Caesar. It's how the church in Eastern Europe overcame communist persecution in the twentieth century. It's how many churches in China and elsewhere meet even today.

Scripture gives us several examples of godly people who resisted the ungodly tyranny of rulers who hated biblical truth. Under a despotic Pharaoh, the Hebrew midwives "feared God, and did not do as the king of Egypt had commanded them" (Exodus 1:17). Elijah opposed Ahab and was labeled "troubler of Israel" because of the stance he took (1 Kings 18:17). John the Baptist rebuked Herod to his face and was ultimately killed for it (Mark 6:18-29).

Western evangelicals now need to have that same resolve—and prepare ourselves for more pressure from the government and more persecution from the rest of society. When COVID has run its course (if it ever does) other crises are already lined up for government officials to exploit, claiming "emergency powers" to assert more and more regulatory authority over the church. Fears over climate change, the campaign to normalize sexual perversions, imaginative applications of "social justice," and a host of other major ideological shifts have speedily and dramatically changed the climate of virtually every Western democracy already. Some of the people who now wield power for making public policy believe the gospel and its truths are a form of "hate speech." Churches in this part of the world have already lost much of our civic freedom.

Now is not the time to forsake our own assembling together. The church must be the church—a pillar and buttress for the truth. We cannot cower in fear. We cannot hide our light under a bushel. We are not called to feed the fears of a world that is perishing. We have been commissioned to "go into all the world and preach the gospel to all creation" (Mark 16:15), and we are soldiers in a spiritual war. "The weapons of our warfare are not of the flesh, but divinely powerful for the destruction of fortresses. We are destroying speculations and every lofty thing raised up against the knowledge of God, and we are taking every thought captive to the obedience of Christ" (2 Corinthians 10:4-5).

It is past time for the church of Jesus Christ to confront the prevailing falsehoods of a depraved society and show hopeless people the way to true hope and abundant life. We are the Lord's ambassadors, and we must stand confidently in that role, with joy and not fear, in bold unity—and all the more as we see the day of Christ drawing near.

APPENDIX C

SAMPLE RELIGIOUS EXEMPTION LETTER

We believe that the Triune God who revealed Himself in His dealing with the people of Israel, and then most particularly in the coming of the Son of God, Jesus the Messiah, and today in the ministry of the Holy Spirit in His Church, made mankind in His image, and gave to man dominion over the world as His steward and representative. In opposition to the assertions of secularism, we assert that man's life has transcendent value because of this act of special creation on the part of God. God's law, therefore, is the highest standard by which man, God's creature, is called to live and abide.

For this reason we condemn as a blatant act of rebellion and murder the destruction of the lives of unique pre-born humans in the womb. The plague of abortion brings God's judgment upon any nation or people who would place their self-claimed sexual liberty above that of the value of human life as God has proclaimed and defined it. Obedience to the commandment to preserve life is multi-faceted and provides a broad and deep understanding of how Christians are to seek to honor God by honoring life itself.

We also assert that while we are to preserve life, we are to do so in accordance with God's will. God's law provides for freedom, for liberty of conscience, and these realities are to be exercised by mankind in light of God's revealed will that man is to live for His glory always recognizing his own mortality and the briefness of life. We are not to live in constant fear of death, and indeed it is for this reason that the gospel removes our dread of death and gives to us life eternal.

Christians therefore proclaim Christ's Lordship over all realms, for, as He claimed, all authority has been given to Him in heaven and upon earth (Matthew 28:18). In light of His Kingship, we assert that men and women have the right to refuse mandatory medical procedures, actions, medications, or injections, whether these actions are ordered by the highest government authorities, or lesser authorities, such as an employer or local magistrate. They may do so when they are convinced that these medical procedures could threaten their life, their future health, their future fertility, and their wellbeing. Further, parents have the right and responsibility to make said decisions for their children as well, without external interference.

We believe and assert that a Christian's conscience can properly and validly submit to medical procedures, such as in the taking of tested and proven medications and vaccines, giving thanks to God whose ordering of His creation has allowed such wondrous advancements. At the same time, we believe and assert that many sound bases may exist for a Christian to refuse similar treatments, such as when they lack long-term safety information, have deleterious and dangerous side-effects, possible unknown impacts upon pre-existing medical conditions, and originate from fetal stem cell lines via abortion. Likewise, one may be convinced that the demanded procedure arises not from a public health concern, but from political machinations and activities that are opposed to God's truth and ways, and hence are to be resisted. We assert that the conscience cannot be coerced, and that all such attempts to do so are in opposition to divine truth.

Therefore, we assert in the name and authority of our Lord Jesus Christ that we and our members have the right and the responsibility to research fully the issues relevant to all such medical matters; that free flow of information must be guaranteed and protected; and that we have the right to refuse such experimentation and mandatory procedures, including vaccination, upon sound religious grounds. We likewise call upon all governmental agencies, businesses, schools, employers of all types, to respect these deeply held religious conclusions and convictions, and to honor our religious liberty and freedom by granting religious exemptions as requested.

To Whom It May Concern:

The eldership of Apologia Church is writing on the behalf of _______________ to confirm that his/her sincerely held religious beliefs prevent him from receiving a mandatory COVID-19 vaccination. Our church, for ourselves and our congregants, affirms the right to take religious exemption against mandatory vaccination by governmental authorities and/or employer. Our congregation has also issued a statement confirming this right according to our doctrinal standards and Scripture.

____________ application for religious exemption is, therefore, not merely a matter of personal opinion or preference, but of bona fide religious conviction with the support of his/her church. We appreciate your understanding in this matter.

Sincerely,

APPENDIX D

RELIGIOUS EXEMPTION APPEAL
TO A SOUTH AFRICAN UNIVERSITY

Dear Sir or Madam:

For the reasons outlined below, the leaders of Antioch Bible Church ("the church") are requesting an immediate exemption for our members – **[church member]** from your restrictive policy based on coercing a person to inject biological agents[252] into their own bodies.

We request that reasonable accommodation needs to be made for our church member, especially if our member does most or part of their work or studies online, or conducts most activity outdoors.

The church advances two fundamental objections:

1) Our church member cannot submit to the coercion that you are forcing on them and their fellow students. By forcing them and fellow students to be injected against their will, (by your restriction of access to university), which said restriction and coercion is a gross violation of our Religious Beliefs.

---

[252] We *prefer the term "biological agent" - as unlike other "vaccines" which are based on "attenuated "and "dead" viruses, the C19 injections are a bolus of mRNA active pathogenic spike proteins.*

2) The development of mRNA vaccine technology, it is beyond doubt that "human fetal cells" were used for “proof of concept.” (Showing how a cell could take up mRNA and produce the SARS-CoV-2 spike protein) or to characterize the SARS-CoV-2 spike protein. Antioch Bible Church totally forbids the use of aborted (or otherwise) human baby cells. Therefore, it is an unconscionable act to force our member to use these so-called "vaccines" that have been tested on human babies.

The above two points are our main argument. Yet here are further sincere concerns:

3) You are also violating what we and many have fought for in Africa and that is, a basic individual human right to education, by discriminating between students, much like the tyrannical Apartheid System of the past.

But primarily, our most fundamental objection is that this person Christian who is a member of Antioch Bible Church, who cannot go against what is taught by his/her spiritual leaders (Hebrews 13:7). They cannot subscribe to the loss of their God-given freedom (Gen. 1-2) as taught in the Bible and goes against the terrible use of human fetal tissue, according to the religious precepts that they uphold in our church. You are coercing and forcing them to go against what is taught by this church and the Bible and their God-appointed spiritual leaders of this church. This would mean that you are forcing them to violate their conscience.

Our member states that they hold to the Religious Tenants of this Church:

Statement from our member

We **[church member]** hereby state that my fundament religious belief, faith and conviction, is what is taught by my church Antioch Bible Church and I am bound by the Word of God to obey my leaders (Hebrews 13:7) - and this is what I/we hold to in my/our faith: (as outlined in my pastor’s book, *A Christian Response to Covid Tyranny*, Essay #2)

Antioch Bible Church Religious Confession 1: *Freedom is from God*

Antioch Bible Church Religious Confession 2: *Freedom is Defined By Scripture*

Antioch Bible Church Religious Confession 3: *We are God's Image Bearers*

Antioch Bible Church Religious Confession 4: *Resistance to tyranny is obedience to God.*

Antioch Bible Church Religious Confession 5: *Human life begins at conception.*

Any harvesting or use of human baby tissue from the womb, is a crime against God's creation. Each person from the womb is entitled to a burial intact to honour God's theological view of the body. Abortion in any form at any term, is therefore considered by Antioch Church as murder.

Please take my very strong religious convictions and beliefs into consideration. This objection is against the fact that you are coercing and forcing me against what I hold and believe, using biological agents developed on human babies, against my church, against my spiritual leaders. Please note my/our further and yet secondary considerations in the Appendix below:

The elders of Antioch Bible Church
310 Boundary Rd, Honeydew

____

Signature/s of Impacted Member/s

ADDITIONAL CONCERNS

My main objection is stated in previous pages. What follows is additional considerations, but this does not detract from or add to, in any way from my fundamental religious objection as stated in the above body of this letter.

If the University is requiring me as part of my role as a student to be vaccinated with the new mRNA biological agents, or discriminating me together with other students requiring me to be tested each week, then it is fair to ask for the University to take full liability for any adverse effects and loss of livelihood or any expense incurred from testing? If the University is not prepared to take this risk, then I question their right to require students to undergo a highly debatable medical procedure.

1. <u>Authority and Risk</u>: In terms of this South African legal framework, where now many court cases are being brought against vaccine coercion.

(a) Section 187(1)(f) of the Labour Relations Act, 1995 (the LRA) which prohibits dismissals that discriminate against employees based, inter alia, on their religion, conscience, belief, political opinion or culture.

(b) Occupational Health and Safety Act (OHSA) 85 of 1993 – Employer required this after submitting study and full OHSA approval, and medical testing inherently required the employer pays for it.

(c) Employment Equity Act (EEA) no. 55 1998 - <u>Section 7</u> – Medical testing of employee testing prohibited, unless there is legislation -our legal regulation.

Currently there is <u>no legislation</u> in South Africa making vaccination mandatory - it does not exist. Clearly even the vaxed carry and spread virus - no distinction in the science and current condition (See Gibraltar; Israel, Singapore, Cayman Islands, UK where over 90% even 100% people are vaccinated and they are the main spreaders of the virus. Therefore to distinguish between the unvaxed and vaxed is simply workplace baseless discrimination.

(d) EWN vs Pharmco Distribution Pty Ltd - 2016 precedent - Labour Court Case - employer cannot require medical procedure, conditions.

(e) Compliance with POPI regarding privacy of information.

I find no legal or moral authority that would allow you, as an employer, to require me to submit to an experimental drug treatment as a condition of my employment. If you are aware of authority that allows you to require me to submit to a request to allow an invasion of my body with a drug treatment and experimental drug product for which I bear all the risk and the seller/purveyor of the product bears no risk and has legal immunity, please provide this authority. There are also Worker Compensation issues involved as well. And in terms of this Act I would also request you to pay for any doctors examination which shows that I would not be subject to any adverse effects based on my health, and that medical practitioner guarantees my health in such a letter.

If you are unwilling to assume the risk that the vaccine producers refuse to accept, please explain why you will not accept this risk? If you are able to provide some authority for your vaccine request, in your response also please explain how and why your authority applies to the present situation? All data that I have seen indicates that the mortality risk–the IFR (Infection to Fatality Ratio)relative to the 2020 seasonal flu (aka Covid-19) is no different than any other prior seasonal flu.

2. Informed Consent: My conscience, worldview, and religious value system informs me that I cannot consent to an intrusion into my body without fully knowing the risks. The risks of getting the 2020 seasonal flu (aka Covid-19) are known and negligible for all demographics. This is the IFR referred to above.

Please additionally note that the IFR may overstate the known risk because the PCR test used to identify the 2020 seasonal flu (aka Covid-19) is an inductive, not deductive, test in which the sample is mixed with other genetic material and does not isolate the allegedly harmful virus.

Further PCR "results" are magnified as many as 45x to determine the presence of some genetic material (in a soup of genetic material) that correlates with (does not cause) the 2020 seasonal flu (aka Covid-19). The existing PCR tests therefore do not satisfy Koch's Postulate which requires: (1) complete isolation of danger/bacteria/virus; and (2) definitive and reproducible proof of causation (factor A produces result B).

The risks associated with the vaccine you request, on the other hand, are largely unknown and may be unknowable for many years. Many esteemed doctors and health professionals advise against accepting the vaccine. In addition, there are many anecdotal adverse outcomes associated with the vaccines. These include Guillain-Barre Syndrome (paralysis) and myocarditis. Because we do not know whether or how many recipients of the experimental vaccines are receiving placebos and because adverse outcomes many develop many years down the road, it is impossible to assess the total risk associated with taking the vaccine. Meanwhile the vaccine producers, who presumably have done some testing and are aware of the risk, refuse to accept the risk and demand legal immunity from risk.

In addition have you examined the VAERS and EUDA databases which both point to nearly 50,000 deaths and hundreds of thousands adverse events as a result of the vaccine? These databases are grossly understated such that the current C19 shots, have more deaths and adverse events that every single vaccine the world has ever produces, and it is debatable whether or not they are indeed "vaccines" since they confer no infection immunity. Informed consent in these circumstances is thus impossible.

3. Epistemology: Epistemology is the question of "what can man know and how can he know it?" All epistemological questions ultimately boil down to the question of "who is in charge here?" and lead to the dualistic choice of

whether our time-space experience is under the control of men or a Sovereign God. Your vaccine request, for which I am very grateful because it has caused me to ask these questions, has also led me to conclude that I am better to put my fate in the hand of my Triune God I believe in than I am to putting it in the hands of shamelessly dishonest and self-interested men.

All of the points above are reflected in various constitutions, laws, statutes, and the Nuremberg Code. I say "reflected in" because I do not rely primarily on law or "rights" written by man for my position. My position is based on an epistemological worldview–God is in charge here. If there are laws that accord with this worldview and my faith and you believe that such laws require that you cooperate with me, then please follow such laws. This will benefit both of us.

My religious objection against tyranny and coercion is my main objection. But here are further objections to which I hold as a citizen of South Africa:

4) <u>Ethical objections</u>:

The Bill of Rights – The Constitution of South Africa guarantees several rights to each citizen. You have made mention of these in your document (2.3). Specifically, Chapter 2 of the Bill of Rights addresses such matters. Clause 9 concerns Equality, and subsection 4 explicitly states that "no person may unfairly discriminate directly or indirectly against anyone on one or more grounds in terms of subsection 3".

I suggest that the proposed vaccine mandate violates a person's right to not be discriminated against based on their conscience. Your proposal attempts to answer the provision of subsection 5 of this section ('fair discrimination") by arguing that the broader public interest is reasonable, justifiable and rational. However, mandating the use of a vaccine actually fails all 3 of these tests. These failures fatally undermine your attempt at limiting our Constitutional rights.

Mandating a "vaccine" which demonstrably does not prevent infection anywhere in the world, even when boosted by additional vaccinations, is not reasonable. However, here is a clear subset of people who may develop less severe symptoms as a result of having a vaccination. This should surely indicate that the individuals at highest risk should consider vaccinating, not that all must. It is unreasonable to mandate that all people should have the same vaccine when they do not share the same risk profile.

Mandating "a vaccine" without specifying which one, and how many times or how many booster shots are needed to comply with the directive is not rational. If the intent is to promote the health of the University community, surely the assessment of a individual's antibody status is a far better way to assess their risk to the community. Vaccinating without assessing efficacy of the intervention, or ignoring an individual's actual risk profile, seems an irrational action which is unbecoming of a centre of higher learning.

The mandatory use of a vaccine is not justifiable. To make this claim, you need to balance the risk profile of each individual. This means an assessment of their absolute risk of contracting COVID-19, against the purported benefits of whichever vaccine they are offered. Of particular relevance here are the age profiles and co-morbid status' of the vast majority of people who could be affected by the virus. The overwhelming majority of serious cases of COVID have been in older age cohorts; Very, very few of all serious cases do not have underlying medical conditions including those relating to the heart, haematological system, and metabolic issues.

By mandating a vaccine for all rather than targeting the groups that are at particular risk, you ignore the real world epidemiological data. The absolute risk to healthy young people is self-evidently minuscule worldwide. By contrast the real world risk to young people from vaccine related adverse events is not low. Witness the VAERS data which show unprecedented levels of vaccine related harms which disproportionately affect younger people.

Rose & McCulloch 2021 (Curr Probl Cardiol 30 Sept, doi: 10.1016j.cpcardiol 101011) reported "markedly higher" myocarditis rates in people ages 13-23 to be significantly higher, with 80% of these among males. After the first dose, the rate was 19 times higher than the control group. A 5-fold increase was found after the second dose. The authors argue that the vaccines included in the study were "deterministic for the myocarditis cases observed after injection". Taken together - a low absolute risk of symptomatic infection plus an "unprecedented level" of vaccine related injuries, this proposed mandate is clearly an unjustifiable risk to younger healthy people.

5) <u>Freedom & Security of the Person</u>

Section 12.1e includes the right to not be treated or punished in a cruel, inhuman of degrading way. It is difficult to see how your proposed treatment of those electing to not be vaccinated can be seen as anything other than discriminatory and falling foul of this clause.

Section 12.2b&c follow on from the above, and are explicit that individuals have the right to bodily integrity, control of their bodies, and the right to not be subjected to medical experimentation without their informed consent. A mandate would violate these rights.

Note that the proper exercise of the notion of "informed consent' would necessitate that the University explain clearly to each person the risk and benefit of the procedure. This means that the University must be explicit as to why their stakeholders should incur an unacceptable risk to their health.

6) <u>Scientific objections</u>

(a) <u>Relative Risk versus Absolute Risk</u> – Your proposal assumes that all stakeholders carry the same risks of either themselves being infected, or being able to infect others. This is not a scientifically sound position. There is no good data to show that asymptomatic spread of the virus occurs to any significant extent. Symptomatic people - both vaccinated and unvaccinated - are implicated in spreading disease.

(b) Testing: Your punitive proposals for managing the people who choose to not be vaccinated include a mandatory test weekly. This is clearly an intimidation tactic and is again not scientifically valid. There is at present no test of infection or of infectiousness for COVID-19 available for routing use. Neither PCR tests nor lateral flow tests test for live virus. Mandating a useless test is not scientific. Mandating an expensive and useless test at any repeat cycle (you propose weekly - what is the scientific basis for this?) smacks of deliberate coercion.

(c) Vaccine efficacy. The proposal assumes that the vaccines are effective at protecting against COVID infections. This is of limited scientific accuracy. Olliaro et al 2021 doi.org/101016/S2666-5247(21) 00069-0) give the absolute risk reduction for an individual person of each the four major vaccines is as follows:

1·3% (AstraZeneca–Oxford)
1·2% (Moderna)
1·2% (J&J)
0·84% (Pfizer–BioNTech)

This means that the vaccines reduce an individual's risk by those small numbers. Expressed differently, the number of people you would need to vaccinate to prevent a single case of COVID is called the NNT (Number Needed to Treat). An example of an effective vaccine would be that developed to counter the Ebola virus (the NNT is 1) or that for Human Papilloma virus which protects women from genital warts (NNT of just 8). For the same COVID vaccines as above, Montrastruc, et al 2021(doi.org/10.1111/fcp.12715) have collated the NNTs previously published:

83 (AstraZeneca–Oxford)
91 (Moderna)
149 (J&J)
141 (Pfizer–BioNTech)

As can be seen, the COVID vaccines are significantly less effective than what would normally be acceptable for medical intervention.

(d) Further Research on Masks: N95 masks for both symptomatic and asymptomatic people at all times. The CDC recommends that N95 respirators be reserved for use by healthcare practitioners directly caring for patients. They are not needed outside of the acute healthcare setting. Use outside of the appropriate setting will reduce the supply of N95 to Health care practitioners. This is irresponsible in a South African context. The CDC also expressly do not advise that masks be used when outdoors. Your proposals on masks are therefore not based on good science, but in point of fact are positively advised against by the best available guidelines.

APPENDIX E

Declaration of Christian and Civil Liberties

(February 2022, by Tobias Riemenschneider of Germany, Steven Lloyd of N. America, and Paul Hartwig of S. Africa)

In the course of human events, it sometimes becomes necessary for people of good faith to speak out against the abuse of power. This should be done only after serious and prayerful deliberation, and even then, in an attitude of humility and with respect for the authorities that have been established by God. Such protest should be expressed in the hope that civil authorities who are found to be eroding rights and liberties may yet fulfill their responsibility as their rightful guardians.

A few ordinary yet concerned Christians from different countries, moved by the rise of an emergent totalitarianism of the State over all realms of society, and particularly the Church, joined in common cause to craft a solemn declaration that would clearly identify this threat faced by the Church in our day, and respond to it with the timeless affirmations of God's Word. The following declarations and denials, derived from biblical principles, we put forth for consideration by all Christians and relevant authorities, in the hope that this document will give light and strength for faithful witness to Jesus Christ in our day.

Article 1
God as Sovereign Creator and Judge

We affirm that the Triune God, Father, Son, and Holy Spirit, is the personal Creator of the universe, the blessed and only Sovereign, and the ultimate Lawgiver for all human conduct. We believe that He has revealed in the Holy Scriptures the nature of good and evil conduct for all people at all times, and has appointed a day on which He will judge the world in righteousness by a man, the risen Lord Jesus Christ. To him be honor and eternal dominion. Amen.

We therefore deny that impersonal matter is the final reality behind all things and the belief that secularization serves human welfare. We deny that human conduct is a merely sociological or biological phenomena, and that any earthly authority has the right to define, independently of God's revealed will, what is good and evil human conduct. Since God is the ultimate Lawgiver and Judge, no earthly authority can make themselves an absolute moral standard and require unconditional obedience from their subjects.

Article 2
Truth and Morality

We affirm the character of the Christian and the Church as individuals and communities of truth derived firstly from the Holy Scriptures and secondly from any facts which can be credibly verified. These Scriptures reveal to us a morality and life that is rooted in the nature and character of God, and also in His original purpose for mankind which is restored in Jesus Christ. We believe that evil exists, and that its pervasive power corrupts all human thoughts, actions, and institutions separated from the grace of Christ.

We therefore deny that human governments always know or want what is good for their citizens, and that their policies and decisions should be unconditionally obeyed. We reject any indoctrination, deception, or coercive fear-mongering by the State and mass media, and all reporting on critical world issues which is selective, instant, and biased. Since the modern State's secular humanism and relativistic ethics has no transcendent basis for human behavior or morality, we have good grounds to doubt their ethical pronouncements and moral vision.

Article 3
Mankind as the Image of God

We affirm that every human being is created in the image and likeness of God and therefore has inherent dignity and certain inalienable rights and liberties. These rights and liberties extend to their personal and embodied relationships, vocational employments, and include the right to marry in a public gathering, to witness the birth and dedication of one's child, to comfort the dying (especially of their own family), to attend funerals and engage in honorable employment. We also affirm that governments should recognize that each individual is responsible for their own bodily well-being and should also uphold the right of people to refuse medical treatment.

We therefore deny the dehumanizing actions of a State or any human authority to subject any person to psychological manipulation and intimidation, which also fosters suspicion of others as potential threats to the common and individual good. We likewise oppose indiscriminate social distancing and mask-wearing, the State's legislation and mandating of medical decisions for its citizens, and all criminalizing, enforced segregation, and vocational disempowerment of persons who out of good conscience cannot comply with its medical policies.

We thus reject all forms of medical tyranny, including the implementation of vaccine passes, and any restrictions on individual freedoms or surveillance on human movements for people who who have not been clinically diagnosed with a highly contagious and life-threatening disease. Global trends toward technological tyranny over human beings and their movements we also oppose since they undermine the human agency so fundamental to our God-given calling.

Article 4
Sphere Sovereignty

We affirm that all earthly authorities derive their authority ('the right to be obeyed') from God, who is over all. We believe that He has established their different spheres of responsibility and in doing so has set limits to their authority. God has delegated authority to civil governments for the purpose of rewarding good and punishing evil, and to protect the God-given rights and freedoms granted to all men. We believe that He has delegated a unique authority to the Church in its various expressions, particularly to make disciples of all nations and establish redeemed communities of faith living under the authority of Christ. We also affirm that God has delegated authority to the family as the basic unit of society, for the purpose of fostering societal cohesion and sexual fidelity, and to raise children in the fear of the Lord to be good citizens. We affirm our right as citizens, parents, and Christians to freely self-determine our beliefs and behaviors based on these truths.

We therefore deny totalitarian ideologies of governments which do not recognize the boundaries of their authority and extend their jurisdiction over the Church or family sphere. In particular, we reject the socialist tendencies of governments to centralize the beliefs and conduct of their citizens by creating a thoroughly secular and authoritarian society in which the State is absolute. Such totalitarianism and statism are built on beliefs that have fundamentally redefined good and evil and the nature of human beings. The effect of these beliefs is to enslave individual freedoms in general and religious freedoms in particular, and engender an ideological intolerance which seeks to silence, cancel, and re-educate those who think otherwise.

Article 5
Worship

We affirm that the Church of the Lord Jesus Christ belongs to Him at the cost of His life and that it is accountable to Him alone in all matters of faith and practice. We believe that Christ's command for His Church to give to Caesar (i.e., the civil authority) what belongs to Caesar and to God what belongs to God establishes for us the functional independence of the Church from the State. We declare that Christ, who is Lord over all, invites all without distinction of any kind to freely and regularly gather together in His Name in local congregations to seek and serve Him in truth and love. We affirm that the activities of the local church which are essential acts of worship are to be regulated by Christ alone.

We therefore deny that any other authority, secular or religious, has jurisdiction over the local church to regulate any of its affairs in matters of faith and conduct, or to downgrade its activities to a non-essential status. We thus repudiate all actions of the State that impose coercive measures over the church and criminalize, inhibit, or regulate any of her activities which are undertaken as acts of service toward her Lord. Lastly, we resist the trend of digital platforms in Christian worship and ministry to become substitutes for the congregational and embodied means of ministry that are so essential in our faith.

Call for Respect, Repentance, and Resistance

We commend and express our gratitude to those civil authorities who respect the essential nature of these Christian beliefs and practices and who have a high regard for individual and religious freedoms. To those civil authorities who have disregarded these freedoms, we call on you to repent and to again become the protectors of liberty and of the rights that God has given to all men.

To those civil authorities who desire to compel us to obey the secular State, like the three Hebrews who refused to worship Nebuchadnezzar's golden statue, we respectfully, but firmly say, "We have no need to answer you in this matter. The God we serve is able to save us from you, and He will rescue us from your hand. But even if He does not, we want you to know that we will not serve your gods or worship the idols you have set up" (Dan. 3:16-18).

To our brothers and sisters in Christ around the world we say, "Take courage, stand up, and stand firm together, and prepare for persecution." It appears that the world may well be entering a time of testing, not only for the Church, but for everyone who believes in freedom and who opposes tyranny. Let us stand in solidarity with those who are being arrested or forcefully isolated because they have chosen to obey God rather than men. Let us stand in solidarity with those who have had their churches forcefully closed or been exiled from their congregations.

Let us help and support in practical ways those who have been fined or who have had to forfeit their employment for the sake of Christ. And we ask our brothers and sisters who have lived under persecution all their lives to pray for us, that God would give us the grace to bless those who persecute us and to pray for them; that God would give us the courage to stand firm in our faith as His witnesses; and that He would give us the strength to remain faithful and persevere to the end. Amen.

APPENDIX F

WHAT IS THE WAY OF SALVATION?

Why do we stand against tyranny and for liberty? Supremely for this reason: That we might freely proclaim the glorious gospel of our Lord Jesus Christ (1 Tim. 2:1-7). Here is the greatest news in the entire universe – a brief summary of the biblical gospel, of what it means to be a Christian, of the only way to true and lasting freedom:

Being a Christian is more than identifying yourself with a particular religion or affirming a certain value system. Being a Christian means you have embraced what the Bible says about God, mankind, and salvation. Consider the following truths found in the Bible.

God Is Sovereign Creator
Contemporary thinking says man is the product of evolution. But the Bible says we were created by a personal God to love, serve, and enjoy endless fellowship with Him. The New Testament reveals it was Jesus Himself who created everything (John 1:3; Colossians 1:16). Therefore, He also owns and rules everything (Psalm 103:19). That means He has authority over our lives and we owe Him absolute allegiance, obedience, and worship.

God Is Holy
God is absolutely and perfectly holy (Isaiah 6:3); therefore He cannot commit or approve of evil (James 1:13). God requires holiness of us as well. First Peter 1:16 says, You shall be holy, for I am holy.

Mankind Is Sinful
According to Scripture, everyone is guilty of sin: There is no man who does not sin (1 Kings 8:46). That doesn't mean we're incapable of performing acts of human kindness. But we're utterly incapable of understanding, loving, or pleasing God on our own (Romans 3:10-12).

Sin Demands a Penalty

God's holiness and justice demand that all sin be punished by eternal death (Ezekiel 18:4; Romans 6:23). That's why simply changing our patterns of behaviour can't solve our sin problem or eliminate its consequences.

Jesus Is Lord and Saviour

Romans 10:9 says, If you confess with your mouth Jesus as Lord, and believe in your heart that God raised Him from the dead, you shall be saved. Even though God's justice demands death for sin, His love has provided a Saviour who paid the penalty and died for sinners (1 Peter 3:18). Christ's death satisfied the demands of God's justice, and Christ's perfect life satisfied the demands of God's holiness (2 Corinthians 5:21), thereby enabling Him to forgive and save those who place their faith in Him (Romans 3:26).

The Character of Saving Faith

True faith is always accompanied by repentance from sin. Repentance is agreeing with God that you are sinful, confessing your sins to Him, and making a conscious choice to turn from sin (Luke 13:3, 5; 1 Thessalonians 1:9), pursue Christ (Matthew 11: 28-30; John 17:3), and obey Him (1 John 2:3). It isn't enough to believe certain facts about Christ. Even Satan and his demons believe in the true God (James 2:19), but they don't love and obey Him. True saving faith always responds in obedience (Ephesians 2:10).

(https://www.gracechurch.org/about/gospel)